Everyday Belonging in the Post-Soviet Borderlands

Everyday Belonging in the Post-Soviet Borderlands

Russian Speakers in Estonia and Kazakhstan

Alina Jašina-Schäfer

LEXINGTON BOOKS

Lanham • Boulder • New York • London

Giessen dissertation, Faculty of Language, Literature, Culture (FB05).

Chapter 3 and 4 reuse some of the previously published materials with the permission of rights' holders. The section "Enacting Interiority in Narva" and "Becoming Culturally Intimate with Kazakh" in Chapter 3 reproduce excerpts from: Jašina-Schäfer, Alina and Ammon Cheskin. 2020. "Horizontal Citizenship in Estonia: Russian Speakers in the Borderland City of Narva," *Citizenship Studies* 24(1): 93–110 and Jašina-Schäfer, Alina. 2019. "Everyday Experiences of Place in the Kazakhstani Borderland: Russian Speakers between Kazakhstan, Russia, and the Globe," *Nationalities Papers* 47(1), 38–54.

In chapter 4, some of the materials are being reused from: Jašina-Schäfer, Alina. 2020. "Of Homogenous 'Freaks' and Heterogenous Members: Cultural Minorities and their Belonging in the Estonian Borderland." *New Diversities* 22 (2), 9–22 and Jašina-Schäfer, Alina. 2019. "Everyday Experiences of Place in the Kazakhstani Borderland: Russian Speakers between Kazakhstan, Russia, and the Globe," Nationalities Papers 47(1), 38–54.

Published by Lexington Books
An imprint of The Rowman & Littlefield Publishing Group, Inc.
4501 Forbes Boulevard, Suite 200, Lanham, Maryland 20706
www.rowman.com

6 Tinworth Street, London SE11 5AL, United Kingdom

British Library Cataloguing in Publication Information Available

Library of Congress Cataloging-in-Publication Data

Names: Jašina-Schäfer, Alina, 1989- author.
Title: Everyday belonging in post-Soviet borderlands : spatial narratives of Russian
    speakers in Estonia and Kazakhstan / Alina Jašina-Schäfer.
Description: Lanham : Lexington Books, 2020. I Includes bibliographical references and
    index.
Identifiers: LCCN 2020039201 (print) I LCCN 2020039202 (ebook) I
    ISBN 9781793631381 (cloth) I ISBN 9781793631398 (epub)
    ISBN 9781793631404 (pbk)
Subjects: LCSH: Belonging (Social psychology)—Estonia. I Belonging (Social
    psychology)—Kazakhstan. I Russians—Estonia. I Russians—Kazakhstan. I
    Education, Bilingual—Estonia. I Education, Bilingual—Kazakhstan.
Classification: LCC HM1033 .J37 2020 (print) I LCC HM1033 (ebook) I
    DDC 302.5/4094798—dc23
LC record available at https://lccn.loc.gov/2020039201
LC ebook record available at https://lccn.loc.gov/2020039202

To my parents, Rezida and Aleksandr

Contents

List of Figures

Note on Translation and Transliteration

All translations from the Russian, including the interview excerpts, have been made by the author, unless otherwise specified. Throughout the text, for Russian words a BGN/PCGN romanization system is used.

Acknowledgements

This book is based on my doctoral dissertation which took shape in the walls of the International Graduate Center for the Study of Culture (GCSC), Justus Liebig University (JLU) Giessen. I would like to thank GCSC for their intellectual as well as generous financial support for my research, fieldwork, and the attendance of numerous international conferences, which helped me grow and progress as a scholar.

In many ways, I owe this book to all the people who supported and inspired me, who guided, and encouraged me throughout the years full of exciting new revelations but sometimes also frustrations. This monograph would not have been possible without the tremendous support and valuable comments I received from my doctoral supervisors Monika Wingender and Ammon Cheskin. I am also thankful to my peers and senior scholars from the research groups *Global Studies and Politics of Space*, *Cultural Memory Studies* and the sociology colloquium at the JLU for challenging me and contributing immensely to the development of various parts of this book. My special words of gratitude are directed at Bernardo Teles Fazendeiro, Ana Ivasiuc, Mateusz Laszczkowski, Andreas Langenohl, Ekaterina Pankova, and Lenneke Sprik for their detailed reading of some parts and chapters, for their comments and advice that helped develop my thoughts, ways of knowing and seeing. I owe much to Sofia Kouropatov who read my final draft and helped me present my work in a coherent and a reader-friendly manner. I am furthermore indebted to the anonymous reviewer and the editorial team at Rowman and Littlefield, Eric Kuntzman, Alexandra Rallo, and Kasey Beduhn for helping finalize this manuscript. Thank you for your motivation, attentiveness, and active participation.

Parts of this research have been previously presented at the 2017 Annual Convention of the Association for Slavic (ASEEES), East European and

Eurasian Studies in Chicago; 2018 conference on 'Space in Peace and Conflict' in Marburg; 2019 convention by the Association for the Study of Nationalities in New York, during the annual conference on Russian and East European Studies in Tartu and the summer ASEEES convention in Zagreb. I would like to thank all the discussants and participants for posing challenging question that significantly shaped my angle of analysis. I am also grateful to European Centre for Minority Issues in Flensburg, especially Tove Malloy and Caitlin Boulter, for inviting me to discuss my findings and conclusions. This event generated a lot of valuable feedback that brought me substantially further.

Each of my research participants deserves a separate thank you. Without your personal stories, your feelings, and experiences, which you were so kind to share with me, this monograph would have never taken shape or seen the light. Your hospitality, your friendship, your willingness to let me into your lives and share your knowledge significantly affected me and the course of my research. In Petropavlovsk, I am especially grateful to A. whom I once met by chance on a train. Two years later he became a tremendous source of support during my research stay, providing the first insights into the colorful life in the city. In Estonia, I would like to thank the former director of the Narva College Kristina Kallas for offering me valuable contacts and re-directing me to Jelena Nõmm and Olga Burdakova, local researchers who have been working extensively on the topic of Narvan identity. I would like to thank each one of you for supplying me with useful materials about local traditions that informed several pages in this work. For the cover picture of the book that represents the everyday life flow at the Narvan Promenade I am thankful to a local photographer and my dear friend Maria Kanevskaja.

This project would not be possible without my husband Timo whose kind, gentle, and selfless support helped me through the most challenging phases of my work. Our long discussions on the most complex issues helped me systematize my, at times confusing, ideas and thoughts. Your patience and integrity, for which I am immensely grateful, inspired confidence in me. Finally, I would like to end at the beginning of it all, by thanking my parents who fostered the curiosity in the questions I pursued for this research. Throughout the years, your unconventional love, understanding, and trust nurtured me, enabled me, and brought me to where I stand now. It is to you, my dearest parents, that this book is dedicated.

Chapter 1

Introduction

The collapse of the Soviet Union, the world's largest multiethnic federation, constituted both an opportunity and serious challenges for tens of millions of former Soviet citizens. Having secured sovereignty and reorganized socio-political structures, the newly independent states embarked upon national-izing projects that not only sought to reshape cultural practices and recreate national identities but also to strengthen and empower core ethnonational groups. For some people, those changes symbolized the (re)birth of their national identities, the return of their cultural symbols, promotion of their languages, and political hegemony over their now successfully independent states. For others, however, independence brought with it numerous political and sociocultural struggles.

Growing up in Tallinn, Estonia, I became a witness to the unique dif-ficulties that fell upon the Russophone population, which had to reconcile themselves to their new minority status. As a formerly privileged group in the Soviet Union, Russian speakers experienced what we could call a migra-tion of borders—a process that almost overnight turned them into minorities with disputed memberships. The disappearance of the Soviet Union and the movement of borders implied the obliteration of their established orders, bonds of belonging, and familiar daily routines. The new trajectory of the successor states, which sought to homogenize previously heterogeneous populations and spaces, erase the vestiges of the Soviet past, and radically redefine community memberships, often only strengthened these uncertain-ties. This peculiar situation subsequently generated diverse political and scholarly questions, starting with inquiries into the new possible identities of the Russophones (Who are Russian speakers? How do they live in this new spatiotemporal order? How do they negotiate their new position within these societies?) and continuing with the exploration of their complex spatial

1

affiliations, politics of belonging, and their relationship with their alleged homeland, Russia.

As a child from a Russian-speaking family, I was confronted with these questions not from afar but right at the playground in front of our house. Growing up surrounded exclusively by other Russian-speaking children, our everyday worlds seemed to have formed in parallel to Estonian speakers, who went to different kindergartens, different schools, and different after-school activity centers. We were seemingly separated by the insurmountable historical, political, and cultural divisions that erupted as the Soviet Union collapsed. Among my peers and teachers, I heard numerous stories of struggling to fit into a larger society that accepted policies which ostracized the vast majority of Russian-speaking Soviet-era settlers—stories of exclusions and inequalities based on the language one practiced at home, stories filled with contempt for these injustices. In my own family, both of my parents struggled to understand their new positions in independent Estonia. My father, who was born in Tallinn in the late 1950s into a mixed Russian-Estonian family, was particularly affected by having to undergo the naturalization process to obtain citizenship.[1] Once, he even told me that, whether we want it or not, we will always remain the second-class citizens in a country that "privileges and values ethnic Estonians only." However, strange though it may sound, the stories of my parents and other Russian-speaking friends are filled equally with warm feelings for Estonia, emphasizing it repeatedly as their only home. As I recollect now, my father often told me how much he loves the country, how every tree in the Pirita area, the place where he was born, reminds him of his childhood and of his friends, some of whom were Estonian speakers: "I am a son of this land no matter what."

Motivated first by personal experience and later by researching the lives and practices of Russian speakers in a broader context, this book attempts to better understand the complex meanings of everyday belonging within and outside the post-Soviet borderlands. How do minorities define their surroundings and practice belonging? How do they respond to political and sociocultural exclusions? How do they reconcile claims of being excluded with attempts to call places like Estonia their home? Finally, what are the broader implications of these processes for the spaces and societies that Russian speakers live in?

Situations in which linguocultural minorities feel themselves to be on the outside of the imaginary line of the nation are certainly not unique to post-Soviet countries. In an era marked by increasing transnational mobility and interconnectedness, the understanding of who "we" are and who is a part of the community becomes particularly important. The resurgent nationalism and nativism as well as increasing socioeconomic disparities between and within societies lead to profound questions about what belonging (or not belonging) means, how it is differently enacted through competing claims to and performances of insidedness, and what are its implications for individuals and societies at large (Wright 2015; Yuval-Davis 2006). These questions constitute some of the most difficult issues confronting all of us today; it is a new arena of political and cultural contestation that necessitates a careful reconsideration of the complexity of belonging as a theory, practice, and a mode of being (Halse 2018).

The term "belonging" is fundamentally important in people's lives and pervades our everyday speech, academic articles, book titles, and songs. It has the ability, as Sarah Wright (2015, 391) notes, to "change lives, to make communities and collectives, to bring together and to separate in the most intimate, loving, accepting, exclusionary or violent ways." Yet, despite its power, belonging has managed to escape the level of rigorous theorization applied to many other foundational terms. Sometimes treated as flexible and self-evident, slippery, and axiomatic, it tends to be left undefined. More often belonging is used as a synonym of other concepts like "citizenship"[2] (Bhabha 1999; Ho 2006; Jackson 2015) and "identity,"[3] in particular when referring to the ethnic and national domains (Bond 2006; Hernandez et al. 2007; Meinhof and Galsinski 2005; Warriner 2007). In other cases, however, scholars consider belonging to be multidimensional, at once encompassing citizenship, nationhood, gender, ethnicity, and diverse attachments (Antonsich 2010, 645). With these scholarly disagreements in mind, how can we understand the analytical and theoretical specificities of belonging? How can we avoid glossing over its multiple meanings, uses, and inconsistencies in favor of problematic labels and categories, like what already occurred with other terms, for example, identity?[4]

To this end, this research synthesizes previous studies in anthropology, human geography, and political science that engage with belonging in detail (Anthias 2002, 2006, 2013; Bennet 2014; Lähdesmäki et al. 2016; May 2011; Miller 2003; Pfaff-Czarnezka 2011; Pollini 2005; Wright 2015; Yuval-Davis 2006) and focuses on the underexplored spatial qualities of belonging in the everyday, which reflect the relations not only between people but also between circulating objects, artefacts, and changing social, political, and cultural landscapes (Lefebvre 1991; Low 2017; Soja 2000). With this multitude of entangled aspects, the space-sensitive approach helps to imagine belonging as a "rhizomatic network" (Youkhana 2015, 15) characterized by a dynamic and heterogeneous movement between "inside" and "outside," situated within quite specific sociopolitical, material, historical, and hegemonic settings that order and condition people's lives, that include and exclude them.

Focusing on the lives of politically yet not physically "displaced" Russian speakers and their visions of space and community within two different countries (Estonia and Kazakhstan), this book expands the debates on the everyday manifestations of "inclusion" and "exclusion." Over the last few decades, these have become defining words in both political speeches and academic research on belonging. However, their meanings, their character-istics, and relationship lack a clear shape, leading scholars like Aboim et al. (2018) as well as Tiesler (2018) to ask: How is the border between "in" and "out" proclaimed and negotiated? Are inclusion and exclusion necessarily the opposite sides of the coin or can they be approached as a continuation of the same process? To unpack these questions productively requires not only shift-ing our attention to broader political discourses, but to the micro-level prac-tices that were sourced here through ethnographic engagement with Russian speakers in the borderland cities of Narva in Estonia and Petropavlovsk in Kazakhstan. Instead of viewing these borderland cities through the frame-work of securitization and marginalization, as has been frequently done before (this will be discussed later; for critique, see Makarychev 2018), here I approach them as places of contradiction that offer particularly interesting angles into the analysis of inclusion and exclusion and the complex dialecti-cal relationship thereof. As places that integrate conflicting cultural codes and lifestyles, borderlands help to tease out more clearly how different spatial scales of the global, national, and local, as well as the Soviet and post-Soviet temporalities become implicated in the practices through which Russian-speaking populations negotiate their belonging and move between different versions of "inside" and "outside."

This movement will be developed more clearly in the empirical chapters and conceptualized as a practice of *exterior interiority*: a practice that can-not be defined by either a concrete spatial fixation or a clear dividing line. In other words, it is neither a state of clearly opposed positions—"inside" and "outside"—nor simply a middling state of liminality. Rather, to think with exterior interiority very basically involves a thorough understanding of belonging as a constant relation, a spiral play of boundary crossing, whereby every process of displacement and exclusion from something entails trans-formation and inclusion into something else. Hence, it is at once a dialectic of movement and transgression from one position to another as well as cer-tain static state that gains "a recognizable 'pattern'" (Thomassen 2012, 32) through the continuous demarcation of difference between the foreign and domestic worlds (Andrews and Roberts 2012).

Unlike other concepts, such as cultural hybridity, which has been increas-ingly criticized for celebrating "all too quickly both the blending and bor-derlessness of global relations" (Bachmann-Medick 2016, 122, see also Andrews and Roberts 2012; Marotta 2008; Massumi 2002; Werbner 2015), exterior interiority emphasizes the importance of boundaries and local background structures that in many ways continue to define the palimpsest, seemingly rootless, and ambivalent identities of contemporary existence. In this regard, Vince Marotta (2008, 309) highlights how, even in moments of sameness, people "search for foundations and use social, cultural, and political boundaries to guide them through fluidity of contemporary life." Georg Simmel (1997, 174) notably reminds us how a human being is necessarily "the connecting creature" that "cannot connect without separating." As such, the task here is not only to inscribe the agency of the subaltern by mixing and overcoming binary thinking, as usefully sought by many studies on hybridity (Bhabha 1994), but essentially to understand who and what is left out of this fusion and how different forms of exclusion are produced and overcome.

Furthermore, unpacking belonging through the lens of exterior interiority could usefully extend the literature on the Russophone communities, which, according to Andrey Makarychev and Vladimir Sazonov (2019), despite its breadth, still lacks a more nuanced picture. Extant studies often represent the dichotomous accounts of Russian speakers either as an integrated part of the so-called "host" society or as alienated from it based on their "Russianness" (see, for example, Barrington et al. 2003; Duvold 2006; Laitin 1998; Nimmerfeldt 2011). In contrast, this research uncovers the ambiguity, complexity, and plurality of individual movements between separation and incorporation. It begins by first revisiting the debates that shape the studies on Russian speakers and shows how this monograph engages with and contributes to them. The introductory chapter subsequently turns to a brief discussion of the methodological underpinnings of this research, mapping the key themes and directions of the book.

Before proceeding, I must, however, caution the reader that *Everyday Belonging in the Post-Soviet Borderlands* does not offer a final word on the positionings of Russian speakers, nor does it develop a synthetic typology of belonging across countries. Given the complexities behind people's practices, a quest for generalization would not only be undesirable but also, quite frankly, impossible. Rather, the empirical chapters represent a refreshing look into belonging as a continuous movement between different versions of exteriority and interiority, thereby going beyond unproductive binaries, which overemphasize the importance of boundaries, or the notion of in-betweenness, which dramatically underplays them. By reflecting on the different sociopolitical, historical, and economic conditions in Estonia and Kazakhstan, the book reconstructs belonging as a concept in translation that, despite wide circulation across countries, is anchored in quite concrete lifeworlds and local histories. This anchorage, in turn, opens up an array of local, national, and transnational narratives that Russian speakers use to navigate their daily lives.

RUSSIAN SPEAKERS: COMPLEX PHENOMENA

One of the motivations to write this book was to rethink the many overgeneralized assumptions about Russophone communities that are reproduced in both academic writings and political accounts. To date, a wide range of academic research is already available into the lives and practices of the so-called Russian speakers in the context of the post-Soviet sociopolitical order. An attempt to grasp who Russian speakers are and what relationship they have with Russia or with their state of residence has been translated into rigorous research of a diverse spectrum of themes, including political and economic deprivation of Russian speakers (Hallik et al. 2001); migration from the post-Soviet countries (Pilkington 1998); loyalties of nontitular populations (Linz and Stepan 1996; Smith and Wilson 1997); as well as the impact of post-Soviet language reforms on the identities of Russian speakers (Braun and Wingender 2015; Pavlenko 2008). Numerous studies have also been conducted examining interethnic relations (Korts 2008; Lauristin and Heidmets 2002; Vallimäe et al. 2010; Vihalemm 2007); nation-building and minority integration (Kolstø 1999a); and, more recently, in response to Russia's annexation of Crimea, the potentiality of their political mobilization and secession (Diener 2015; Grigas 2016; Trimbach and O'Lear 2015). Considering such a plethora of themes, how do we decide what falls under the broad term of "Russian speakers" and how did it come to be used as a unit of analysis by earlier research? In fact, this term, like the others mentioned above, entails a problematic homogenizing feature and will therefore be used here cautiously.

Following the collapse of the Soviet Union, scholars began to use the terms "Russian speakers" or the "Russophone population" to connote an imagined ethnosocial community of ethnic Russians and other Russian-speaking populations that emerged as "beached diasporas" (Laitin 1998) in fourteen newly constituted national states. Historically, during the Russian Imperial as well as Soviet periods, extensive Russophone settlements developed in areas traditionally populated by non-Russian people. Especially during Soviet times, the intermixing of nations in the regions that we nowadays commonly refer to as the Baltic states and Central Asia was taking place en masse. Forms of and reasons for the movement of people differed greatly—from voluntary to forced, from a movement of a single person in search of a better life to movements of entire "nations in the echelons" (Shukurov and Shukurov 1999, 202). Apart from the representatives of the Slavic nations, such as Russians, Ukrainians, and Belarusians, a considerable number of other nationalities— such as Germans, Tatars, and Armenians—found themselves in foreign territories, diluting the ethnic composition of the preexisting populations. Separated from their original homelands, these typically non-Russian people preferred to join the dominant Russian "culturescape." Although by the time the Soviet Union collapsed it became practically impossible to draw a line between ethnic Russians and other Russian-speaking populations, one must emphasize numerous differences within this vast community: Russian speakers considerably diverge in their degree of integration into the "host" country and in their economic well-being, political rights, and future plans (Zevelev 2001, 92). The task of combining such a diffuse assemblage of people into a meaningful homogeneous group is therefore rather difficult.

The inevitable diversity that nowadays defines so-called Russian speakers notwithstanding, several factors provide scholars with significant ground for conceptual research on these groups of individuals. The emergence of this population as a "beached diaspora" that shares common ancestry, social roles, standings, and orientation towards the historic homeland of Russia spurred much research into the identities of the Russophones. However, this anchorage did not come without serious limitations for the conclusions that the scholars drew. In the most extreme cases, Russian speakers came to be associated with ethnic Russians as a more or less unified social group (e.g. Wlodarska-Frykowska 2016).

Despite the common—and arguably unbreakable—bond with Russia, the different lines of research highlighted multiple identity trajectories and ruptures among this "diasporic" community. Pal Kolstø (1996, 607), for example, argues that we cannot expect Russian speakers' "adherence to a given diaspora community by dint of their ethnic extraction." In fact, according to him, millions of individuals saw themselves (and were seen by others) as both "Russian" and "non-Russian" at the same time. In a similar vein, David Laitin, who conducted a thorough study in Estonia, Latvia, Ukraine, and Kazakhstan, proposes a new category—"Russian-speaking nationality"—as an alternative to their assimilation with the titular population or mobilization as Russians (1998, 263). Being neither "Russian" nor "non-Russian," Russian speakers were nevertheless unified based on their common historical, cultural, and especially linguistic features. Instead of addressing the ruptures and diverging practices among this vast community in meaningful ways, researchers simply replaced "ethnicity" and shared ancestry with culture and language as the "most salient markers" of Russian speakers' group identity (for critique, see Cheskin and Kachuyevski 2019, 4). To date, extant literature often represents Russian speakers as "those members of the minority community who declare Russian as their mother tongue or as their second language" (Schulze 2010, 363). Anastassia Zabrodskaya (2015, 218) also indicates that, for example, in the case of the Baltic states, Russian-speaking communities construct their common identity mainly by means of the Russian language without distinguishing between their different ethnic backgrounds.

While these dynamics might seem to make Russian speakers a fruitful unit of analysis, we must be aware of the homogenizing effects of focusing on ethnicity, language, and a seemingly monolithic culture. The conceptual problem, according to Rogers Brubaker (2013), is even greater when we take, for example, linguistic or cultural affiliations as independent factors that influence human behavior. This carries a risk of foregrounding one frame of reference at the expense of alternative and equally relevant frames that define and structure individual belonging. Despite Brubaker's (2006) warning against "groupism," most of the research that has delved into the lives of Russian speakers has been nevertheless determined to group them into different categories of identification (e.g. host country-centered, fragmented, extraterritorial, confused; see Vihalemm and Masso 2003). Quite unsurprisingly, these practices produced public knowledge of Russian speakers that feeds off their categorical representations as people who have either integrated themselves into the new structures of their states or still struggle to find a place of their own (see, for example, Veser 2015).

A constructive point of departure has been offered by Kevin Platt (2019) and later by Makarychev and Sazonov (2019), who suggest reconsidering the Russophone community, or rather communities, as complex phenomena that engender a broad variety of narrative and performative practices that vary across time, space, and social environments.[5] This kind of approach advocates for a shift in seeing Russian speakers as a group connected through either ancestry, language, or cultural orientations toward their spatially enacted practices of de- and rebordering between their "own" and "alien" spaces, between belonging and not belonging. Placing spatial practices at the center of our analysis, we can cast a new light on the ways Russian speakers constitute themselves and are constituted by the local sociopolitical landscapes. The geographical and historical situatedness, in turn, allows us to account not only for ruptures across different countries, but to remain aware of numerous shifting meanings and experiences among Russian speakers within the same local social environment. It enables us to go beyond the static vision of the lives of these people to see how they perform and creatively engage with their sociopolitical realities in order to claim a place for themselves. However, exploring these diverse spatial practices ethnographically entails revisiting the notion of belonging from a decentered perspective afforded by the peculiarities of Russian speakers' positionalities in Estonia and Kazakhstan in the past and present.

UNCOVERING BELONGING SPATIALLY

Subsequently, what do we exactly study when we study the belonging of Russian speakers? While there are different theoretical approaches to belonging (some of which are utilized here), the point of departure of this book is spatial.[6] As Eva Youkhana (2015) rightfully notes, in order to reflect upon changing belongingness, sociospatial production processes must be better integrated into our conceptual thinking. According to her, belonging "arises by means of multiple and situated appropriation processes" (Youkhana 2015, 16) and describes "alterable attachments that can be social, imagined, and sensual-material in nature" (Ibid.). Other scholars, like Floya Anthias (2006, 2013) and Marco Antonsich (2010), also stress the importance of the spatial reference of belonging, whereby belonging, they argue, is not merely comprised of community affiliations or memories thereof but also the social places as well as spatiotemporal "contexts from which belongings are imagined and narrated" (Anthias 2006, 21). To think of belonging spatially means, therefore, to see it as a "circuit of action and reaction" (Wright 2015, 393) of different activities—the so-called institutionalized "regimes of belonging" (Pfaff-Czarnezka 2011) and the repeated everyday practices of people.

The contention that all social phenomena, social networks, structures, and relations occur in space is by no means new. Following the so-called spatial turn in humanities and social sciences during the 1990s and early 2000s, the study of place and space has undergone a profound and sustained resurgence. In this process, the understanding of space has shifted dramatically from a mere neutral setting against which life unfolds to a constitutive dimension of social life (Lawrence and Low 1990; Lefebvre 1991).[7] Academics in various fields came to appreciate the central role of space and place in social organization, social relations, and personhood, acknowledging that "it is not just that the spatial is socially constructed; the social is spatially constructed too" (Massey 1984, 6; see also Fuller and Löw 2017). Although some scholars would perhaps insist that such a focus on spatiality is by its very nature anti-progressive and represents solely a sense of "being" to which a range of epithets, such as local, specific, concrete, descriptive, and immobile are attached (Bachelard 1994; Heidegger 1962), Massey (1991, 1994) importantly reminds us how space, too, by its very definition as an intersection and interaction of "concrete social relations and social processes" (Massey 1994, 138) is dynamic and changing.[8]

Our current understanding of space has been driven in many ways by the previous works of French theorists like Foucault (1995), Lefebvre ([1974] 1991), Bourdieu ([1972] 1977), and de Certeau ([1980] 1984). In his seminal work on the social production of space, Henri Lefebvre (1991), for example, rethinks space as both grounded in social, economic, ideological, and technological factors that lead to the physical production of material settings and as a lived space through which dominated spaces of exclusion and inequality can be reconstructed and appropriated by the inhabitants. Later, Setha Low (2017) summarizes this dialogic process through the notion of "spatializing culture," which complexly links the social production and development of space, nature, and the built environment with the social construction of space and place meanings. According to Low (2017, 7):

> The materialist emphasis of social production is useful in defining the historical emergence and political [and] economic formation of urban space, while social construction refers to the transformation of space through language, social interaction, memory, representation, [embodiment,] behavior and use.

Both layers in combination can uncover social injustices, forms of inclusion, and the reproduction and maintenance of boundaries by the hegemonic political powers as well as the ways people understand the everyday places where they live and socialize. To unveil this layered entanglement in the context of Estonia and Kazakhstan, I begin my analysis by exploring the top-down processes that define space and society. What Nira Yuval-Davis (2006) frames as "politics of belonging" responsible for constructing belonging in particular ways to particular collectivities and Low (2009) calls the "social production of space" will be reconstructed here by drawing on previous studies on nation-building in post-Soviet countries (Agarin 2010; Cummings 2005, 2010; Schatz 2004; Schulze 2018), medial discourses, and my own observations.

By "nation-building," I refer to the most common form of the collective identity formation process, which draws on existing traditions, customs, and institutions to demarcate the margins of a nation and to emphasize its sovereignty and uniqueness. This process can take an exclusionary turn when a particular segment of the population receives privileges over the others, or it can be regarded as more inclusive if the state measures do not encroach upon cultural distinctiveness and extend equal political and cultural rights to all inhabitants. Setting the nation-building policies, peripheralization policies, and boundary maintenance enacted by the Estonian and Kazakhstani political elites into a dialogue, this monograph aims to better understand the forces that shape the countries today. To this end, chapter 2 traces the different and similar ways in which the borderland cities of Narva and Petropavlovsk have been produced by their governments and how the cities have developed since the early 1990s.

At the same time, everyday belonging is also sought in the mundane, habitual activities, and spatial tactics that Russian speakers use to "negotiate their way through or around social structures" (May 2011, 357). Using detailed ethnographic material, this research concentrates on different ways in which individual memories, narratives, and embodied performances are interwoven into a process of belonging, which is often overlooked in the top-down approaches that characterize much of the literature on nation-building and identity formation, especially in the countries of the former Soviet Union.[9]

This work asks how Russian speakers live in and perceive the places wherein they reside. How do they respond to the bordering practices of their states? How do they redefine their positionalities and terms of belonging? In what ways do local experiences challenge national and transnational ideas of space? These questions make up the essence of this book, highlighting the individual agency of Russian speakers to "do" their own belonging as opposed to being simple bystanders of rapidly changing spatio-temporal settings. It is worthy to note, however, that "agency" in this case is not necessarily seen as resistance to the meanings and norms within structures of power or as the desire to break with the context altogether. The agential capacity of Russian speakers, as the empirical chapters will reveal, is rather entailed in their search for stability and continuity, as well as in the creation of new alternative social visions of inclusion by means of transgressing, de- and rebordering previous exclusions.

EVERYDAY REALITIES IN NARVA
AND PETROPAVLOVSK

For a long time, everyday life was utilized by social scientists in theories but ignored as a phenomenon in its own right (Kalekin-Fischman 2013). Earlier research insisted that at its core, everyday life is either too "inauthentic, confused, or mystified" to be studied or that everydayness represents "an uncorrupted life" free of political structures (Colerbrook 2002, 687). As a result, most scientific inquiry instead concentrated on the effects of governments and social structures on social relations, ignoring what meanings these could carry for people in their daily lives (Zerubavel 2006).

Only recently has interest in the study of the everyday began to grow, leading to numerous emergent interpretations of the "ordinary" with different functions in different cultural contexts. Nancy Ries (2002, 732), for example, argues that for ethnographers everydayness is a domain where the ordinary and the extraordinary meet, where "nonalienated, culturally and existentially meaningful productivity occurs." Burials, marriages, communal feasts—they all play a role in establishing a system of social stratification, social relations, and cultural identities. Such quotidian cultural practices can also contain "minor subversion[s] of the official code of behavior" (Boym 1994, 21) and therefore represent a way to undermine centralized power systems (de Certeau 1984; Hartley 2003).

At the same time, everyday life does not always contain elements of resistance to power structures; it is not only an arena of struggle or a form of micropolitics that resists the macropolitics of political institutions. Following Kristin Ross (1998) and Joe Moran (2005), I use the category of the everyday rather as a way for "imagining social change and defusing its politics"

(Moran 2005, 13). In other words, in the case of Russian speakers, the everyday serves as both a creative way to break out of marginalizing political discourses and to reproduce them. Like Moran, I am less concerned with the investigation of daily life per se than with the everyday as a category that brings together time, space, power, and culture in a way that affords a better understanding of the relationship between the public sphere and the belonging of ordinary Russophones.

To examine how the belonging of Russian speakers is alternatively narrated, performed, and imagined, in 2016 and 2017 I emplaced myself for several months in Narva (Estonia) and Petropavlovsk (Kazakhstan). As a "complex imbroglio of actors with different goals, methods, and ways of practice" (Amin and Thrift 2002, 92), cities represent particularly interesting sites for analysis. They are laboratories in which one can observe the dynamism, incoherence, and messiness of everyday life (whereby messiness is used here in a positive sense denoting plurality of connections). Constituted through overlapping subjectivities and identities, which resist any simplifications, messy everydayness is a "'work in progress' contingently assembled by residents and other actors who creatively, and with a lot of effort, draw on local and translocal resources to patch up the social and material fabric of place" (Laszczkowski 2016, 21–22). Narva and Petropavlovsk are, in this regard, not just any cities, but borderlands located at the margins of their states, subject to the bordering practices of both internal and external actors as well as spatial and economic "peripheralization" (chapter 2). As borderlands, they not only depict everyday life as an open-ended, abundant series of actions, but have an "imagined other side" (Tsing 1993, 21) deeply entangled in their consciousness. Hence, Narva and Petropavlovsk are sites of ambivalences and diverse projects of self-definition, sites of "creative cultural production" (Rosaldo 1989, 208) defined by the divergences and convergences that guide us towards the "intersection of power and difference" within and across nations and local communities (Tsing 1993, 21).

Petropavlovsk (figure 1.1) or Petropavl (Kazakh spelling) is a city of 217,205 people (Passport of North Kazakhstan region 2016), roughly 70 per cent of which are ethnic Russians and other non-titular Russian-speaking residents. Founded in 1752 by Tsarist Russia to extend Russian settlements, the city consequently grew under the resettlement policies of the time, Stalin's deportations in the 1930s and 1940s, and the development of the Virgin Lands under Khrushchev. Nowadays, Petropavlovsk represents the most northern point of the country and is therefore commonly referred to as the "Northern Gates of Kazakhstan." My second fieldwork destination, Narva (figure 1.2), while smaller in size, with a population of only 60,383 (Siseministeerium 2016), serves as a good case in which to look for alternative practices of belonging. Narva is located directly at the border with the

Figure 1.1 Map of Kazakhstan. *Source*: Created by the author via https://www.scribble maps.com/create, June 2020.

Figure 1.2 Map of Estonia. *Source*: Created by the author via https://www.scribblemaps .com/create, June 2020.

Russian Federation and seen an even greater daily cross-border movement of people. Similarly to Petropavlovsk, the residents of Narva are predominantly Russian-speaking, making up over 90 per cent of the local population (Narva City Government 2013). Most of the inhabitants arrived in Narva during the reconstruction years following the end of World War II, as the city was almost completely destroyed by the ground warfare and the Soviet bombardments in 1944. The large flow of newcomers from Russia and other parts of the Soviet Union considerably shifted the ethnic composition of the city's population, turning ethnic Estonians into the minority group.

Politically and geographically speaking, Petropavlovsk and Narva have both been perceived as a potential security threat for their newly independent nation states. There is a persistent belief that most of the population in these cities associate themselves with Russia rather than their own countries of residence (Burch and Smith 2007). Some politicians and thinkers from the Russian side also contribute to these concerns. For example, prominent Russian nationalist Aleksandr Solzhenitsyn (1995) openly disputed the "artificial" borders between Russia and Northern Kazakhstan, insisting on including the historically defined "Russian zone" into the Russian Federation. With the annexation of Crimea by Russia, the fears of possible dissent in these cities, as well as of Russia's potential attempts to include them as a part of its territory, grew exponentially. Since 2014, numerous newspaper articles have expressed concern over this theme: "Is Putin 'rebuilding Russia' according to Solzhenitsyn's design?" (Coalson 2014), "North Kazakhstan isn't the next Crimea—yet" (Kucera 2014), "*Baltijskij put.* Estonia—*rodina*, Putin—president" (Baltic way. Estonia—homeland, Putin—the president) (Boldyrev 2015), and "Why Narva is probably not next on Russia's list" (Coffey 2015) are just a few examples.

Remaining aware of the broadest commonalities that make research into these two cities particularly interesting (Cheskin and Kachuevski 2019), we must also understand that everydayness in Narva and Petropavlovsk is structured considerably differently by internal and external forces. The juxtaposition should, therefore, avoid essentializing and overplaying possible similarities and differences. Although Estonia and Kazakhstan are both home to large numbers of Russian speakers and have both implemented nationalizing policies that prioritize the titular nationalities at the expense of minorities, we should not infer that these countries follow the same patterns of development. There are numerous differences in the political and cultural practices, transnational orientations, and economic situations that define them today (see chapter 2 for more). Furthermore, historically too, Estonia and Kazakhstan had very different profiles prior to the imposition of the Soviet rule and very different experiences of socialism itself (Stenning and Hörschelmann 2008). This concurrently has led not only to the different ways in which the governments deal with diversity and define the contours of the core community, but, as will become visible in the empirical chapters, to the different ways in which Russian speakers negotiate images of their borderland cities as well as meanings of inclusion and exclusion. Thus, when I use the term "post-Soviet" across the book, I merely refer to the geographical area occupied by the states that comprised the former Soviet Union.

ASSEMBLING A COLLAGE OF BELONGING

In her book, Svetlana Boym (1994, 21) reflects on the complexity of studying the elusive context of the everyday that is at once "too near us and too far from our understanding." Indeed, how should we scrutinize people's implicit behavior? How can we account for numerous divergent practices while remaining context sensitive? How can we avoid reducing the lives of Russian speakers, which are bewildering in their layered complexity, into singular, or clear-cut categories? These questions are by no means unique to this study and have preoccupied numerous scholars, who express growing dissatisfaction with the ways in which research often prioritizes a particular method, aimed at studying seemingly clear, definite objects (Feyerabend 1993; Latour 2005; Law 2004; Mol 2002). In his sharp critique, John Law (2004, 5), for example, argues that research methods often tend to work on the assumption that the world should properly be understood as a "*set of fairly specific, determinate, and more or less identifiable processes*" (emphasis in original). The practices of institutionalized methods favor fixed, static, and self-contained taxonomies, hierarchies, and structures over the movement, transformation, and heterogeneity that exist on the ground. To escape this postulate of singularity and to instead see the world creatively as composed of the contrary but related experiences of "the real," Law suggests following the so-called method assemblage that favors multiplicity and fractionality.

Following this idea, snapshots of scenes of ordinary life were sourced here in different ways. Living in Petropavlovsk from August until mid-October 2016 and in Narva from February until April 2017, I started my ethnographic research by collecting photographs which contained images of Russian speakers' favorite places. According to Richard Stedman et al. (2014, 113), images communicate "something different than 'words and numbers' approaches" traditionally used to collect data for studies on place attachment; they convey ways of inhabiting places by human bodies, of moving through or being situated in urban spaces (Datta 2012). In this regard, photographs are useful not only for capturing what is/was there but also to uncover meanings attributed to phenomena situated in cultural, historical, and political contexts (Stedman et al. 2004).

The visuals of places and stories related to them were combined with the spatial narratives of individual life in these two cities.[10] Similarly to Margaret Somers and Gloria Gibson (1994, 38), I consider narratives to be a constitutive feature of social life through which people make sense of what has happened and is happening to them and of potential inequalities, oppressions, or other practices of power. Whether verbal or written, Milena Komarova and Liam O'Dowd (2016, 271) usefully note, competing and interweaving stories of daily lives are always constructed "within, and with reference to, specific places, performed through associated spatial practices, and given form by the material and visual city." Such stories were collected here through twenty-four semi-structured interviews in Petropavlovsk and twenty-seven in Narva with Russian speakers between eighteen and sixty-six years of age. Most of my interlocutors were city-dwellers who came from working-class, middle-class, and upper-middle-class backgrounds (insofar as these classifications are applicable to the society in Kazakhstan—see Daly 2008).[11] I was particularly interested in participants' situated telling or versions of their lives in relation to place, that is, how Russian speakers position themselves in relation to place, how they refer to different categories of place in their speech, and what aspiration for a sense of place they have with regard to the future.

The ethnographic knowledge of everyday belonging was equally gained through so-called walking tours and dwelling alongside my interlocutors. From a phenomenological point of view, our knowledge of the world "is not just a matter of thought about the world but stems from the bodily presence and bodily orientation in relation to it" (Tilley 1994, 14). Through movement and walking the pathways, we become aware of the environment around us, as the making of routes mobilizes all our senses (smell, touch, vision), reconnecting us with both the physical world and the moral order inherent within it (Ingold 2004). Ethnographically, Tanya Richardson (2008, 139–70) provides a good example of how this method works. Participating in walking tours along the streets of Odessa, Richardson reveals the initially hidden histories the locals ascribed to those streets and buildings, reconstructing the city as a different kind of place than that which emerged in the interviews. Compared to Richardson's research, however, in my approach I was more concerned with mundane walking that was self-initiated by my respondents, rather than organizing the groups to deliberately walk together and act out histories. I was interested to see how they interact with the sociospatial environment and to understand how the surrounding landscapes are woven into their lives.

Assembling different, often seemingly incompatible, elements emerging from the field into a larger whole, I do not claim that this collage of Russian speakers' belonging is conclusive. Instead, I call to consider different practices that produce different realities as well as our own "unavoidable complicity in reality-making" (Law 2004, 153). I remain aware of the problems that arise from my own positionality and the influence my located "self" exerts upon the ethnographic comparisons conducted for this research. Indeed, as Marilyn Strathern (2004, 7–8) notes, an ethnographer cannot "pretend to be a neutral vector for the conveying of information" nor can she claim to translate her observations "into an authentic representation of the 'culture' or 'society.'" As an individual who already has a certain point of view, positionality, and geocultural belonging, I do not attempt to "represent" another society or culture but rather provide a reader with a "partial connection" to my ethnographic case studies (Picker 2017; Strathern [1991] 2004), acknowledging the mutual, dialogic production of a narrative. Only this way, Haraway (1991, 190) argues, can scholarly perspective "be held accountable for both its promising and its destructive monsters."

This connection is partial insofar as there is no organically bounded wholeness of Russian speakers' experiences across the two countries. It is also partial because my own geocultural belonging as a Russian speaker from Estonia has resonated differently with my interlocutors and led to different narratives about their own belonging. Was it perhaps my own background as a resident of Tallinn that strengthened the desire of Narvans to reinscribe themselves into the national narrative (chapters 3, 4, and 5)? To what extent did the perception of my Estonianness and Europeanness elevate the transnational lens through which Petropavlovsk inhabitants sought to tell me about their lives (chapter 4)? Was it accidental that my Petropavlovsk interlocutors guided me mostly to places that represented to them the so-called new urbanized lifestyle? Pointing out these questions should not stifle the research, but rather emphasize my close entanglement in the production of perspectives and realities that this monograph represents. It should also offer possibilities for other researchers to "play" with different methods and uncover their versions of exterior interiority, thereby strengthening our understanding of belonging not as a clear-cut product, but as a process that encompasses a variety of co-existing modes of ordering space and time.

STRUCTURE OF THE BOOK

What remains now is to outline the content of the chapters that follow. Chapter 2 represents the first empirical glimpse into the manifestations of exterior interiority among Russian-speaking minorities. It begins by providing the macro-level, sociohistorical, political, and economic context that serves as a frame of reference for the following chapters and especially for the benefit of readers unfamiliar with Estonian and Kazakhstani contexts. Drawing on secondary literature, policy documents, and my own embedded observations of material settings in Narva and Petropavlovsk, this chapter reconstructs how since 1990s the borderland cities have been dislocated from the national discourses as potential "Russian enclaves" (Pfoser 2017). The more totalizing views of the cities that this section represents are then entangled with the lived experiences and subjectivities of Russian speakers. This is done to explicate how the state-produced dislocation feeds into the narratives of everyday exteriority and exclusion. Further on, the chapter also begins to sketch out the differences that emerge between Estonia and Kazakhstan both at the level of the state and individual experiences of dislocation.

Continuing the empirical exploration of belonging, chapter 3 focuses exclusively on the individual spatiotemporal transgression of "exteriority" through practices of de- and rebordering. In other words, by drawing on diverse embodied "spatial tactics" (de Certeau 1984), I highlight how Russian speakers rework their positions within their cities and countries, subvert the narratives of "otherness," and create alternative inclusionary social visions. This chapter largely follows scholarly approaches that work with the concept of "embodied space" and locate the body in the center of all place-making activities (Csordas 1994; Low and Lawrence-Zúñiga 2003; Sen and Silverman 2014). To uncover the embodied practices of interiority among Russian speakers, the first part mainly discusses their memories of life in the borderlands, how they relate to the past and present while describing their localities, and how they emphasize geographical and temporal continuity or rupture to substantiate or renounce received notions of territoriality, and to construct different forms of inclusion. Alongside memory work, localities also take on the meanings which people assign to them through the process of living there (Ryden 1993). The second part then dissects how Russian speakers construct subjectivities and negotiate personal terms of belonging through habitual routines that regularly happen in a place. In particular, attention is given to the relationship of Russian speakers to the wider community in their countries of residence.

Chapter 4 turns to investigate the role of material and natural spaces in their capacity to mediate the dialectic relationship between exclusion and inclusion. In the same way as the space can serve to exclude (chapter 2), spaces are also enabling and can be used to alter conventional meanings. They create room for interpretive freedom for individuals to work out their disagreements symbolically, politically, or personally. In this chapter, I attend to the entanglement of human beings with, what Bruno Latour (2005) calls, "non-human actants" and view both the artefacts in public spaces (buildings, streets, squares) and the natural environment as more than bystanders in the processes through which Russian speakers negotiate their belonging and positionality within collectives. Instead, I reconstruct the material and natural landscapes as the "architects of sociability" (Tonkiss 2005) that actively mediate and facilitate the encounters of individuals and groups. They open up possibilities to Russian speakers to overcome marginality and to create new forms of interiority grounded in the amalgamation of different "cultural styles" (Ferguson 1999). By looking into the mechanisms of how Russian speakers find different ways of being in the city and in nature or how they stitch together different narratives to "make" spaces, this chapter contributes to the broader debates on the "affective geographies" (Navaro-Yashin 2012) that highlight the interrelation between an outer environment and interior human selves.

To understand the role of the external spaces in the practices of belonging among my interlocutors, chapter 5 shifts the focus to the external actor, Russia. In the context of post-Soviet borderlands, it is important to note that the dynamic feelings of belonging do not only intersect with the unraveling bordering practices of the states Russian speakers inhabit; their experiences are complicated further by Russia's attempts to create competing senses of belonging. To draw a more comprehensive picture of everyday life of Russian speakers, here I attend to discursive practices that Russia employs to "diasporize" the Russophone community outside of its territory. At the same time, I examine the attitudes and expectations my Russian speakers have towards Russia. Further extending the bricolage of cultural practices discussed in chapters 3 and 4, here too I demonstrate how Russia emerges as different spaces at once enmeshed into the relational spatial constitution of the localities in question. As an "outside" space of difference and an "inside" space of cultural-historical commonality or economic aspirations (especially in Petropavlovsk), Russia is actively used in the process of boundary negotiation between domestic and foreign, between "in" and "out."

Chapter 6 focuses on the notion of *rodina*, considering both the more intimate meanings of home among Russian speakers and broader demarcations and manifestations of a sociopolitical homeland. The chapter explores the multiple geographies of home that "traverse scales from the domestic to the global in both material and symbolic ways" (Blunt and Varley 2004, 3), thereby adding new insights to previous studies which mainly focused on *rodina* as a bounded and confining location. In contrast, I argue that *rodina* does not always connote a concrete geographical place but represents an "entity in becoming" (Nowicka 2007, 77) that reflects a dynamic negotiation between inclusion and exclusion through the narratives of marginalization and insidedness, of acceptance and recognition. In the same vein as the rest of the book, this chapter therefore highlights how people's belonging is never finished but is always actively performed.

NOTES

1. The 1992 citizenship law granted citizenship only to the historical inhabitants of the country and people who were able to trace their direct ancestry to individuals

who were Estonian citizens in 1940, right before the Soviet occupation. In turn, official citizenship was denied to almost all Soviet-era settlers and their descendants who could not prove ancestral links to the pre-war republic. Individuals who were unable to prove such ancestral links were forced either to apply for the citizenship of another country or to accept their legal status as resident "aliens."

2. Notably, only a few studies consider the emotional dimension and micro-practices of belonging as an underlying dimension of citizenship. Instead, citizenship continues to be dominated by the liberal conceptions promoted by political science theories, which treat the notion exclusively in normative and institutional terms as the rights and responsibilities of individuals before the state, or, if linked with belonging, citizenship is approached predominantly through the macro lens of a nation state.

3. Pfaff-Czarnecka and Toffin (2011, xvi), for example, argue that belonging encompasses the notion of identity, yet differs from it in its meaning and scope. While identity focuses predominantly on the positioning of the individuals vis-à-vis the other, belonging, on the other hand, is a multidimensional experience that implies a relationship not only with people but also with places and things (May 2011, 370). Thus, it simultaneously interweaves many aspects of human existence in the world.

4. For further critique, see Anthias 2006, 2008; Brubaker and Cooper 2000; Niethammer 2000.

5. The complexity of the Russian-speaking world that cannot be reduced either to exclusive territorial, linguistic, or ethnic terms has been well demonstrated in *Global Russian Cultures* edited by Kevin Platt (2019). This complexity can be especially traced in the context of Central Asia, where the Russian language and culture became largely a transethnic phenomenon, the fundamental givens of a Sovietized urban lifestyle not only among Russians but also among members of local ethnic groups—Kazakhs, Kyrgyz, and Uzbeks. Although this book does not focus on the everyday practices of the Russified titular populations (a theme that deserves a book of its own) I will elaborate on the transethnic quality of the Russian culture in the context of Kazakhstan in chapters 2 and 3.

6. To understand how and when people belong, Nira Yuval-Davis (2006), for example, proposes three intersecting levels of analysis which help redefine belonging as a dynamic process that is constructed along the power axis of difference and is influenced by different historical trajectories and social realities. According to her, belonging can be approached, first of all, through individuals' social locations, which relate to a particular age group, kinship group, or a certain profession. Her second analytical level entails individuals' identifications and emotional attachment to various collectives and groups. In the stories people tell themselves and others about who they are, they directly or indirectly produce images of what being a member in particular groupings and collectivities might mean. At the same time, however, constructions of belonging can be forced on people by ethical and political value systems that determine whether and how the societal boundaries should be drawn. Very similar analytical dimensions can be found in the research of Pfaff-Czarnezka (2011), who, however, calls to study not only the perception and performance of commonality or a sense of mutuality but also material and immaterial attachments. While Pfaff-Czarnezka's first two dimensions are particularly related to the idea of

Zusammengehörigkeit (belonging with), which considers belonging in terms of one's attachment to social groups in which people share common values, experiences, memories, and cultural forms like language, religion, and lifestyle, her third analytical level concentrates on the less researched attachments to material and immaterial worlds.

7. This is not to suggest that no understanding of the notion of space/place has existed before. The first explicit philosophy of place already emerged in the works of Plato and Aristotle, who gave place a particularly powerful position in the lexicon of ideas (on the genealogy of place, see, for example, Cresswell 2015, 25–30).

8. Time or temporality should be, therefore, considered as a salient dimension of our spatial understanding. Although space and time appear and manifest themselves differently, they are inseparable: time "takes on flesh" and becomes visible; likewise, space "becomes charged and responsive to the movements of time" (Bakhtin 1981, 84). In the same way as the social uses of space can redefine the meanings of various periods and temporal experiences (Wunderlich 2010, for example, argues that time is place-specific), so can the qualities of time affect the individual perception of space.

9. Much of the previous scholarship on Russian speakers is structured by Brubaker's (1996) framework on the triadic relationship between the nationalizing post-Soviet states, the external national homeland of Russia and national minorities (Russian speakers). In the first decades following the collapse of the Soviet Union, approaches using this framework focused overwhelmingly on the top-down nationalizing policies and discourses of the independent states, on the relationship between those states and Russia or the policies of Russia with regard to its so-called diaspora abroad. Little attention was paid to the micro-practices of Russian speakers themselves and their everyday attitudes, feelings, and experiences. Although more recent studies expand the nexus and provide a more granular approach to Russian speakers across different countries (e.g. Cheskin 2016; Rees and Burkhanov 2018), the focus remains predominantly on Russian speakers' perceptions of the two bounded spatialities: the state and the external state. In this research, however, I am interested in the interrelated narratives about different spatialities, be they Russia, the state, boundless nature, or a concrete local building, and how these narratives, in turn, structure individual belonging.

10. To analyse the fieldwork data, I turned to a narrative thematic analysis (NTA), most basically understood as a method for "identifying, analyzing, and reporting patterns (themes) within data" (Braun and Clarke 2006: 82). In my research, I was primarily interested in the content of the told stories rather than on the aspects of "telling." In other words, language was viewed merely as a resource to express one's own feelings and to position oneself in relation to the surrounding landscapes, rather than a separate topic of inquiry. For the data analysis the interviews were first transcribed in the Russian language and then anonymized by giving my interlocutors different Slavic names.

11. In the early 2000s, following Kazakhstan's economic growth, a professional middle class began to emerge in the country. Privatization policies of state-properties and reforms of the educational system were directed at strengthening the middle

class and enabling its representatives to secure the basic necessities, such as housing, transport, and higher education (Daly 2008). However, the sudden prosperity was soon replaced by economic challenges, hampering further development of the middle class. As a result, Gulmira Ileuova, the president of the Center for Social and Political Research *Strategiya* (Strategy), notes that in today's Kazakhstan we ought to speak about *bazovyi sloi* (basic layer) rather than a "middle class," in the Western sense of the word (cf. Nastyukova 2018). Based on the surveys conducted by *Strategiya* in 2018, 48.3 per cent of the population in Kazakhstan is represented by those who "have enough money for food and clothing, but struggle to purchase items for a durable use, such as a TV-set or a fridge" (Ibid.).

Chapter 2

Cities of Enduring Dislocation

The mundane encounters of people never take place in a space free from history, material conditions, and power (Valentine 2008, 333). No matter how complex the "interior response" to it, a landscape "remains a social and political fact, designed, owned, and manipulated by people" (Riley 1992, 31); it is a landscape of wider political projects and discourses, framed as politics of belonging, that maintains or reproduces the boundaries of the community in many different ways. All politics of belonging necessarily involve the making of borders and boundaries that are driven by the logics of division or difference and serve as major instruments for governing space as well as controlling social diversity (Fuller and Löw 2017; Low 2017; Tonkiss 2005; Yuval-Davis et. al 2017). These boundaries manifest themselves spatially in numerous social (and economic, cultural, administrative, and political) practices which spread into the whole of society by drawing a line between "inside" and "outside," "us" and "them" (Paasi 1999). In her book, bell hooks (1984), for example, provides striking images of how her life has been conditioned by bordering practices and discourses of spatial exclusion that denied entry of black Americans into the regular world and instead left them at the margins of society:

> To be in the margin is to be part of the whole but outside the main body. As black Americans living in a small Kentucky town, the railroad tracks were a daily reminder of our marginality. Across those tracks were paved streets, stores we could not enter, restaurants we could not eat in, and people we could not look directly in the face. Across those tracks was a world we could work in as maids, as janitors, as prostitutes, as long as it was in a service capacity. We could enter that world, but we could not live there. We had always to return to

the margin, to cross the tracks, to shacks and abandoned houses on the edge of town. (hooks 1984, ix)

Like in many other countries, bordering practices in Estonia and Kazakhstan have been central to the processes of nation-building that followed the collapse of the Soviet Union. Albeit in different ways, the overt nationalization of urban space is ubiquitous in both countries, which sought to reassert the national identity, language, demographic position, economic flourishing, and political hegemony of the nominally state-bearing nation. The efforts to create specific cultural and political narratives were reflected, on the one hand, in exclusionary citizenship and language laws in Estonia that sought to renew its vision as a part of Europe distant from both Russian and Soviet influence, and in Kazakhstan through ambiguous language and education policies aimed at diluting the influence of Russian language and culture. On the other hand, the specific discourses of national identity crystallized spatially through the replacement of the street names and the creation of historical landmarks that commemorate specific national narratives while forgetting or trivializing the narratives of local minorities.

This chapter begins by examining the effects of the political projects of national revival upon everyday life in the borderland cities of Narva and Petropavlovsk. Looking at how the cities have evolved, especially since the 1990s, I uncover the markedly different ways of dealing with social diversity and defining the contours of community belonging in these two countries. Despite the broadest of commonalities described in the Introduction, the contemporary direction taken by each central government is significantly different in terms of geographical and temporal imaginaries that are used to direct national policies. The varying degrees to which the rhetoric of a "return of the nation" has been reinforced and the divergent perceptions of "Russianness" and the Soviet period in general by the Estonian and Kazakhstani elites produce different conditions within which the Russophone populations dwell, experience, and give meaning to their places. In what follows, I demonstrate how the essentialized ideas of Estonian identity and exclusive political boundaries temporally dislocated Narva as an underdeveloped periphery. It became marginal in terms of physical location on the edge of the country, as a cultural landscape in relation to dominant narratives of nationhood, and in the sense of serving as a natural container for people considered potentially disloyal to the country. The radical discontinuity with the past and reconfiguration of space that the state authorities have pursued feed increasingly into the narratives of isolation and inherent exteriority of Narva among the Russophones. In Kazakhstan, the nation-building policies have been rather ambiguous, moving between the construction of a supraethnic Kazakhstani nation that provides a common sense of belonging and a tendency to reinforce ethnonational rhetoric that alienates the large non-Kazakh population. While such ambiguity reinforces a sense of disadvantage and exteriority of the Russian-speaking dwellers of Petropavlovsk, this exteriority carries a substantially different meaning from that in Narva.

Enmeshing the practices of the Estonian and Kazakhstani political elites with the spatial narratives of my Russian-speaking interlocutors, this chapter reconstructs exteriority as both a historically grounded and geographically responsive notion. It is a social, political, and economic strategy by which people are displaced from the confines of a larger "imagined community" as well as the personal experiences of this displacement. Situated in the animating forces of contexts, it manifests itself as an affective "zone of stasis" (Roberts 2002, 82) defined, in the case of Narva, through a negative experience of marginality that reinforces the state-produced boundaries; or, as crystallized in the narratives of Petropavlovsk inhabitants, it can carry positive meaning as a space that provides a sense of a known superior cultural order and security against the socially coded "other." Although exploring the lines of separation in space would make little sense without understanding how spatial connection might occur, as the two represent a part of the same process (Simmel 1997), it is necessary to grasp the ways in which the political production of material and social conditions make exteriority possible in the first place (Thomassen 2012).

NARVA: 'A FORGOTTEN PERIPHERY?'

Narva's story is one of contradictions, a story that blends heterogeneous narratives and imaginaries of inclusion and exclusion, of construction and deconstruction. Throughout its history Narva has demonstrated all merits and disadvantages of being a border settlement. Situated on the margins of different European powers, Narva has been a crossroads of cultures, a marketplace and battlefield for different Western powers, such as the Knights of the Germanic Order and the Swedish and Russian monarchies. At the end of the fifteenth century, Russian Tsar Ivan III ordered to expand Narva castle to the eastern side of the river Narva, which led to the creation of another settlement that received its prosaic name of Ivangorod (the city of Ivan). Until the break-up of the Soviet Union, Narva and Ivangorod functioned as a single composite settlement, with people working in one town and living in another. In the present day, however, the river Narva divides not only the fortresses of two towns, but two countries: Estonia and Russia.

Narva as we know and see it today is almost completely unrecognizable from the one that existed prior to World War II. Previously characterized as the "baroque jewel" of northern Europe, in 1944 it was devastated and reduced almost to rubble by the fierce fighting between German and Soviet forces (Burch and Smith 2007). Its population at the time was only 6,600 people, in comparison to 22,400 in 1939 (Nikiforova 2005, 5). Previous inhabitants that had been evacuated by the Nazi regime were not allowed by the Soviet successor to return to Narva and the population was instead replaced by workers from other neighboring Soviet republics. This decision largely explains why today Estonians make up less than 5 per cent of the overall town population.

After the war, the city was remodeled entirely on the Soviet plan, with only two historic buildings—the town hall and the castle—being restored to the way they were. Seeking to raise the industrial potential of Narva and to restore the city, the authorities encouraged migration from all over the USSR. As a result, Narva became a major prestigious industrial center in the northwest of the Soviet Union's western borderlands. It also offered relatively high living standards and access to goods unavailable elsewhere, which attracted a lot of workers not only from the neighboring republics of Russia, Ukraine, and Belarus, but from the whole of the Soviet Union. Thus, by the end of 1980s, the post-war reconstruction and industrialization turned the region into a largely "Russian-speaking working-class environment" (Pfoser 2017, 2). Consider, for example, the recollection of the family history of one of my respondents, a 34-year-old housewife, whose parents moved to Narva during Soviet times and remained there:

> When my parents came here, it was their conscious choice. For example, I ask my mom, why did you guys even come here? She tells me that back then she had a choice between going to Pskov or Leningrad or to this big industry in Narva. But precisely Narva was famous for being very young. A lot of young people came here; my mom was only fourteen years old. She says, they came here because the city was young, developing, under construction, a city full of jobs. And the conditions were good and the social package too. No one could ever think that this all will end. (Sveta, interview with the author, March 15, 2017)

What does Narva look like today and what changes has it endured since 1991? In the post-Soviet period, the local economy of Estonia's Ida-Virumaa (the northeastern region of which Narva is a part) has been severely affected by deindustrialization and the privatization of old factories, which resulted in a large number of dismissals and consequently high unemployment rates and poverty. At the same time, the investment flows and Western subsidies that became available as a support to the "nationalizing" Baltic states have omitted the Russian-speaking "enclaves" with questionable reputations and, at least potentially, separatist sentiments (Nikiforova 2005, 7).

Scholars like Bohle and Greskovits (2007) connect the internal peripheralization of Narva, visible through economic disparities, unemployment, as well as a lack of local urban development, with the nation-building process in Estonia. In their comparative analysis of the capitalist transformation of Central and Eastern Europe, Bohle and Greskovits argue that the radical socioeconomic restructuring in the subregions of the Baltic states has been intrinsically linked to the agenda of nation-building, which aimed at an impetuous departure from the Soviet past and served the purpose of forging an Estonian national identity.[1] In this context, whereas the majority of ethnic Estonians associated the collapse of the Soviet Union with a "benchmark episode" that allowed their return to a European community, the official state discourse has largely displaced Russian speakers from this "new" spatiotemporal ordering as a "leftover" of the undesirable past.

Seeking to secure the rights and position of ethnic Estonians in the country, the citizenship policy excluded everyone who moved to Estonia after 1940, thereby hoping that Russians would eventually return to their ethnic homeland (Ehala 2009). A similar line of thought was followed by the education and language laws, which sought to prioritize the Estonian language as a way of securing cultural identity, leaving the majority of Russian speakers outside the public space. However, the exclusionary policies that the country has implemented failed to solve the social situation and deep segregation of Estonian society that stretches from the Soviet past. Quite on the contrary, they have reinforced the existence of parallel societies—Estonian and Russian— where both groups have very little or no interaction with each other. For Russian speakers, this situation produced numerous problems associated with economic "stability"[2] and self-identification as well as numerous grievances, reinforced through public discourses that tend to present them as a threat to national cohesion (Seliverstova 2018).

These radical socioeconomic and political transformations have clearly materialized themselves in the urban space of the city. When I first came to Narva, I was struck by the presence of empty houses and streets, conveying a sense of marginality. Taking a stroll through what once was one of the most populated areas in the city, Krenholm, I could not avoid noticing the emptiness of this place: abandoned houses, broken windows, decaying walls. In fact, Krenholm could be regarded as an artefact of hardships that the city has endured since the early 1990s. Located on the western bank of the Narva River, the Krenholm factory has been part of the city since 1857. It was the largest textile factory of the Russian Empire and, during Soviet times, provided employment for a considerable share of Narva's population. The Krenholm area was also one of the liveliest parts of the city, with its own library, *dom kultury* (culture house),[3] hospital, schools, kindergartens, and housing for the factory workers. However, following the break-up of the USSR, the main factory owners soon started experiencing serious financial problems and struggled to sustain the company. Despite financial support from the World Bank, production in Krenholm eventually declined, followed by its full closure in 2011 (Martinez 2018, 163).

What is now left of Krenholm are not only ruins which mark the absence of industrial activity in the city but also growing negligence and state disengagement. Empty apartments, crumbling buildings, decaying parks represent the "phantomic spaces" (Navaro-Yashin 2012, 7) which serve as a reminder of the prosperous Soviet past while simultaneously transmitting a sense of discontinuity, present ruination, alienation, and marginality that spread all around (figure 2.1). The brokenness of places like Krenholm can be, therefore, considered as a form of peripherality (Martinez 2018, 164), a situation of dispossession which symbolizes "withering of Narva" as some of my research participants put it. To some scholars, such distortion or even erosion of the public spaces compounds "the dwindling of a public sense" (Tonkiss 2005, 73), which significantly affects how the city is conceived and experienced by local citizens. Once the cradle of progress and Soviet modernity, the post-Soviet borderland city of Narva was turned by the central government into a crumbling place, an adjacent element that consists of "not comfortable elements" (Martinez 2018, 177). Although in the past years there have been several state attempts to rebrand Narva from the most Russian city in the European Union (EU) into an Estonian space through a

Figure 2.1   The Abandoned Building of Krenholm Factory. *Source*: Author's photograph, July 2020.

series of cultural projects and the development of environmental and sports tourism (Makarychev 2018), these more positive changes continue to coexist with rather negative official narratives that still question the belonging of Russian speakers. How this "out-of-placeness" and Orientalization feed into the general trajectories and the dynamics of everyday exclusion among the Russophones frames the discussion of the next section.

"I AM A LITTLE BIT ASHAMED OF THIS TOWN"

Sipping on his cup of tea and pensively staring outside the window, Dima, a forty-two-year-old Narvan businessman, tried to explain to me how his city acquired a marginal position within Estonia and what this position meant to him personally. The enduring mental perception of the borderland as a part of the whole yet persistently outside of the main body has dramatically affected Dima's life, who still has an "alien" passport, does not speak Estonian, and carries a feeling of being "foreign" when visiting other Estonian cities. Dima told me that Mart Laar, the former prime minister of Estonia, recently acknowledged that abandoning Ida-Virumaa was a big mistake: "These words contain the fates of my generation. You sit like a fool and watch how this old man confesses that politicians did not pay attention to your region. You sit and understand how this decision affected your life. He confessed, way to go. But our fates already took a wrong turn" (Dima, interview with the author, February 15, 2017).

During my fieldwork, a sense that Narva was exteriorized from the rest of the country as a backward periphery was present in most of the narratives shared by my interlocutors. What was once a "showcase of socialism," a center full of jobs and opportunities that attracted people throughout the Soviet Union, is now the site of a depressing socioeconomic situation, with the lowest average net incomes and the highest figures for unemployment and relative poverty (Kalvet 2010, 6). In my interviews with Russian speakers, such drastic changes were often reflected through the narratives of spatial "deconstruction," a process through which Narva was dislocated from the Estonian political, cultural, and economic mainstream. Zinaida, a kindergarten teacher in her fifties, spoke, for example, about the tremendous input of Russian speakers into the development of Narva and how it was laid to waste in the 1990s. After playing a central role in Soviet times, Zinaida notes, Narva was turned into a peripheral place, with people who toiled in the industries becoming "useless" for the state:

> The nineties, they have bulldozed the lives of people. Well, the whole city, the whole population here. For Narva it was a big kick because everything started

from here. Because Narva, and I repeat again, was a city of workers. Everything was concentrated here—Baltic, Estonian hydroelectric stations. All these were developed by Russians here. But now no one even tries to build here anything, so that people could work. Schools are closed down, in the Krenholm area they have now decided to leave only one school. It used to be three. (Zinaida, interview with the author, March 14, 2017)

Another research participant, Sveta, whom I already mentioned earlier, also had difficulties coming to terms with the dramatic changes in the city. As a child, she spent her time in the Krenholm area: attending kindergarten, going to school and dance courses, playing with her friends in Gerasimov Park. Now these places represent a mere memory (figure 2.2):

The Gerasimov Culture House, I cannot look at it without tears. It is a wreck, even the windows are all knocked out. Nothing is left of this place. Once this culture house used to be surrounded by a beautiful park with fountains, full of kids. All parades and celebrations in the city used to take place there, 9th of May, 1st of May. Numerous cultural events, gymnastics and music classes all used to take place at Gerasimov. There was life and it was vibrant. What we see now is a few shabby columns and slowly, quietly corroding swings of

Figure 2.2   The Abandoned Culture House, DK Gerasimov. *Source*: Author's photograph, July 2020.

the demolished amusement park. (Sveta, interview with the author, March 15, 2017)

For Sveta, the despair around the Gerasimov Culture House represents a form of "interrupted temporality" (Navaro-Yashin 2012, 7), a rupture between the good life of Soviet prosperity and the present decline, insecurity, and loss of jobs. The disappearance of familiar cultural geographies happened through the creation of new symbols of territoriality, which manifested themselves in the form of new monuments, as well as in the renaming of social spaces by using Estonian names and key figures. This manifestation of state narratives at the level of everyday life, coupled with the corrosive projects of "ruination" of old Soviet spaces which produced in Narva numerous sites left to decompose, left its inhabitants with uncertainty over the ongoing redefinition of identities and turned the city into a so-called zone of abandonment (Stoler 2013, 9, 23).

These deconstruction and temporal ruptures are often not seen as one's own failures to adapt to the new realities and developments in the country, the way it is commonly framed by political and medial discourses (Malloy 2009). It is rather depicted as a deliberate attempt of the state to abandon the city and position Russian speakers as "other." Vera, a social worker in her forties, tells me directly that Narva was "consciously and deliberately imbued with a negative image" (interview with the author, February 16, 2017). She recalls reading an article about Narva which left her with a bitter aftertaste. Vera was appalled by the words of a journalist from Tallinn that still echo in her head: "Heavy-laden clouds move over Narva, a crowd of tired and wrinkled women go to toil at Krenholm at 6 a.m., where they will spend the next eight hours without straightening their backs." She assured me that every city has the sun and the clouds, hard work and happy hours, but Narva is always singled out, "left somewhat apart, somewhat isolated." These remarks are very similar to that of Natalya, a fifty-three-year-old museum employee:

Natalya: In the past twenty-five years they have destroyed the whole city.
Author: They who?
Natalya: I don't exactly know who, I won't . . . Local government is nothing without the state. I am not strong in politics, I can only talk to you like that at a kitchen level, how I see it from below. From atop it all looks fine. Our average salary is 1000 Euros. But who has it? When they closed all factories, I became unemployed. This city was so hardworking. How many factories, sewing fabrics did we have? People would go to Krenholm in three shifts. The street that leads there, formerly Lenin Street, was always full. Everyone was occupied, people were earning, were setting goals. Now we are the city of beggars, we don't have any work here. When we have work, the salaries are delayed. People

go *v sotsialku* (to social services), sign up for disability benefits, drink, use drugs. Already a third generation full of problems. But they didn't come up with this life. And now Estonia can't stand Ida-Virumaa. It is like *yazva na tele Estonii* (an ulcer on the Estonian body). (Natallya, interview with the author, March 21, 2017)

To demonstrate the internal "otherness" of Narva and its dwellers, Natalya uses the medical term "ulcer"—a painful sore in the stomach lining in need of urgent treatment. The specific demographic situation in Narva and its direct proximity to the Russian border is a present-day reminder for Estonians of the "evil" socialism under which its population had suffered and which it seeks to carve out (Kesküla 2015). The attempts to Estonianize or to "cure" the city by inscribing new national narratives into the urban landscape are complicated by the presence of local minority identities, memories, and practices, which often manifest in divergent perceptions of urban iconography and spatiality. Injection of the Estonian language into the body of Narva is also only partially successful, as its use remains limited. As a result, such failed efforts to homogenize national narratives only strengthen the image of Narva as "not quite Estonian" (Pfoser 2014, 273), as a place that looks "eastwards towards Moscow rather than westwards towards Tallinn" (Burch and Smith 2007, 920). This way, the exclusion of the Russian-speaking working class, associated with the "socialist mentality," was often seen as a justified measure by the national politics seeking to safeguard the western orientation and the liberal economy of the state (Kesküla 2015, 99). As Dima sums up: "We are kind of in Estonia, but we are foreign. And it is not us who have drawn this line, but them" (Dima, interview with the author, February 15, 2017).

The horizontal interaction with fellow ethnic Estonians often seems to strengthen such perspectives. As the conversation with Vera progressed, she expressed her unease of not being taken as *svoi*,[4] as a rightful part of the Estonian community. Belonging to a larger collective would in this sense require subsuming one's own language and culture to a dominant discourse that privileges the language and culture of ethnic Estonians. Those who fail are often left outside the Estonian national community (Kruusvall et al. 2009). However, scholars like Zabrodskaya (2015) argue that even when Russian speakers decide to move along the road of cultural and linguistic integration, the younger Estonian titulars still demonstrate unwillingness to accept them as their "own people." This is clearly evident in the narrative of Vera:

The feeling of being *svoi sredi chuzhikh i chuzhoi sredi svoikh* (*svoi* among the strangers and foreign among *svoikh*) still prevails. I have Estonian citizenship, which I received about seven years ago. And I don't really speak Estonian so well, maybe on a B2-level, though I want to. I consider Estonia my country, not Russia or any other country. But I don't feel myself *svoei*. Despite being able to vote, I always feel my inferiority because of the language. If I want to write any official letter, I would have to do this in Estonian. And if you have an appointment somewhere, there will be a different attitude to you when you speak Russian. (Interview with the author, March 16, 2017)

While much has been written here on the political techniques of exclusion and the dramatic effects it had on the everyday lives of Russian speakers, it is also necessary to attend to the ways in which the dwellers might themselves participate in the exclusionary discourses and practices. On the one hand, my respondents expressed unease with the negative labeling of Narva and their own marginality within the context of Estonia; on the other hand, however, the process of externally enforced dislocation was entwined with the process of the internalization of this dislocation. Thereby, Narva was self-constructed as a place of inherent exteriority, as different from the rest of the country. Natalya, who blames "them" at the top for neglecting Narva and turning it into an Estonian ulcer, herself draws a clear line between Narva and the rest of Estonia. She used to live in Tallinn, but then due to personal reasons moved to the borderland to be unpleasantly surprised by the amount of disorder:

When I was in Tallinn, I wasn't Estonian. Then I came here and I understood that I am not Russian either. I got so used to the Estonian mentality, culture, way of life. Estonians, they are law abiding, we can't deny that. And then here, this national *razgil'dyaistvo* (slovenliness). [. . .] I have been living here for fifteen years, but the feeling is always there, that it's only temporary—that I am here temporarily, and not forever. Why? I have somehow distanced myself from everything and with every occasion tell people that I am not Narvan. I am a little bit ashamed of this town. I don't like that people living here despise it. (Natalya, interview with the author, March 21, 2017)

Dima, who feels dramatically affected by living at the borderland, also highlights how many of his friends started positioning themselves in opposition to Estonia:

People here are *zatiukany estonskim yazykom* (being hit by the state again and again with constant quibbles about the Estonian language), about the fact that we are foreign here, saying 'train station—suitcase—Russia.'[5] Of course, people start drawing conclusions. They are angry in silence, carry this anger in them and then react accordingly by saying that we are separate. Estonia should come here more often. (Dima, interview with the author, February 15, 2017)

Research by Zabrodskaya and Ehala (2010) highlights that the numerous grievances and discomfort that Russian speakers experience leads them to construct their region as a "significant, mentally imagined place, a small fatherland, where they can 'hide' from the rest of Estonia." Although the experiences of "dislocation" and practices of self-Orientalization certainly point in this direction, in the next chapters I demonstrate both the resilience of Russian speakers to present Narva as a continuously Estonian place and their agility in constructing positive alternative images of the city. However, to understand how the process of multilayered belonging occurs, it was necessary to first comprehend how exteriority comes into being. This exteriority, as this section highlighted, manifests itself through the narratives of spatial deconstruction, temporal discontinuity, and the perception of one's own uselessness in the new post-Soviet context. It is in many ways different from the dynamics of inclusion/exclusion in Petropavlovsk.

THE NORTHERN GATES OF KAZAKHSTAN

Throughout the past years, research on Kazakhstan has expanded considerably, focusing on the elite schemes for ruling and transforming space and society (e.g. Brubaker 1996; Diener 2016; Kolstø 1998); on the state- and nation-building strategies of the government (Cummings 2005, 2010; Schatz 2004); questions of nationhood (Dave 2007; Peyrouse 2007); language and identity (Kosmarskaya 2013; Wingender 2015); as well as ideas of modernity, progress, and urbanity in the major cities of Almaty and Nur-Sultan (previously Astana) (Bissenova 2014; Koch 2010, 2014; Laszczkowski 2016). At the same time, borderland places like Petropavlovsk have remained largely beyond academic attention. Prior to my field trip, I could, therefore, only draw on online newspaper articles to gather preliminary information about the city. These articles depicted Petropavlovsk as the "Northern Gates of Kazakhstan"—a place where Kazakhstan gradually ends and Russia begins.

My own encounter with the "Northern Gates" started when I disembarked from the train and confusingly found myself at the railway station belonging to Russia. Until recently, the Petropavlovsk branch of Russian South Ural railways even resembled a separate state, a *gosudarstvo v gosudarstve* (country in another country) (Brezhnaya 2016), which had its own kindergartens and schools for the children of railways employees, culture clubs, the Lokomotiv sports stadium, a hospital, housing, dormitories, and even their own telephone utilities. While to an outside observer this spatial layering might be confusing, the train station is, in fact, a very symbolic representation of the transnational entanglements between Kazakhstan and Russia which, in many ways, define the city today.

Founded in 1752, Petropavlovsk was thought to serve as a military fortress of the Novo-Ishim defensive line of the Russian Tsarist Empire in the south of Siberia. Pressured by the devastating raids of the Dzungars on the nomadic Kazakh tribes on the West Siberian borders, the Russian Senate saw the urgent need to construct a new Ishim line that would stretch from the natural border of *Zverinaya Golova* (Beast Head) on the Tobol River to the Omsk Fortress on the Irtysh River. In the summer of that year, on the feast day of Saints Peter and Paul, military servicemen and local peasants laid the fortress around which the city consequently grew, receiving its name in honor of Peter and Paul: Petropavlovsk.

In the nineteenth century, while preserving its military and strategic importance, Petropavlovsk became a major center for trade and economic and spiritual contact not only between the Kazakh and Russian people but also beyond. The city that emerged near the walls of the fortress lay at the intersection of caravan routes from Russia through West Siberia to the far regions of Central Asia. One of the first documented *torg* (trade bargains) in Petropavlovsk, where Russian merchants exchanged goods with merchants from China, Mongolia, Tashkent, and Bukhara, dates back to 1773 (Kikimov 1998). Such trade relations have, in turn, contributed to the gradual transformation of the fortress into a prosperous city, of which many historical landmarks have been preserved until today (Dysenov 2017).

After the October Revolution in Russia, a whole series of administrative and territorial transformations took place, making Petropavlovsk first a part of the Omsk Province, and from 1936, a part of the newly formed Kazakh Soviet Socialist Republic (Kazakh SSR). During the early years of Soviet rule, the north-central steppe saw successive famines, purges of Kazakh leadership, and the subsequent flight of the Kazakh people to the east.[6] However, from the 1930s until the early 1950s, the population in the city was bolstered under the resettlement policies and Stalin's deportations of people deemed threatening to the state, including *kulaks* (landowners), "bandits," "nationalists," ex-prisoners of war, and repatriated persons (Diener 2016, 3). During the Virgin Land Campaign in the 1950s–1960s, around two million (mainly) Russian, Ukrainian, and Belarusian "volunteers" surged to the territory of today's Kazakhstan, considerably diluting the ethnic Kazakh population (Peyrouse 2008, 2). Though reshuffled within various administrative units, a large population of Russians and other Russified groups remained in the northern borderlands of Kazakhstan and played profound roles in shaping local culture.

These historical economic interdependencies, peculiarities of the demographics, and cultural entanglements, which originated even before the Soviet cultural transformation and intense linguistic Russification, explain in large part the particular course that independent Kazakhstan took with regard to its nation-building project. This course represents a markedly different response to the end of the Soviet Union than that of Estonia, which sought to distance itself from both the Soviet past and its Russian-speaking inhabitants—the reminders of the oppressive colonizing regime. Although in the wake of independence Kazakh elites supported a postsocialist "return of the nation" and chose an ethnic state name, the narratives of the nation are rather more complex (Diener 2016).[7] On the one hand, the elites engage with the new modes of identification through ethnonational rhetoric; on the other hand, they highlight the need for a national identity that exceeds ethnic, cultural, or political differences (Diener and Hagen 2013).

Given the challenges of potential Russian separatism[8] that could undermine the territorial integrity of the newly independent state and rising Kazakh ethnonationalism that demands the state promote an ethnically and ethnolinguistically determined Kazakh identity, Kazakh elites face a dilemma: whether to submit to the ethnonationalist aspirations and to alienate the large non-Kazakh population or to promote more inclusive forms of identity (Rees and Williams 2017, 2). This dilemma has led to a rather ambiguous process of nationalization (Kadyrzhanov 2014; Kudaibergenova 2012) that walks a fine line between reviving ethnic Kazakh tradition and forming a unified nation out of its polyethnic and polyconfessional population. Thereby, the government delicately balances between a transnational "Eurasian" cultural identity and a more inclusive "Kazakhstani" civic identity, while simultaneously promoting the Kazakh ethnonation (Diener 2016b).

As noted by Isaacs and Polese (2015, 373), the underlying ethnic diversity and the geographical concentration of minorities in Central Asian countries, including Kazakhstan, meant that the region's elites could only maintain their power and political stability by constructing a "common-sense of belonging" and "groupness." This contributed to the formation of the definition "Kazakhstani" and "Kazakhstaniness" as an ideal of a supraethnic identity widely used by state authorities since 2007. It was meant to be a "blueprint for strengthening the inter-ethnic harmony of Kazakhstan for years to come" that acknowledged the claims of all people to a home within its territory (Diener 2016b, 140; The Doctrine of the National Unity). The construction of civic-identity-based society in Kazakhstan, united by common history, culture, and language, became, for instance, the dominant idea of the recent Patriotic Act, called *Mängilik El* or "eternal state" (Sharipova et al. 2017, 206). While ostensibly any citizen of Kazakhstan can claim membership in this supraethnic group, additional criteria have been identified by the state; central among them is knowledge of the Kazakh language (Rees and Williams 2017). In this context, despite the potential inclusivity of these nation-building policies, the inhabitants in cities like Petropavlovsk, where daily life is dominated by the Russian language, regard the focus on Kazakh as increasingly pejorative.

It is seen as an element of ethnonationalization that seeks to underprivilege Russian speakers (Laruelle and Peyrouse 2007).

Tendencies to construct totalizing narratives of national identity, while simultaneously supporting ideas of a "return of the nation" are clearly embedded in the urban landscape of Petropavlovsk. The nation-building program is expressed especially through the ambiguous engagement with Soviet artefacts and entrenched commemorative practices of the past (Cummings 2010). Since Kazakhstan's independence, government officials have pursued several campaigns to renegotiate the contours of national identity and belonging through urban space by erecting new monuments of Kazakh historical and cultural figures, or by renaming streets to reference Kazakh culture. So, for example, *Kommunisticheskaya* Street is now *Zhumabaeva,* honoring Soviet Kazakh writer, publicist, and founder of modern Kazakh literature Magzhamn Zhumabaev. What is now *Zhabaeva* (carrying the name of a Kazakh national *akyn*—an improvising poet and singer) used to be *Kirova. Dzerzhinskogo* was renamed into *Altynsarina* in honor of another Kazakh writer, Ibrai Altynsarin, and famously *Lenina* into *Konstitutsiya,* honoring the constitution of the independent Kazakhstan.

The official attempts to create discontinuity in the "old" narratives of the city and to construct new national histories are, however, often complicated by the resilience of minority identities and people's everyday practices and habits. For example, following the decision of the town planning council, in 2011 the last Lenin monument was dismantled and replaced by a cartoon figure, Captain Vrungel, to advertise a soon-to-be-built water park. The decision provoked overwhelmingly negative reaction among the local population, forcing the government to reinstall the monument in one of the central squares of the city.[9] Bearing these complexities in mind, the nation-building policies of the Kazakhstani state could not be regarded as outright denying or seeking to marginalize the nontitular Russian-speaking population. In fact, Diener and Hagen (2013) note how despite the efforts to develop an ethnonational identity and to emphasize the Kazakh language and traditions, several localities still genuinely appreciate Russian culture in the postsocialist period. "Russianness" in the northern regions of the country is, thus, a part of a broader concept of Kazakhstan. It is both the "core" and the "other" at the same time (Diener 2016, 13).

In stark contrast to Estonia where the Russian language and culture are seen as symbols of repression that need to be ousted from public space, Russification under Russian/Soviet rule in Kazakhstan produced different effects. For Kazakhstan, being first a part of the Russian empire and then under the rule of the USSR created a great incentive for further development of the region. Advances in cultural modernization, including the increased level of literacy of the local population, led to the considerable Russification of the native Kazakh community many of whom came to associate the Russian language with the promises of an urbanized lifestyle and prestige (Kosmarskaya 2013, 4). In this process, a special population segment took shape of Kazakhs who, according to Natalya Kosmarskaya and Artyom Kosmarski (2019, 76), were sharply distinct from "their provincial, largely rural coethnics in form of life and language preferences." This population has relegated the Kazakh language to second place, becoming gradually the bearers, consumers, and, in some cases, producers of Russian culture.

The historical formation of a Russified community in Kazakhstan, especially in the north of the country, contributed to the construction of solidarities above ethnic boundaries, whereby the Russian language and culture ceased to be the exclusive properties of ethnic Russians only (see more on that in chapter 3). Indeed, bordering and "othering" practices in Kazakhstan run more often through other moral geographies and tend to carry a non-ethnic character. In a series of articles, Natalie Koch (2012, 2014, 2015) thoroughly demonstrates how Kazakhstan's social spatiality figures in popular imaginaries through the urban/rural and north/south dichotomies. The rhetorical production of this moral geography becomes visible through the public discourse, in which southerners and Kazakh nationalists, for example, frequently portray the north as urban, "modern, culturally and linguistically Russified and civilized" (Koch 2014, 437). In contrast, the northern urbanites and Russified Kazakhs code the south as rural, "traditional, uncivilized, and culturally and linguistically 'Kazakh'" (Ibid.).[10] The dividing line is also closely tied up with class divisions (as urbanites and northerners have historically been in the privileged economic and political positions), race (whereby the poor are marked by their skin color and ascribed to the rural and provincial space), and levels of nationalization (with the southerners being represented as "retrogressive nationalists") (Ibid., 437–38). Although such regionalisms and binary visions of society reveal numerous social cleavages, they also highlight the persistent support for—and the high level of prestige of—Russian in some parts of Kazakhstan. Russianness remains thereby a legitimate component of the state.

As such, we could argue that despite numerous state attempts to Kazakhify the urban spaces, iconography, and identity of Petropavlovsk, the state does not deliberately seek to marginalize Russian speakers through the process of "othering," as is often the case in Estonia. The bordering line in Kazakhstan runs instead more commonly through other spatial geographies, reflecting the inequalities between the rural and urban worlds that already existed under socialism. In this sense, the economic decline and relatively high unemployment rates that Petropavlovsk has been experiencing since the early 1990s should not necessarily be seen as a deliberate peripheralization of the region based on the ideology of national revival and discontinuity with the past.

Rather, scholars like Alima Bissenova (2017) connect the deurbanization and deindustrialization of cities like Petropavlovsk to a poor distribution of state fiscal resources, which are directed at the continued urbanization of Nur-Sultan, Almaty, as well as a few other regional centers, such as Shymkent and oil-rich Atyrau and Aktau.

THE "RUSSIAN-SPEAKING SPACE" OF PETROPAVLOVSK

"*My vstrechaemsia na Lenina*" (we meet on Lenin Street) was a typical reply to my question when arranging a meeting with my Russian-speaking interlocutors. In fact, I quite frequently overheard the local inhabitants calling streets by their old Soviet names, avoiding references in Kazakh, which, as Anssi Paasi (1995, 48) and Joma Nazpary (2002, 151) note, can point towards a gap between socialist and postsocialist authoritative visual representations of the city and the everyday perceptions among ordinary residents.

The undesired Kazakhization of urban landscapes in Petropavlovsk was indeed a prominent theme in numerous conversations that I had with Russian speakers. When recounting life in Petropavlovsk, many of them blamed Kazakhs for monopolizing urban spaces, state posts, and places in higher education to the disadvantage of the Russophone population. For example, Anton, a 31-year-old audio technician who works in a concert hall, said that he was unable to finish university as his grant was given to one of the *oralmans*. From the Kazakh language *oralman* is translated as "returnee"—a Kazakh repatriate (I will come back to the perception of the new Kazakh migrants in the city later in this section). Another research participant, Toma, a woman in her late twenties, expressed her intentions to emigrate because she is concerned for the future of her child:

> You know, we live in a country where the Muslim society with different traditions dominates. So, the language—I mean, I know that my child won't be able to speak Kazakh. She won't be able to understand it well at school and get a decent education. To get a good job here or anywhere in Kazakhstan, for example somewhere in the government where they have good benefits, will be simply impossible. (Toma, interview with the author, September 15, 2016)

Nastya, a young graduate from a medical college in her early twenties told me that she could not find a job because she is Russian:

Well, when I was trying to get into a college . . . I had good grades and was certain that I would get a scholarship. But they decided to provide scholarships only to a Kazakh group. And that was it, I had to pay for my studies. Then, when I started looking for a job, it took me months. I would come to a hospital and they would ask me, 'Do you speak Kazakh?' I would say no. And they would answer, 'Well, too bad.' And would hire—and they hired only Kazakhs. And us only afterwards to fill the leftover positions. . . . In Kazakhstan, they prioritize Kazakhs. (Nastya, interview with the author, September 6, 2016)

The peculiar language situation and a perceived disadvantage compared with Kazakhs led Arsen, a student and a freelance photographer in his thirties, to conclude that he lives "not exactly in his place," but rather "out of place":

Arsen: Somehow, I usually forget that I live in Kazakhstan.
Author: How come, where do you live then?
Arsen: Well, in some kind of, I don't know. . . . In some kind of Russian-speaking space, I would say. I sort of understand, that it's not Russia here, but Kazakhstan. But Russia is somehow more in my consciousness, Russian culture, Russian language, Russian people. Therefore, I somehow forget about it. (Arsen, interview with the author, August 24, 2016)

What is particularly interesting here is the conception of being "out of place" mentioned by Arsen. "Out of place" is not equivalent to the experiences of exteriority in Narva. It is not about being ousted from a public space and being neglected and marginalized, nor does it necessarily carry a negative connotation. Rather, it symbolizes the grounding disjuncture between the diverse landscapes that Russian speakers inhabit in Kazakhstan.[11] According to Arjun Appadurai (1996), people simultaneously inhabit numerous dimensions of cultural flows, which he terms ethnoscapes, mediascapes, technoscapes, financescapes, and ideoscapes. All of these landscapes represent the building blocks of the "imagined worlds" constituted by the "historically situated imaginations of persons and groups" (Appadurai 1996, 33). In this sense, the local ethnoculturalscape, which Arsen and other respondents view as "Russian," is challenged by the internal rural to urban migration from the south. The arrival of southerners leads, in turn, to a physical compression of the Russophone cultural space, contributing to the conception of out-of-placeness among the long-term city dwellers. The local scape also coexists uneasily with the ideoscape directly linked to the state ideology and the vision of the "proper" Kazakh nation understood especially through the knowledge of the Kazakh language.

Although the language was not a precondition for acquiring citizenship in the new state, it did become one of the key criteria for defining the supraethnic Kazakhstani nation. It also became a formal precondition for getting or keeping a job in the public sector. There are further inconsistencies and ambiguities which correspond both to the real domination of Kazakh in the state and its nominal identification with all ethnic groups, such as the ambiguous wordings of the constitution, which both identifies the state with the people and opens possibilities for an interpretation which may award Kazakhs a privileged position, and the speeches of the former president Nazarbayev, which prioritize Kazakh language on the one hand, and emphasize the importance of Russian on the other hand (see also Nazpary 2002, 146–58; Dave 2007).

As a result, there is a growing unease with administrative Kazakhization, leading people like Arsen to distance themselves from Kazakhstan and argue for living in an exterior "Russian-speaking space." In this sense, the reproduction of a Russian-speaking space in individual narratives is a way to create a place of stasis that is legitimately and continuously dominated by the Russian language and culture, as well as to protect themselves from the sociocultural expectations of the new state that they cannot necessarily meet. For example, Ruslan, an IT-specialist in his thirties, describes Petropavlovsk as a Russian city precisely because of the Russian language that can be freely practiced here:

> So, I consider, at least in the near future, Petropavlovsk to be a Russian city. . . . Here you can easily speak Russian, and no one will look at you askance, unlike, for example, how it can be in the southern regions of Kazakhstan, as I was told. But I have a feeling that the local authorities are systematically trying to change it. For example, they rename the streets and other objects into Kazakh, establish university quotas for southerners, thus taking away the scholarships from the locals. The local population endures so many things. They show their resentment briefly online and that's it. The local government does not consider our opinion. Perhaps, the only thing that the local population won't allow to do is to rename the city, for example, to Kyzyl Zhar. The city was named in honor of Saints Peter and Paul. Yes, so far Petropavlovsk is a Russian city for me. Will it ever cease to be such? Probably, but for this, numerous years must pass. (Ruslan, interview with the author, September 12, 2016)

Perception of Petropavlovsk as a Russian-speaking space is thus strengthened through the notion of the shared Russian language, common traditions, history, and solidarities beyond ethnic boundaries. As crystallized in the narratives of my respondents, the Russian language especially is regarded as a vital and intimate dimension of belonging to a place and community. Alongside a deep connection to the Russian language comes resistance to learning Kazakh from both the nontitular population and the urban ethnic Kazakhs themselves. In the accounts of Nazpary (2002) and Sebastien Peyrouse (2007, 2008), the emotional relationship of some urban Kazakhs to the Russian and Kazakh languages is very complex and contradictory. Although they lack the knowledge of Kazakh and blame it on the Soviet colonial policies of Russification, they are more attached to Russian emotionally and inscribe Kazakh with a stigma, as the language of rural people. The continuity of this stigma then indicates Russian cultural hegemony, which provides the basis for Russians and other non-Kazakhs to feel at home in their localities despite the Kazakhization policies of the state (Nazpary 2002, 156).

Petropavlovsk has been, therefore, often constructed as Russophone in order to maintain moral geographies where Russian speakers, as well as other urbanized Russian-speaking ethnic Kazakhs, are "in place." In this sense, the arrivals of Kazakh migrants from the southern rural areas of the country and *oralmans* from Uzbekistan, China, Turkmenistan, Russia, and Kyrgyzstan, as a part of Kazakhization, are seen as transgressive acts that erode the urban lifestyle and threaten to demodernize the city. Some nationalist accounts have earlier noted that demographic, migrational, and social Kazakhization will provide the cities with a good portion of Kazakh traditionalism, helping to overcome the rural-urban imbalances of the Soviet times (Gali 2004). However, scholars like Bissenova (2017) and Mateusz Laszczkowski (2016), who conducted a thorough research in Almaty and Nur-Sultan, argue that, quite on the contrary, the longstanding urban dwellers of the cities often hold Kazakh traditionalism to be responsible for numerous problems in Kazakh society, state, and cities—from corruption scandals to urban disorders—and Kazakhization in general is equated with the ruralization, Orientalization, and backwardness of the country.

In this light, several of my respondents have expressed discomfort with the increasing numbers of arriving southerners, who arguably "dress like *kolkhoznik*,"[12] speak accented Russian or no Russian at all, and are "uncultured." My roommate, a man in his twenties, with whom I stayed over the course of my entire fieldwork, on several occasions emphasized his Russianness, defined by the richness of Russian history, while at the same time distancing himself from Kazakhs with diminishing words like *mambety* (a derogatory term meaning poor, uneducated, and often predisposed to crime).[13] Furthermore, he stressed his love for the Russian "kitchen," the space which, according to Svetlana Boym (1994, 147), during Soviet times was actively used by people as a site of rituals of private conversation about the most important matters of public concern. While the tradition of long kitchen conversation seems to have an afterlife in the post-Soviet period, the meanings of it have shifted. It is now being used by my roommate as a way to draw boundaries between Russians or Russified ethnic Kazakhs and rural ethnic Kazakhs:

> I mean the abstract understanding of it, where we have vodka, where the secrets are held, where the new thoughts are born. Particularly the 'Russian kitchen'

and not the one where *Beshparmak* [a traditional Kazakh dish] is being cooked, a kitchen that symbolizes Russian spirit and culture. (Andrei, a personal conversation with the author, March 2016)

With the arrival of Kazakhs from the south comes the contestation for control over certain public spaces like universities, public squares, and clubs. Living in Petropavlovsk, I heard numerous stories of (and also observed) confrontations between Russian speakers and Kazakh migrants. In these stories, my conversation partners often placed themselves into a superior position, depicting themselves as the socially coded opposite of the rural southerners—more cultured, more civilized. The arrival of migrants was connected to disorder which represents a threat to law-abiding citizens. In her research on the experiences of rural Kazakhs in Almaty, Saulesh Yessenova (2003, 164) similarly highlights the desire of the urban dwellers to protect the known intellectual and cultural order of their space by marginalizing recent rural migrants and positioning them as the "urban underclass." Moya Flynn and Natalya Kosmarskaya (2014, 12) also argue that such salient anti-migrant discourse, which is present not only in Kazakhstan but also in other postsocialist contexts, became a convenient tool for the long-term urban residents to blame migrants from primarily southern rural areas for the wider difficulties of post-Soviet contemporary life. Commonality in such bordering practices across the country only reinforces the idea that Kazakhstan's moral geography is rather more often split between urban/rural and north/south dichotomies than simply between different ethnicities.

GEOGRAPHIES OF EXTERIORITY

The collapse of the Soviet Union shattered an overreaching ideological framework, economic structure, and system of relations between people, creating numerous problems and uncertainties (Alexander and Buchli 2007; Bös and Zimmer 2006). Since the 1990s, Estonia and Kazakhstan have been dealing differently with these uncertainties, drawing different boundaries to create order out of the chaos that emerged as a result of attempts to forge new social links and define new communities of belonging. These divergent directions feed into markedly different experiences of exclusion and meanings of exteriority among the Russophone populations. In Estonia, the ethnic, linguistic, historical, and spatial boundaries were formed clearly against the Russian "other." This led to visible social and ethnic segregation across the whole country as well as the spatiotemporal exteriorization of the borderland city of Narva, which came to represent an adjacent periphery that was allegedly disloyal and insufficiently socialized into the larger whole. As such, with time the "otherness" of Russian speakers has been perpetuated rather than removed, which feeds into a self-Orientalizing image of the city characterized through the notions of alienation, abandonment, and marginalization. Thereby, Russophones themselves experience the difficulty of creating a sense of belonging in a place marked as inherently on the outside. In Kazakhstan, the predominantly nonethnic character of the numerous social divisions as well as a general sense of cultural affinity with "Russianness" among the urbanized segments of society (including ethnic Kazakhs) give shape to a different representation of exteriority that does not necessarily separate the core and the rest of the society. Rather, it is a moral geography that emerges in response to the undesired Kazakhization and safeguards the known everyday order against a backward, Oriental rural "other."

In both cases, an existential sense of dislocation becomes centralized in the everydayness of Russian speakers, establishing itself as normality. Having said this, the boundaries of exteriority are not indefinitely fixed, and are open to possibilities for change, transformation, and perpetual negotiation between "in" and "out" in the complex spatial system. More than that, there is no "outside" without "inside," the two being part of the same relational process. Both are strategically complicit in the mutual constitution (Roberts 2002). According to Simmel (1997, 171), separation would have no meaning at all if we had not earlier connected two distinct spaces in our practical thoughts, our needs, and our fantasy. As such, narratives of dislocation coexist and develop alongside alternative attachments on multiple levels: local, national, and global. They are, therefore, not pregiven but emerge anew with specific "dispositions and sensibilities" being developed through the process of dwelling and orienting ourselves in relation to surrounding places (Ingold 2000, 153).

In the next chapters I demonstrate, therefore, how Russian speakers simultaneously internalize multiple, overlapping scales of identification with their places of residence, despite seemingly cemented feelings of disadvantage and marginalization. While boundaries can be dividers, they can also enable the construction of new relationships (Cohen 2000). They do not necessarily entail the outright dissociation of Russian speakers from their neighboring Kazakhs and vice versa but provide connections and opportunities for engagement. Against this background, studying belonging can fruitfully benefit from shifting the analytical focus from the notions of dislocation and "otherness" towards transgression and change.

NOTES

1. The effects of the transition to a market economy upon the lives of Russian speakers are also noted in an article by Alena Pfoser (2017), wherein she briefly

discusses how the economic recession of 2009 and 2010 has strongly affected the working-class population, which in Estonia consists largely of Russian speakers. She notes that class-related marginalization intersects with ethnicity and is further intensified by the nationalizing policies of the Estonian state.

2. The language and citizenship laws as well as economic restructuring have ensured that the members of the Russian-speaking community find themselves with lower incomes, higher unemployment rates, and a lower life expectancy that ethnic Estonians (Leping and Toomet 2008).

3. In the USSR, *dom kultury* was a specialized cultural and educational organization, which included diverse amateur groups, sports sections, a cinema hall and so on.

4. Since *svoi* is a grammatical form that does not have an equivalent in English (the closest meaning would be "being a part of" or "being accepted"), I will from now on keep the word in its original Russian.

5. "Train station—suitcase—Russia": This slogan was often used particularly in the 1990s by some political and medial discourses, indicating that Russian speakers who are unwilling to adapt and integrate into the new state should return to their original ethnic homeland, Russia.

6. It is important to note the role collectivization played in the demographic catastrophe for Kazakhstan. As Shirin Akiner (1995, 45–46) estimates, over 40 per cent of all Kazakhs died as a result, which "extended to the annihilation of a whole culture" and became a major source of anti-Russian sentiment and Kazakh nationalism during the late Soviet period (Wolfel 2002).

7. The literal translation of the state name Kazakhstan is the "land of Kazakhs."

8. See, for example, Michele Commercio (2004) on the "Pugachev incident" that occurred in 1999 in Ust'-Kamenogorsk. Kazakhstani authorities arrested twenty-two individuals, charging them with an attempt to violently overthrow local branches of government and to create an autonomous Russian Altai Republic. In her article, Commercio (2004, 88) highlights the disproportionate reactions of the authorities, who sought to convey the message that "Kazakhstan will not tolerate opposition to its nationalization program" and to stop Pugachev's group from drawing local and international attention to the position of Russians in the country.

9. Interestingly, the story comes in contrast to the fate of the Lenin monument in Astana, which had been first displaced from the Central Square to another less prominent location and later disappeared from the cityscape altogether, "providing material foci for uncertainty over the ongoing redefinition of public values and identities" in the city (Laszczkowski 2016, 84).

10. Yet, it is worth mentioning that while during the Soviet Union "Russianness" carried a certain cultural capital, a sense of prestige attached to a person, in the post-Soviet times some Kazakhs came to associate "Russifiedness" as a pejorative feature of 'otherness' (see more on this in Laszczkowski 2016, 121–26).

11. Note that ethnic Kazakhs, especially in the northern parts of Kazakhstan, also inhabit numerous cultural dimensions that often intersect with those of nontitular Russian-speaking groups. For example, in their study of contemporary Kazakhstani identity, Kristoffer Rees, and Aziz Burkhanov (2018) usefully note how, for the ethnic Kazakh long-term dwellers of the city Oskemen, the Russian language and culture represent essential elements of their own identities.

12. In the Russian language *kak kolkhoznik* means having no appropriate style in the way of dressing him/herself, literally translated as being "like a farmer."

13. Laszczkowski (2016, 58–59) provides a good analysis of the term *mambet*, which is stereotypically associated with southern Kazakhs, stemming from poor rural areas. According to some of his research participants in Astana, *mambet* was not only determined by one's economic standing but also had to do with rude and "uncultured" behavior. The term was arguably predominantly used by Russians and Russified Kazakhs to depreciate Kazakh culture and language, as well as to delineate themselves from rural migrants.

Chapter 3

Transgressing Exclusion

We might boldly assume that nothing good can grow out of exteriority and that this liminal space becomes a cage with firmly fixed boundaries.[1] However, to apply such a perspective to the everyday experiences of Russophones would be, at best, to overlook a narrative gestalt in which the spatiotemporal exteriority—the experiences of separation and distance—actually become reconstituted by individual practices of interiority, proximity, and attempts at reconnection (Roberts 2002; Wright 2015). Therefore, in this chapter I ask what interiority means to Russian speakers in my ethnographic sites, what alternative meanings they give to their places of residence, and how interiority is, in turn, crafted and achieved out of exteriority. The attention to these questions does not solve the riddle of what it is to belong, but rather provides a glimpse into the "multivocality and multilocality" (Rodman 1992) of belonging simultaneously enacted in the process of dwelling across all spatial scales, from local through national to global.

Central to our discussion here becomes the notion of "transgression," which, according to Julie Allan (2008, 85), enables individuals to challenge "disabling barriers and find new selves, new ways of being in the world." Transgression emerged prominently in Michel Foucault's (1977) writings on ethics as a subversive tactic of crossing boundaries, which "plays on and with a terrain imposed on it and organized by the law" of power (de Certeau 1984, 37). Blow by blow, step by step, these tactics open up cracks in the constituted spaces, trespass onto them, and transgress them. For Foucault (1977, 35), transgression is engaged in a constant interplay with the "limit," or, in case of this book, with models of dominating culture: "Transgression, then, is not related to the limit as black to white, the prohibited to the lawful, the outside to the inside, or as the open area of a building to its enclosed spaces. Rather, their relations take the form of a spiral which no simple infraction can exhaust."

Importantly, Foucault's interpretation of transgression implies the incessant crossing and recrossing of boundaries, whereby a transgressed line does not irredeemably sink into oblivion but is always brought back. This remark is particularly useful from the perspective of this research, which does not seek to oppose exteriority in favor of interiority or to substitute one for the other. Rather, the attempt is to highlight their simultaneous coexistence, complicity, and mutual constitution. In other words, as this chapter demonstrates, the process of transgression, here in the form of critically challenging the state-enacted configurations of social relations and creating new alternative modes of belonging, is often closely entangled with returning to old boundaries or drawing new ones.

Seeking to make places habitable while defying prefabricated meanings of space, individuals or groups often turn to clandestine tactics expressed in both material and less material acts (Low and Lawrence-Zuniga 2003). Dwelling, moving about, speaking, remembering—these are all activities of the "weak" which are used to invert the experiences of exclusion and disadvantage within the established order by the "strong" (de Certeau 1984, 40). In the following sections, I consider these subversive tactics in two particular ways: through *memories* of the past and *rhythms* forged through performative daily encounters (Amin and Thrift 2002). As such, the focus is, on the one hand, on the acts of remembering one's own place, thereby exploring how Russian speakers filter their memories of life in the borderlands for their present purposes and how they relate to the past to substantiate or renounce received notions of territoriality and space; on the other hand, I reflect on different local performances which people consciously (but, more often, unconsciously) undertake to position themselves vis-à-vis the larger community. These small everyday acts enable individuals to develop new forms of sociality in both material and symbolic terms and are, therefore, integral for understanding the ways in which interiority plays out across different settings.

Before we proceed, I must caution that the episodes from the ethnographic accounts are to be read as a fragmentary collage rather than an organized sequence composed into one coherent plot. To an outside observer, these episodes might seem out of sync, even messy, moving between frames of synthesis and differentiation, yet so is the very fabric of the everyday life constructed out of spaces which are "cross-cutting, intersecting, aligning with one another, or existing in relations of paradox antagonisms" (Massey 1994, 3).

REMEMBERING PLACE

Cities constitute complex sites of perception and memory. Urban spaces like monuments, memorials, buildings, and public squares provide an important material and symbolic context for personal and collective memory work as well as the embodied practices of remembering (Fortier 2000). The past lives of these places represent the "invisible identities of the visible" (de Certeau 1985, 108) that press on the experiences of the present (Tonkiss 2005, 120).

Numerous studies indeed consider memory and memory-making to play an important role in the social construction of space and a sense of place (Casey 1987; Lewicka 2014; Low 2017; Manzo 2003). Through memories, places acquire symbolic meaning and help understand the present, the "here and now." Remembering is, however, not a "straight transcription of events from an earlier life but an act of imagination in the present" (Tonkiss 2005, 121). It is a creative process of putting together the experiences of the past, which has "the capacity for endless interpolations into what has been" (Ibid.). In the work of memory, cities become vivid spatial formations that are not only a matter of hegemonic constructions of histories in the name of the nation or collective meanings but also a matter of individual perception that substantiate and repudiate the received notions of territoriality (Low 2017).

Individual memories, central to this study, are regarded as a "glue" that emotionally connects people to their places (Lewicka 2014, 51). By remembering or telling stories about past experiences, people construct images of the place itself, its borders, and its shape, as well as images of their own and others' position within that place (Liebscher and Dailey-O'Cain 2013). These individual narratives, however, do not always easily coexist with a larger framework of meaning that selectively constructs or commemorates national histories in artificially created sites (Nora, 1989; Rowles 1990; Taylor 2010). In Estonia and Kazakhstan, the official attempts to narrate new versions of national history are often negatively received by local minorities. Following the collapse of the Soviet Union, the newly independent states sought to reinterpret their urban landscapes by "returning to history" which would glorify one's own nation. This entailed the renovation and reconstruction of historical monuments and buildings, the production of new historical sites, the renaming places while, at the same time, enacting an "active forgetting of certain experiences deemed inconsistent or incomplete with official identity narratives" (Diener and Hagen 2013, 497). Against these wide-ranging measures to reconfigure space and time, as Laszczkowski (2016) and Pfoser (2014) note, there exist the established daily routines and individual narratives of Russian speakers that complicate state "efforts to solidify new official narratives" (Diener and Hagen 2013, 501).

It is precisely on these local memory-making practices that the next section concentrates, uncovering the complexities and ambivalences of individual remembering as well as the ways in which memories are used to challenge one's own position of exteriority within the new social order. This endeavor necessitates that we focus not only upon the ways in which the Russophone communities in Narva and Petropavlovsk remember their cities but also on the ways they contest or align with the dominant representations of space and time that seek to turn lands into ethnoscapes and root particular ethnic groups in the "national soil" (Pfoser 2014, 270). What emerges once again is a dramatically divergent way in which Russian speakers construct bridges to or close doors behind dominating cultures. Moving differently between Soviet, Russian, Estonian, or Kazakhstani (as well as European) scale effects, they reconfigure exteriority differently and thereby produce different meanings of interiority itself.

Memories of Narva

Most of the literature on memory politics positions the narratives of the Soviet past among Estonians and Russian speakers in opposition to each other. What Estonia sees as a loss of independence and occupation by the communist regime that brought suffering to Estonian people, many Russian speakers consider as a "personally meaningful time," a time of post-war reconstruction, industrialization, and prosperity (Pfoser 2014, 277). This antagonistic polarization and the mutual accusations of having false collective memories became particularly visible during the relocation of the Bronze Soldier monument in Tallinn in 2007 and the subsequent "memory wars" that broke out between Estonia and Russia (Brüggemann and Kasekamp 2008). Seeking to externalize the socialist past linked to suffering, Estonian political elites presented the period of communist rule as a "rupture" and discontinuity of national history and private biographies (Kõresaar 2004). Through the restorationist narratives, the country turned away from the Soviet past to reestablish continuity with the interwar period of independent statehood and to return to its European course of history. In this process, however, the state elites have excluded all the Soviet newcomers from the state-building memory community and created boundaries against those who did not share the "alleged common experience" (Brüggemann and Kasekamp 2008, 426). As a result, Karsten Brüggemann and Andres Kasekamp write, Russian speakers are likely to harbor alternative memories grounded in positive representations of the Soviet past and their own Russianness. History becomes thereby "the main borderline dividing the two communities" (Ibid., 441).

Although these divisions remain important in the context of Estonia and contribute to the experiences of exteriority among Russian speakers (see chapter 2), more recent literature is rather critical of such a simplistic juxtaposition of narratives about the past. The accounts that follow the assumption of divided memory (adopting a static and bounded conception of memory) often dismiss the fact that memories are fundamentally "grounded in lived experiences" and human interactions and are, therefore, dynamic, unstable, and ephemeral (Assmann 2008, 55; Bell 2008). Indeed, the latest empirical research on the memories of Russian speakers in the context of the Baltic states emphasizes the complexities of remembering and place-making, whereby the socialist past serves as both a resource for dissent and a way to claim personal belonging (see, for example, Cheskin 2012; Pfoser 2014). The plurality of memories about past experiences was also clearly visible in the narratives of my Narvan interlocutors. While many talked about the city as a Russian or, to some extent, a Soviet place (I will return to this point in chapters 4 and 5), it is particularly the representation of Narva as historically Estonian that came to dominate the individual narratives, symbolizing a departure from the (self)Orientalizing perspectives discussed before.

The historical embeddedness of Narva within Estonia, or, in other words, the connection between the seemingly ruptured spatialities of local and national, was achieved by drawing a line and distancing themselves from Soviet and post-Soviet Russia, with which they are often associated. In fact, Nadezhda, a kindergarten teacher in her forties, remembered clearly that Estonianness was always an integral part of the local life. Already in Soviet times, many places in the city carried Estonian names, marking a clear boundary of where Estonia begins and ends:

> How I remember it now, in the Soviet times we had a cinema—*Punane Täht*, it was directly written there. Or *Kalaputt*. Already in Soviet times, everything was in Estonian. My granddad had a Moskvich car with a number plate EAH . . . and with the E you could understand that we were from Estonia. When we would go to Vologda [a place in Russia]—my grandad was from there— everyone would think that we were rich. Well, in comparison to Vologda, we were indeed living stylishly. We would come, and everyone would look at us like we were foreigners. (Nadezhda, interview with the author, February 16, 2017)

The differences were, however, not simply limited to the place or street names but ran across the living standards, very visible to those who traveled to and encountered other parts of the Soviet Union. For example, Zinaida, whom I already mentioned in chapter 2, was shocked by the deplorable living conditions that spread across Pskov, where she was relocated to work after finishing school in Narva:

Although Pskov is a big city, nothing could force me to stay there . . . . I lived in
such bad conditions, in a dormitory with a stove. For me it was *diko* (barbaric).
Diko. Conditions were so horrible. Super tiny music school, shops were empty.
In the meantime, Narva had products. Living standards in Narva were different,
considerably better. So, I came back and haven't thought even for a second of
going back. (Zinaida, interview with the author, March 14, 2017)

As another interlocutor remarked, Narva and the whole of Estonia were not
only economically better off than the rest of the Soviet Union but had more
freedoms. When reminiscing about school, Vladimir, a pensioner in his late
fifties, acknowledges that already in the 1980s Narva, and Estonia as a whole,
was far more 'Western' and more advanced than the rest of the Union:

Our teachers at school were freer. For example, my wife studied in Saint Petersburg
and every morning they would sing the Soviet anthem. And I would say, you
know, this is *diko* (barbaric) for me. Stinks like China. China, Mao Zedong, that's
really bad. No, our teachers here were free, they gave us freedom to think.

Although such biographical accounts do not directly contradict the Soviet-
Russian ones and often exist alongside them, they are simultaneously used
by people to construct alternative narratives of place, marking it Estonian
and different to Russia, which is/was considered backward both in terms of
living standards and political freedoms. This, in turn, illustrates how personal
memories often ran counter to the binary opposition between what is Estonian
and what is Russian in the polarized national discourses (Pfoser 2014, 279).
Appropriating discourses of Estonianness and telling stories about Narva as
a cultured, modern, and developed place were often integral for highlighting
overall changes in their mentality as well as the personal and collective identities that came thereof:

Our tastes are now different, after living here. That's why I am telling you that I
can't live in Russia. This tastelessness still prevails there. Russian people were
brought up differently. They like brightness, loudness, crowds. Of course, it's
not foreign to us, we are somehow Russian people too, but we were still brought
up in a different environment. Although there are few Estonians in Narva, the
atmosphere is still different from Russia. (Zinaida, interview with the author,
March 14, 2017)

For many, the appropriation of certain Estonian cultural traits (*obestonits'ia*)
symbolized their departure from Russia as a geocultural space. The experiences of differences are then not linked to the Soviet past only but are
also widely used when describing present-day experiences and feelings.

Regardless of the ways in which Russian speakers are treated in Estonia, those who feel marginalized by the state (see chapter 2) find life in Russia both to be foreign and impossible:

> Both life and customs there [in Russia] are unacceptable to me. Since I accustomed myself so much to Estonia, Russia *budet dlia menia dikost'iu* (would be barbaric to me). Not that I am entirely European. I was eighteen years old when the Soviet Union collapsed, so my education is Soviet. But the rest developed for me already here, in our country. We received an Estonian education, everyday way of life. Whether it is good or bad doesn't play a big role. (Dima, interview with the author, February 15, 2017)

In essence, ascribing particular attributes, negative or positive, to geographical locations helped people like Dima to transgress the exteriority and marginality of the city due to its cultural connection with Russia, demonstrating the continuous cultural superiority of Narva and themselves over Russia. In the process of remembering, Russian speakers drew new territorial and cultural boundaries to subvert the state visions of the borderland as an "enclave" detached from the Estonian political and cultural mainstream (Makarychev 2018) and to create their own alternative cultural geographies of belonging to the geocultural space of Estonia. Importantly, however, the interior relationship of Narva to Estonia did not only develop out of pragmatic economic grounds, which is something that has been earlier proposed by Laitin (1998). In their complex place- and memory-making strategies, people often drew on cultural association and symbols of Estonianness—particular life modes, morals, and everyday culture—to strengthen their interiority within a larger national collective.

Remembering Narva as interior to Estonia, my interlocutors often took a few steps further to include the city into the broader framework of a European space, thereby transgressing its internal otherness within Estonia, as well as the EU, as the "most Russian of all cities" (Makarychev 2018, 11). Consider, for example, Inga, a kindergarten teacher in her sixties, who reconstructs Narva both in the past and present as European. When Inga moved from Nalchik to Narva during Soviet times, she landed in the West:

> When I first came here, my immediate thought was that I landed somewhere abroad, in the West. I visited a lot of places across the Soviet Union, but nowhere was like in Narva—nature, people, opportunities . . . . Even our kids now don't want to go anywhere else. [. . .] I think Narva has developed for the better. It's thanks to the EU, of which we are a part. There are sufficient funds to build and renovate the roads and, you know, our roads are so much better than even in Saint Petersburg. (Inga, interview with the author, March 24, 2017)

The vision of Narva as "the West" through its distinct historical heritage and consumer culture during the Soviet period has been extended into the present discourse of being European people within a European space. As another research participant, a young student, Yuliya, emphasized there are further differences that exist between Narvans and Russians, with the former being more European and more civilized. According to Yuliya, Russian speakers have good habits, like fastening their seat belts, wearing a reflector in the darkness, or crossing the street where and when appropriate—traits they share with fellow ethnic Estonians and other Europeans. The behavior of Russians, in turn, reminds her of the famous Russian fairy-tale figure—Ivan the Fool, very disorderly and chaotic (from the interview with the author, February 17, 2017). Such narratives of "becoming" or even already "being" European were used by Russian speakers like Yuliya to reconstruct their interiority grounded in both Narva's spatiotemporal continuity in the West and its cultural superiority over disorderly Soviet and post-Soviet Russia (see also chapter 5). Interestingly, earlier research into cultural differences between the Estonian majority and the Russian-speaking minority in Estonia has indicated a shift in the socialization environment following the collapse of the Soviet Union (Vihalemm and Kalmus 2009, 110). Especially Estonia's constant economic growth and international integration have facilitated the emergence of new common cultural templates for the younger Estonian generations: from consumerism to openness to the West, from adherence to the rules to basic family and personal values. Already in 2003, opinion polls indicated that Russian speakers started to pursue the same goals as ethnic Estonians: "material wealth and an interesting life" (Lauristin and Vihalemm 2009, 17). These are the resources on which both ethnolinguistic groups equally draw when making their place in Estonia.

The brief examples here demonstrate how Russian speakers filter personal memories of life in the borderland and negotiate their position at the Estonian margin. Reconstructing Narva and themselves as both Estonian and European against the Russian "other" is one potential spatial strategy to transgress the social boundaries imposed by the nation-building policies of the state. Furthermore, it is also a strategy to shape interiority associated with their inherent geocultural belonging to Estonia.

. . . And of Petropavlovsk

By now we should be aware that post-Soviet Estonia and Kazakhstan have chosen very different ways of reordering space and time. These divisions are equally present in the official interpretations of their national histories. In contrast to Estonia, where the Soviet past has been presented by the titular elites as a vivid manifestation of an ethnic split that runs through language, cultural, and memory practices, Kazakhstani official narratives and the national historiographies are shaped by greater continuity with Soviet times and present-day Russia. The numerous achievements of the Soviet period are still recognized and viewed as episodes of a shared past. For example, despite attempts to emphasize a distinct Kazakh national history, the main Soviet holidays still found their proper place in the calendar for state holidays, including the Victory Day and International Women's Day, to name a few. This official historical continuity plays an equally important role in the individual narratives of Petropavlovsk inhabitants that entangle images of Russia and Kazakhstan as a logical continuation of one another in a mental, cultural, and geographical sense. This entanglement strengthens the representation of Petropavlovsk as a Russian-speaking space grounded in a certain Russian mentality, language, and memories of the Soviet past. While in Estonia the border with Russia is often viewed as a clear line between the past and present and between two civilizations—the East and the West—the perception of border and space by Russian speakers in Petropavlovsk remains rather ambiguous (Kosmarskaya and Savin 2018, 10).

The Soviet and pre-Soviet nation-building policies largely contribute to the explanation of such differences: in contrast to the territory of the Kazakh SSR, where the borders were arbitrarily drawn by Soviet ethnographers, Estonia had experienced, albeit briefly, independence during the interwar period which clearly demarcated its territorial and national boundaries. In fact, according to Kasekamp (2000), already under Tsarist Russia in the first decade of the twentieth century, ethnic Estonians were able to strengthen awareness of an Estonian ethnic identity, form an Estonian urban bourgeoisie, and win control of several city councils. This was not the case in Kazakhstan, where even today the northern parts of the country do not have a clearly established perception of Russia as the "other side," with the region being continuously viewed as uniform (Grigorichev 2007, 20). For example, a nineteen-year-old Lera, who works in a flower shop, told me on several occasions that Petropavlovsk is not really Kazakhstan, but represents to her a part of Russia. Several other interlocutors were also troubled by calling Kazakhstan their home:

I don't associate myself with Kazakhstan. I live here, I am a Kazakhstani citizen, but I don't associate myself with it, it doesn't fit into my mind. I am told that this is my home, but I don't feel comfortable with it. Petropavlovsk has been historically a peculiar city; it is a borderland with a large Russian-speaking population. (Arsen, interview with the author, August 21, 2016)

Although Kazakhstan is my home, Russia is closer to me mentally, Russian spirit. I know a lot about Russian history, but almost nothing about Kazakhstan.

And you know, it's actually a shame that the Soviet Union collapsed. It was a great time I heard, when we all used to live together and shared the language, the culture, and the same past. (Nastya, interview with the author, September 6, 2016)

These attempts to reinstate a sense of unity with Russia in the past and present should not be viewed as a passive relic of the Soviet past, as claimed, for example, by Grigorichev (2007). Instead, emphasizing continuity and transparency between the two geographical locations is an active effort to transgress exteriority that emerged in response to the state Kazakhization policies. It is a cultural response to the "alien" which epitomizes the manners and the culture of the rural Kazakh "other" that can corrupt the authentic Russian lifestyle. At the same time, building the bridge to Russia to construct interiority and inclusion into the larger Russian-speaking space goes far beyond ethnic lines. According to Kosmarskaya and Kosmarski (2019, 70), the formation of the "Russophone cultural-linguistic space" on the territories of Central Asia carries a transethnic character, embracing members of many ethnic groups beyond Russians themselves. The Russian-speaking space as a space of interiority thereby becomes a melting pot for people with shared historical destinies and common social roles, interests, and culture, including a Russified and modernized segment of ethnic Kazakhs, for whom the prevalence of Russian in the region is not necessarily seen "a colonial legacy to be overcome, but the richness of one's own [local] culture" (Florin 2011).

The construction of solidarities beyond ethnic boundaries and a sense of cultural affinity, in particular among the Russified urban population that stems from the Soviet Union is strongly connected to the way Petropavlovsk is remembered and perceived by my interlocutors today. In a sense, neither non-titular Russian speakers nor Russified Kazakhs make clear attempts to reject the Soviet past or the Russian language and culture, thereby sustaining the continuity of a Russian-speaking space. Despite the growing visibility of Kazakh history and culture materialized in the landscape (for example, new monuments, memorials, and street names) as a part of the nation-building policy, the inhabitants of Petropavlovsk seem to rarely draw on these symbolic references. Instead, they prefer to keep the boundaries between what is Russia and what is Kazakhstan blurred, reconstructing themselves as the residents of a cultured and a Russified city that carries over continuities from the Soviet past.

That said, this Russian-speaking space is not necessarily a space of nostalgia for the Soviet era, idealized as the era of prosperity. Many have, in fact, distanced themselves from the Soviet past precisely on economic grounds. Consider, for example, Alla, a saleswoman in her fifties, who juxtaposes Soviet existence, characterized by the shortage of goods and a lack of freedoms, to the opportunities and openness that independent Kazakhstan offers today:

> Recently, I decided to open my own business, and I did it. We are like the rest of the world now. Those who want to work and succeed, they work and succeed. Therefore, I think that life now is so much better than it used to be before. We can earn money, afford things which are available in excess, and we can travel. (Alla, personal conversation with the author, August 2016)

Throughout the conversations, other interlocutors too sought to replace memories connected to the shortages of the Soviet Union and difficulties of the 1990s, when "life was scary, and many people lost themselves to this chaos" (Taras, interview with the author, August 31, 2016). Instead, they highlighted the desire for new lifestyles and opportunities that the transnational orientation of Kazakhstan enables today, opening possibilities for different interpretations of interiority to emerge.

PERFORMING PLACE

The meanings that cities carry for individuals are unlocked not only through the acts of remembering, but equally through performative and embodied rhythms (de Certeau 1984; Cresswell 1996; Tonkiss 2005). Through performance, people compose spaces for themselves and transform existing meanings, even if only partially, temporally, and privately. The importance of the performative and lived dimension for an understanding of space was recognized by earlier research, which argued that any place is generated in the process of living through both conscious and unconscious acts. David Seamon (1980), who introduced the concept of "place-ballet," for example, argues that places are performed on a daily basis through everyday movements that have become more or less involuntary. It is, according to Seamon, through familiarity that "existential insidedness" emerges, whereby we as individuals feel that we are a part of the environments surrounding us. For Ray Oldenburg (1999) too, habitual routines regularly happening in a place—crossing the streets, going to work and shopping, playing sports, or celebrating holidays—represent an important foundation for long-term involvement and spatial belonging. These are the accumulative rhythms through which inhabitants frame and order their urban experience and position themselves in structural fields (Amin and Thrift 2002, 17).

These remarks are in many ways fruitful for our understanding of interiority not only as a mnemonic narrative but also as a performative activity, a rhythmical process rooted both in the present circumstances of larger sociopolitical or economic structures and future aspirations. Performativity, however, does not simply relate to routines but also the small practices of transgression that challenge conventional meanings (Butler 1990, 1993). These performances are concerned with the ongoing relationship of individuals with the larger society, their claims on space, and their effective presence (Melly 2010). In this chapter, I approach these urban performances, these rhythms, from a detached vantage point, thereby observing how the small acts take place locally. Without wishing to overstate my own powers of perception and reflexivity, I also inquire into the meanings that such practices carry for Russian speakers themselves. In Narva, as the following section demonstrates, people often seek to overcome their own marginal position by presenting themselves as active citizens. Through the narratives of hard work and contribution, they seek to strengthen their claims to membership in a wider society, to their interiority as Estonian (for similar conclusions, see also Keskküla 2015). In the case of Petropavlovsk, my "spectral distance" (Amin and Thrift 2002, 18) allowed me to uncover more neglected ways in which Russian speakers interact with and accommodate Kazakh traditions. As such, I unveil how interiority emerges not only by constructing Petropavlovsk as a "Russian-speaking space" but equally through close familiarity with and repetition of—at first glance distant and foreign—Kazakh traditions.

Enacting Interiority in Narva

There are numerous creative ways in which Russian speakers seek to claim their interiority and belonging. Some of these activities are more spectacular, like the video clip by the Narvan rapper, Evgenii Liapin (stage name Stuf), which in 2017 became the most popular YouTube song in Estonia. Dressed in the Estonian tricolour, Evgenii sings in two languages that he is Russian, but loves Estonia (*"Olen venelane aga ma armastan Eestit"*), he was born in this country, lives here, and hopes to make it a better place together with fellow Estonians.[2] Other activities involve a more collective performance with clear political aims, like the electoral alliance *Meie Narva* (Our Narva), which was formed in 2017 ahead of the Estonian municipal elections. Consisting of politicians and several local activists, the alliance promoted a message that appeared on the local billboards, reading in two languages: *"Narva on ka Eesti! Narva—tozhe Estoniya!"* (Narva is also Estonia). Tired of the negative images that depict the borderland as a container of social problems inhabited by people who are not fully integrated in Estonia, *Meie Narva* emerged to challenge such entrenched sociopolitical boundaries. Their ideas seemed to resonate with the local residents who helped them secure the second place in the elections with 23.3 per cent of support.

Participation in different public events and celebrations, according to my interlocutors, also helps them transform existing images of Narva and qualifies them for being worthy members of the Estonian community. Anthropological studies commonly argue that social groups and collective identities are constructed and reaffirmed through public celebrations (see, for example, Durkheim [1912] 1995). The absenteeism from and criticism of certain holidays, like Estonian Independence Day, is believed by some Estonian politicians to go hand in hand with the nostalgic idealization of Soviet-era celebrations and a lack of desire among Russian speakers to associate themselves with Estonia. Although indeed only a few of my interlocutors participate in the yearly celebration of Estonian Independence Day and attend the raising of the Estonian flag at sunrise, in 2018, as Estonia celebrated its 100th anniversary, the courtyard of Narva Castle was filled up with Narvans singing the Estonian hymn together, releasing the balloons into the air, and continuing their celebration in cafés, restaurants, or at home. In this way, as my interlocutors later noted, they paid their respects to the culture and traditions of ethnic Estonians, of which they are also a part.

Those who refrain from actively celebrating Independence Day have been involved in other state-organized events, albeit ones that are less politicized. One such event is *Teeme Ära* (Let's Do It), a communal practice of cleaning up forests and different parts of the city, initiated in Narva by the Estonian ministry of culture, the Foundation for Integration, the city council, and the Defense League.[3] Various authors in the field of ecology studies have earlier pointed out that pro-environmental lifestyles can lead towards stronger ties with one's sociophysical environment (Devine-Wright 2013; Manzo and Perkins 2006). Through the efforts to improve one's community and acts of care for the surrounding landscapes, emotional affinity with place arises. Since both Russian speakers and neighboring ethnic Estonians are often involved in those practices, they also help to promote social cohesion in the city and country in general. As Piret Hartman, the undersecretary for Cultural Diversity at the Ministry of Culture, has noted, "Integration begins with experiences and contacts, and a typical day in Narva offers plenty of opportunities for that" (Kultuurministeerium 2017).

There are also less spectacular "banal" everyday activities that are implicated in the process of transgressing marginal positions. Take, for example, the story of Zinaida, a choir singer and a music teacher in a Russian-speaking kindergarten. Zinaida was born in Soviet Estonia to Russian immigrants. Having Russian as her mother tongue and not necessarily being able to "understand" (as she claimed) Estonian culture as ethnic Estonians do, she nevertheless professes a great deal of respect for it. She often feels uncomfortable with the political and media discourses that represent Russian speakers as occupants (see, for example, Malloy 2009): "I am upset by this attitude.

I was born here, no one needs me in Russia, and it seems Estonia doesn't need me here either" (interview with the author, March 14, 2017). Nevertheless, Zinaida proudly performs Estonian songs around the world with her fellow choir members and teaches them to kindergarten children:

> I love Estonian dances, all those polkas . . . 'Kaerajaan, Kaerajaan' or 'Kaks sammu sissepoole, kaks sammu väljapoole.' I teach them to children. They are very accessible and communicative. When you see those dances at the festivals, they are amazing. [. . .] In the choir, each one of us has a skirt and we put them on when we do the Estonian program. [. . .] Although some people say that we are occupants, we live on this land and we enrich the culture too. I cannot say about myself that I make Narva worse. On the contrary, we always perform with respect. We record and preserve these songs. (Zinaida, interview with the author, March 14, 2017)

In the narrative of Zinaida, the idea of belonging and interiority is closely tied with the ability to contribute to Estonian society both in the past and present. As Engin Isin (2002, 275) notes, it is precisely by developing symbolic, social, and cultural practices that people are able to "constitute themselves as political agents under new terms, taking different positions in the social space than those in which they were previously positioned." Russian speakers display their agency by establishing themselves not as "occupants" or "undesired others," but as valuable members of society who significantly contribute to the country's national and cultural development (Jašina-Schäfer and Cheskin 2020, 106). In the above example, there is a clear link between Zinaida's cultural activity and her claims for justice in the asymmetrical context created by the Estonian nation-building process.

The performative activity of Dima (chapter 2) is another good example of how individuals rework the modes of being an outsider. However, these acts have less obvious links with national Estonian culture than in Zinaida's case. On several occasions during our conversations, Dima told me of his participation in sports events across Estonia, including his personal initiative to organize various events in Narva. According to him, such activities help people overcome the question of nationality and the circle of belonging, which is defined in Estonia in narrow ethnic terms. They interrupt the "normal" operation of space by transforming Narva and Estonia into a unitary place, where people exist beyond their ethnicity:

> So, I went to these scout gatherings; Russians rarely go there. So, you walk next to an Estonian person and both of you forget about your nationality. You are united by a common problem and this problem is a long path, and you sit down together and share a chocolate, and the Estonian doesn't care anymore what

language you speak. When you have common goals and common difficulties, these bring nations closer. [. . .] And here too, if we develop a sports structure in the city, people will come out more and socialize with each other. (Dima, interview with the author, February 15, 2017)

The diverse array of both spectacular and more quotidian individual practices, from preserving Estonian songs to participating in sports events, highlight numerous ways in which Russian speakers in Narva create their interiority. Despite the negative developments Narvans faced after the fall of the socialist project, and despite the exclusionary policies of the state that left numerous Russian speakers outside of the Estonian national community, people not only redefine Narva and themselves as inherently Estonian, but interiority emerges simultaneously as a denationalized space that is not shaped by the dominant culture, be it Russian or Estonian, but goes beyond it toward the "enactments of a large array of particular interests," ideas, and goals (Sassen 2006, 179). Striving for inclusion by claiming their legitimate place within Estonia while simultaneously seeking to transgress the confines of nationality and dominant culture should not be seen as a contradiction (Fein 2005). Rather, these examples represent the multiplicity of ways in which people make sense of the place they inhabit and claim their belonging to it.

Becoming Culturally Intimate with Kazakh

From the discussion that we had so far it might seem that, in contrast to Russian speakers in Narva for whom interiority is in many ways connected with the attempts to reinstate their legitimate place within Estonia, the inhabitants of Petropavlovsk are not only less receptive of state-produced Kazakhness within the urban space but also actively defy it as less cultured and inferior.[4] In the past, some observers, for whom boundaries between people represent a natural phenomenon, have assumed an insurmountable ethnocultural gap—even a civilizational chasm—between ethnic Kazakhs and their Russian-speaking counterparts (for criticism, see Dave 2007, 119). In what follows, however, I go beyond these limited accounts to sketch out how interiority for Russian speakers not only connotes a Russified space but is inherently grounded in their intimate experiences and practices of traditionally "Kazakh" culture, helping to cultivate the terrain of a broader commonality. To understand how Russian speakers engage with Kazakh traditions and rituals, the term "cultural intimacy," proposed in 1997 by Michael Herzfeld, becomes particularly useful. According to Herzfeld (2005, 3), cultural intimacy connotes "those aspects of cultural identity that are considered a source of external embarrassment but that nevertheless provide insiders with their assurance of common sociality." Registered through numerous practices and aspects of everyday life, cultural intimacy intensifies the connection to place and allows people to strengthen their sense of belonging not only to a locally rooted community but to the country in general.

Borrowing the concept from Herzfeld, cultural intimacy here serves to emphasize those cultural traits and Kazakh traditions which Russian speakers often claim to be foreign in their narration but those which are made to be permanent fixtures in their lives through regular performances and quotidian, unreflective everyday acts. This section thus examines how performing certain rituals side by side with local ethnic Kazakhs is closely entangled with the process of transgression that grants my interlocutors cultural intimacy with Kazakh culture, and at the same time creates distance from Russia. Paradoxically, this can go along the contempt for the culture of the titular population that often appeared in the narratives earlier.

When I arrived in Petropavlovsk, I was accommodated by Andrei, who introduced me to his circle of friends and family members, took me out to different parties and events in the city, and was in general very kind to share his daily experiences and thoughts over dinners. Throughout my stay, Andrei often claimed his Russianness and drew boundaries between what he considered to be cultured Russian speakers and uncultured ethnic Kazakhs. While these incidents and speech acts through which Andrei positioned himself as a Russian are certainly important (and they found their place in the discussion regarding the Russian-speaking space), so are the quotidian everyday acts through which Andrei incorporated rituals that he regards as Kazakh and therefore inherently foreign.

The celebration of Kurban Bairam (*Qurban ai't*) would be very exemplary here. In 2016, Kurban Bairam, a big worldwide Muslim holiday that took place between the 10th and the 12th of September, was accompanied by numerous state-organized festivities in Petropavlovsk: a big concert at the central square, cooking and sharing traditional Kazakh dishes, the exhibition of yurts. Andrei followed the spirit of public celebration with great enthusiasm. A week in advance, he announced Beshparmak (*Beshbarmaq*), a Kazakh traditional dish, to be on our menu for the first day of the festive celebration. Early Saturday morning I saw him disappear for hours at the market, where he queued with the others to purchase horse meat—the key ingredient. I observed him spending hours in the kitchen and being surprised at my refusal to eat the meat, which, he told me, is a celebratory food. When I asked to clarify why we were eating Beshparmak on that particular day (in fact, it was the only day he cooked it for me) he became perplexed at my question and ended up saying that he is Russian and "just wanted to eat Beshparmak, that's all." Since it is an expensive food, added Andrei, he chose only one day when to cook it. This day fell on Kurban Bairam.

Interestingly, later that year, Andrei and his friends also participated in the celebration of Nauryz (*Nowruz*), which is one of the largest folk spring holidays in Petropavlovsk. The festivities draw on the myth of spring rebirth, Kazakh legends, traditional games (wrestling, swinging on the swing), and seasonal festive dishes (Laszczkowski 2016, 119). Very much like during Kurban Bairam, the essential format includes a big concert in the central park, which is decorated with a stage and numerous yurts, where people can get acquainted with the nomadic traditions of the Kazakhs; numerous smaller concerts across the courtyards; the sharing of traditional Kazakh dishes; and the singing of Kazakh as well as Russian songs. The whole celebration is prepared in such a way as to promote both the "primordial" traditions of the Kazakhs as well as the friendships between different nationalities, calling for harmony. While Peyrouse (2008) and Laszczkowski (2016, 126) argue that Russian speakers are often reluctant to engage with the Kazakh celebrations and insist on their rural character, my personal observations of the locals from Petropavlovsk offer some contrasting points. In fact, many were keen to join this kind of *narodnye gulyaniya* (popular entertainment) and share the rituals with ethnic Kazakhs (figure 3.1). For example, one of my respondents, Lena, a music teacher in her late thirties, told me that she and her daughter always take part in these

Figure 3.1 Celebration of Nauryz in Petropavlovsk. *Source*: Photograph provided by Andrei and reproduced with his permission, March 2019.

kinds of celebrations. There, as she notes, you can really "feel the Kazakh hospitality, the domesticity of their mentality, and respect that Kazakhs have for other ethnicities"—the qualities that Lena finds valuable and desirable for Russians and other Slavs (from the interview with the author, September 15, 2016).

My observations of the active reproduction of Kazakh celebrations by Andrei and other interlocutors point to what Paul Connerton (1989, 72) regards as "incorporating practice," by which people unconsciously transmit messages and reproduce socially habitual memory. In a ritualized bodily performance, we tend to think and act following what is automatically incorporated into our bodies as a habit. The repetitive nature of such practices and rituals, however, impedes clear reflectivity of our actions and could potentially explain why Andrei did not find eating Beshparmak on Kurban Bairam unusual for a person who often diminishes Kazakh traditions. Through repetition, those acts then begin to instantiate a certain familiar order, becoming visible only in situations of confrontation with different cultural codes and unfamiliar contexts. Some scholars have noted that already during Soviet times the repetition of cultural practices had reduced the sociocultural distance between Russians, other Russian-speaking groups, and Kazakhs, contributing to greater social homogeneity (Dave 2007). Yet it is mostly through post-Soviet encounters with other people and environments that such habitual performances were revealed to my interlocutors. When Taras, a beekeeper in his late thirties, found himself outside of his everyday community by travelling to Russia, he experienced a longing for Kazakhstan and ethnic Kazakhs:

> I am so happy when I come back from Russia and see *rodnikh* (our dear) Kazakhs. I have two episodes. Once we went to the theater in Omsk and I started looking around—only Slavs, only pale Slavs. I was looking and looking. Then found a Uyghur—a *rodnoe* (dear) face and clung to him the whole evening. Why did I do that? *Rodnye* (our dear) Kazakhs. Oh, and how much I love the *dombra*.[5] I always put it on at work or in the car. The second episode, I am on a metro in Yekaterinburg and again I look around—only Slavs, only Russians. I felt uncomfortable.

Particularly interesting is the way Taras employs the word *rodnoi* (our, dear, endemic), which in the Russian language stems from the root word *rod* (origin, species) and connotes familiarity, proximity, and a sense of ownership (see also chapter 6). Sharing everyday lives with the Kazakh people became a habit for Taras, a familiar milieu through which the affective and cognitive links with the Kazakh cultural community were strengthened (Jašina-Schäfer 2019, 47). A similar situation was shared by Veronika, a twenty-one-year-old student who moved to Russia to study:

Here, I miss the Kazakh mentality. I am so used to the ads in two languages, to tea with milk and Beshparmak during every celebration. Petropavlovsk is a Russian-Kazakh city. Two cultures are entangled here. There is a lot of Russian habits in the lives of Kazakhs and in the lives of Russians, Kazakh. My mother drinks only Kazakh tea. She can even tell a Kazakh off for preparing it the wrong way and teach him how to make the right one. (Veronika, online interview with the author, September 16, 2016)

Such statements only reinforce the idea that Kazakhness is not only brought into the cityscape of Petropavlovsk and forcefully constructed top-down through the elite-level projects but is incorporated and reenacted freely by people in their everyday lives and customs. While seemingly devaluating the traditions of the dominant nation through the narratives of otherness, Russian speakers are also aware of their difference from Russians in Russia: "Unlike in Russia, here we respect other nationalities and never call the newcomers *churka*"[6] (Alla, personal conversation with the author, August 2016). The contempt for the ethnic Kazakh culture discussed before thus goes along with a pride for having inherited certain positive traits from their fellow countrymen. Consequently, such pride and everyday familiarity opens up a possibility for a different kind of interiority to emerge, one that not only reconstructs Petropavlovsk as a "Russian-speaking space" but also as a multicultural Kazakhstani space, where different cultures are entangled.

MULTILOCAL INTERIORITY

Cities, as Tonkiss (2005, 119–128) writes, are a "spatial riddle" overlaid with different memories, associations, and conscious and unconscious plots. There is no one vision of the place and one's own belonging to it. Rather, it is a matter of multiple spatial practices that both transgress exteriority and simultaneously return to it. It is a constant process of negotiating the boundaries, a process that not only depends on the individual visions of and position within space but also a sense of distance from or proximity to other spaces—local, national, or transnational.

The bricolage of cultural practices that this chapter portrayed may seem contradictory to outside observers; to the people themselves, however, movement within and between plural worlds is part of a complex post-Soviet life. Individual memories and everyday performative activities all serve to highlight that Russian speakers do not simply confront a world "out there," produced by the governments and state authorities, but are agents in their environment who inhabit it rather than "assimilate to a formal design specification" (Ingold 2000, 173). Through everyday acts they draw differences between social categories, position themselves in surrounding environment, and construct a multilocal interiority. As the numerous examples demonstrate, the inhabitants of borderland cities like Narva and Petropavlovsk are not simply a separated community, a community that is neither Russian nor Estonian or Kazakhstani. Instead, Russian speakers simultaneously draw on and juxtapose different narratives to negotiate belonging. How people precisely position themselves between these narratives is increasingly a matter of the spatial order, the sociopolitical and economic structures around them. The differences in individual meanings of interiority in Narva and Petropavlovsk, as we got to see here, arise through the ways the states seek to demarcate the boundaries of community belonging, through the official and popular interpretations of the Soviet past as well as the official images of the Russian language and culture, whereby Russian still represents a part of the "core" in Kazakhstan and inherent "otherness" in Estonia.

NOTES

1. In this chapter, some of the materials (especially the interview excerpts) are being reused and reproduced with the permission of rights' holders. The section 'Enacting Interiority in Narva' reuses interviews with Zinaida and Dima as well as a brief interpretation thereof from Jašina-Schäfer, Alina and Ammon Cheskin (2020) "Horizontal citizenship in Estonia: Russian speakers in the borderland city of Narva", *Citizenship Studies* 24(1): 93–110. The following section "Becoming Culturally Intimate with Kazakh" reuses interview excerpts with Taras and Veronika, which appeared in: Jašina-Schäfer, Alina (2019) "Everyday experiences of place in the Kazakhstani Borderland: Russian speakers between Kazakhstan, Russia, and the globe," *Nationalities Papers* 47(1), 38–54.
2. The YouTube link is available under the following address: https://www.you tube.com/watch?v=PLuwoJ2J02I. Another good example would be a recent song 'für Oksana' sung in two languages—Estonian and Russian—by an Estonian-speaking rapper Nublu and a Russian-speaking rapper Gameboy Tetris. Their collaborative project appeared on YouTube in August 2019 and attracted more the four million views. The song retells a love story between Nublu and his Russian-speaking girlfriend from Narva and has been highly acclaimed by the Estonian population, disregarding the ethnic heritage. Some people even argue that, with just one music video, Nublu has managed to do more for the integration of minorities in Estonia than diverse political and cultural institutions taken together: https://www.youtube.com/w atch?v=fgJqak4BuzQ.
3. "Teeme Ära," which was conceived in Estonia in 2008, turned into a global civic movement (Let's Do It! World) to call volunteers to action for waste clean-up. By 2018 the movement had grown into a network of 113 countries.

4. Chapter 5 conceptualizes in more detail the ideas behind Russian cultural superiority and Kazakh "backwardness," both closely linked to cultural-historical and socioeconomic realities.

5. *Dombra* is a long-necked Kazakh lute and a musical string instrument.

6. An insulting nickname given by Russians to the representatives of the peoples of Central Asia and, in a broader sense, to all non-Russian people, including natives of the North Caucasus and Transcaucasia.

Chapter 4

Landscapes of Belonging

WALKING THE ROUTES, MAPPING EXCLUSION, AND INCLUSION

One warm and sunny day in August, Petr invited me on an explorative stroll through the neighbourhoods of Petropavlovsk.[1] We met at the bus stop nearby the main pedestrian street Konstitutsiya and soon headed towards a courtyard where Petr spent his childhood years. It was a hurried walk, as my companion attempted to show as many places as he could, starting from personal places like the school and the university he attended or where his grandparents used to live, and ending with the many urban sites that he deemed important for the general image of the city. Our wandering from one location to another was always accompanied by Petr's personal life stories, nostalgic memories of the past, and admiration of certain places like Podgora, which revealed a beautiful view of the river Ishim and the lower part of the city. At the same time, he also often expressed distress with the poor upkeep of certain buildings and architectural landmarks. As we continued touring through the urban and natural environments, the *geist* of Petropavlovsk quickly manifested itself as a place of different temporalities and spatialities, different fragments of histories and experiences of sociability that coexist and juxtapose (figure 4.1).

Walking with my interlocutors in Narva and Petropavlovsk was an essential part of this research that sought to explore how Russian speakers sense, read, and narrate their surrounding landscapes and negotiate their belonging in this process. In the past decade, the act of walking in the city has been increasingly employed as a method of urban ethnography in an attempt to better understand how residents experience their own city, order relations, critique the present, and imagine their future (Ingold 2004; Pink 2008; Richardson 2008). According to Ingold (2004, 330–31), walking the pathways is essential

Figure 4.1   Petr's Favorite Area in Petropavlovsk. *Source:* Author's photograph, August 2016.

for grasping the environment around us, as the making of routes reconnects us with both with the physical world and the moral order inherent within it. While in the previous chapter I focused predominantly on the performative rhythms of Russian speakers in the borderlands and memories that the urban environment evokes among them, helping transgress exteriority, the aim here is to further embroil the individual everyday performances in places with the performativity of place itself. As such, the chapter at hand approaches the dialectic of inclusion and exclusion through the lens of concrete places and examines the symbolic connotations that both natural and built sites generate for Russian speakers in the process of walking and taking up different routes.

More recently, scholars began paying due attention to the outside, that is, the environmental, spatial, and tangible material worlds, viewing them not as mere bystanders but as architects of sociability that mediate and facilitate encounters (Hirsch 1995; Latour 2005). In their approaches, concrete places and objects in places represent "non-human actants" (Latour 2005, 76) that hold power over the social behaviour and cultural identities of a city's population. They generate specific meanings, make certain experiences more viable, and draw symbolic boundaries across a society (Cresswell 1996; Martinez 2018). Although in my own research I take cues from these previous scholarly positionings, I do not wish to favor the outside—that is, the object-centered perspective—at the expense of the inside, which grants insight into interior human selves, personal feelings, perceptions, and interpretations. Instead of choosing one or the other direction, similarly to Yael Navaro-Yashin (2012, 24) and her research on the affective geographies of space, I adopt the position of balance that privileges the "embroilment of inner and outer worlds," their codependence, and codetermination. In other words, in what follows, I attend to the entanglement of human beings with the artefacts in public spaces—buildings, streets, squares—and the natural environment, asking what meanings particular places acquire through the lived experiences of people.

As I walked with my interlocutors across their cities and listened to the spatial stories, I drew a cartography of interiority and exteriority, demonstrating how concrete places can be perceived as exclusionary and, at the same time, open up new possibilities for Russian speakers to overcome marginality or to create new forms of inclusion. The first part of this chapter is concerned predominantly with material spaces in the built environment; here this refers, in the broadest sense, to any physical alteration of the natural environment through construction by humans (Cresswell 2011, 241). Relying on empirical examples, I outline the atmospheric quality of spaces: how material spaces reflect the ongoing sociality in Narva and Petropavlovsk, how they motivate interpretations and meanings of belonging among Russian speakers, and how they are involved in the process through which my interlocutors construct alternative images of their cities beyond state-produced notions. In the second part of this chapter, the focus shifts to explore the role of the natural landscapes in the everyday lives of Russian speakers. On the one hand, I dwell on different ways in which the landscape myths are used by the states to map the margins of homeland, which quickly become exclusionary towards those who seemingly do not share the same connections with and historic rootedness in the national terrain; on the other hand, I scrutinize the different meanings that nature evokes for my interlocutors and the ways in which these meanings are used to transgress exteriority. In sync with previous chapters, here I also follow careful comparisons between the spatial narratives and experiences of Narva and Petropavlovsk inhabitants, providing further insights into the different ways through which Russian speakers reinscribe themselves into local, national, or transnational landscapes.

THE CITY FROM THE LENS OF MATERIAL ARTEFACTS

While space is inherently open, heterogeneous, changing, and improvised, it simultaneously carries material concreteness that is "painfully pregnant with a superfluity of meaning" (Buchli 1999, 1). Radical social transformations, as well as their reception, become apparent in the material qualities of surfaces, buildings, and streets, creating urban landscapes that are both aesthetically and historically diverse (Massey 2005). These materialities, in turn, persist and become not only an integral part of the community but enable this very community by inducing specific interpretations of social life, defining the social behavior, and making certain lived experiences of a city's population more pronounced (Darieva and Kaschuba 2011; Heidegger 1971). At the same time, in the process of dwelling, material compositions can acquire new meanings allowing for the cityscape to emerge as a fragmented space that connects multiple temporal and spatial scales that have no clear boundaries and are superimposed on each other (Martinez 2018, 136). Such fragmentation of the cityscape points to the possibility of pluralities, of continuities and changes in the spatial meanings and symbolic experiences of concrete places, as well as the possibility of a relational coexistence of interiority and exteriority as two complementary space logics (Löw 2008, 26).

To understand both the structuring force of material space and the power of individuals to restructure space through dwelling, it is useful to draw here on the work of anthropologists like Low (2000, 2017). In her research, Low juxtaposes and interconnects the ideas of the "production" and "construction" of space (see Introduction). To give expression to the mutual conditionality of production/structure and construction/individual action, Low provides numerous ethnographic examples of how the state, in her case Costa Rica, attempts to monopolize control over public spaces by designing them in particular ways. But despite state ideology deeply penetrating the material structures of cities, Low (2000) demonstrates how local dwellers simultaneously negotiate the meanings of material spaces through symbolic forms and practices such as music, dance, food, decoration, or other activities.

In the cases of postsocialist Narva and Petropavlovsk, we can observe similar tendencies. Following the collapse of the Soviet Union, the newly established states sought to restructure urban spaces, iconography, and identity by projecting specific cultural-political narratives. These narratives either engage ambiguously with Soviet artefacts or seek to erase any physical representation of the Soviet past from the city altogether, creating numerous discontinuities and ruptures within the cityscapes (see chapter 2). Yet, despite the state-projected images of urban landscapes, Narvans and the inhabitants of Petropavlovsk are too integrated into their constitution. Instead of assimilating to formal design specifications, Russian speakers inscribe their own signs into the cityscape and structure it by individual action, dwelling, and social interaction (Appadurai 1995; Ingold 2000).

On this basis, in what follows I demonstrate how Russian speakers are not only passive admirers or adversaries of rapidly changing urban landscapes, but active actors who imbue material places with their own qualities and meanings. In doing so, the aim is to better understand the ways in which changes occur in the cityscape, how exclusions are negotiated through the encounter with different temporal frames, scales, and materialities; as well as how material forms help transgress exteriority and create different visions and forms of inclusion. As I demonstrate, through everyday pathways and encounters with mundane places, a sense of urban landscape is transmitted in which Narva is often conceived as a locality of entanglement of Russian, Estonian, and European "cultural styles" which do not simply overlap but mutate and condition each other. This allows for new layered meanings of interiority to emerge that go beyond the exclusionary narratives of Estonian national identity. Permutations and entanglements are a daily reality in Petropavlovsk too: attuning to the landscapes filled with Kazakh symbolic and historical artefacts that mushroomed in the post-Soviet period, Russian speakers simultaneously reconstruct the city as Russian, as distinct from the rest of Kazakhstan, but also as cosmopolitan, emphasizing the importance of places that help them reinvent the city as a modern, globally interconnected place.

Re-assembling Narva as a Plural World

Throughout my stay, Narva always appeared to me as a city wherein "several mental spaces at once" coexist (Zerubavel 1991, 35). Such coexistence of multiple temporal and spatial scales, historical breaks, ruptures, as well as continuities can be best observed in the material landscape of the cityscape through the lens of erected monuments and buildings. For instance, a centrally located bust honors the famous Russian poet Aleksandr Pushkin, which, as Brednikova (2008, 52) notes, bears two different meanings for the local inhabitants. On the one hand, the poet represents someone "outside of ethnicity," someone who "belongs to the whole world," while, on the other hand, he symbolizes the preservation of Russian culture, which has been under pressure of the nation-building situation since Estonia regained its independence. Close to the bust we can find a monument dedicated to the famous Narva-born ethnic Estonian chess player Paul Keres, who during the 1930s–1960s was among the world's top players. Simultaneously, the city is home to the Swedish Lion monument, which marks the 300th anniversary of Sweden's victory over Russia in the Battle of Narva (Burch and Smith 2007). There is also a statue of Lenin, relocated from the city's central square and emplaced in the courtyard between the thick walls of the Narva fortress.

Another example, which was of particular importance to my interlocutors, is the Tank T-34 memorial (figure 4.2). Located on the outskirts of the city, the Tank is both the agent of memory and a site of alterity. Erected in the 1970s to memorialize the bravery of soldiers who "liberated"[2] the

Figure 4.2 The Tank T-34. *Source*: Author's photograph, July 2020.

city, the Tank has retained its affective power as a place of remembrance, representing a durable form of the past that left its mark on people's lives. As a material historical witness, it is considered to be a cultural heritage, a reservoir of childhood and Russianness. As Artur, a 39-year-old IT-specialist, put it:

> If I ever leave, I will miss my tank. The tank is the best thing that we have here. When I was a child, we would often go by bus with the kindergarten group to Ust' Narva and drive past the memorial. Lucky were the ones who were sitting next to the window and could see the tank. So really this goes from childhood. And if you sat at the wrong side of the bus, you would be considered a loser for the rest of the day. Well, in general, I think every Narvan associates life with this tank. People even come here during the weddings, it is a must, a tradition. [. . .] The tank symbolizes history, different battles that took place here. Narva suffered a lot during the war; it was almost completely destroyed. Everyone here knows this tank. I think it contains some kind of Russianness; I mean, I haven't seen Estonians coming here. It is rather the monument that symbolizes the Russian nation, especially for those who fought in the war and those who lived in the Soviet Union. But I might be mistaken. (Artur, interview with the author, February 21, 2016)

Henri Lefebvre ([1974] 1991, 139) once noted that monumental space constitutes a collective mirror, which offers members of a society a practical and concrete image of that membership, a social visage. For a long time now, the Tank has been a gathering point during the celebrations of Victory Day on the 9th of May, when people come to lay flowers and honor the memory of the fallen soldiers. Visiting the monument is clearly important for local Narvans today. For people like Artur, the Tank highlights the gap between the socialist and postsocialist visual representations of the city. It serves as a cultural heritage that projects the heroic involvement of Russian people in World War II as opposed to the official state narratives of repression and occupation. But it is also a material historical witness that helps to cement the spatiotemporal continuity of Russian speakers embedded in the Soviet past, as opposed to the ruptures and discontinuity promoted by the agenda of nation-building.

However, what for Artur is an eloquent memorial, a symbol of communal Russianness grounded in historical narratives of continuity, for others can be a mute location that remains invisible in everyday life (Jašina-Schäfer 2020). Especially those born in independent Estonia seem to rely less and less on the Soviet World War II memories as a marker of Russianness, thereby redefining the meanings of it altogether. Yuliya notes to me, for example, that she has many friends who do not associate themselves with anything Soviet and even less so with Russia: "There is no place for them in Russia, they don't have their Russian culture [as in the culture of Russia]. Many don't celebrate Russian holidays. Don't talk about Victory Day, what it is. Don't lay flowers next to the tank. This is a different generation" (interview with the author, February 17, 2017). The departure from the Soviet/Russian tradition of which Yuliya speaks does not necessarily strip Russian speakers of their "Russianness," nor should this example suggest the insignificance of the Soviet past for their present experiences. Rather, it serves to complicate our understanding of the socialization environment within which individuals move and interact (Jašina-Schäfer 2020). In the process of dwelling rooted in Estonia and Europe, Russian speaker change their social and political ideas, activities, and behaviors, whereby we witness how "being Russian" becomes highly heterogeneous, attached to and detached from the memories and places that symbolize the Soviet past.

Spatially reinscribing their alterity as "Russian" in no way precludes Russian speakers from a simultaneous desire to transgress this alterity. Numerous barriers separating Russian speakers from the formal and symbolic structures of the Estonian state were sought to be overcome by engaging with public spaces that represent alternative inclusive "Estonianness," separated from its heavily ethnicized meaning. There are future-oriented spaces that do not attempt to mend the past narratives, which in the context of Estonia are still painfully disjointed, nor reject or trivialize the narratives

Figure 4.3   Narva College and the Town Hall. *Source*: Author's photograph, July 2020.

of Russian-speaking minorities. Instead, such spaces are determined to create unity based on progressive thinking and common interests. The new building of Narva College (figure 4.3), opened in 2012, is in many ways an object of such hopeful outlooks. This is underpinned by the peculiar design and location of the college, which entangles different temporalities and spatialities. The modern building is situated at the heart of Narva's abandoned old town, with its facade containing elements that pay homage to the city's demolished baroque-era stock exchange building. The design contains other symbolisms: it has both a café called *Muna* (egg) and egg-shaped furniture elements that symbolize the beginning of a new life in Narva. The building also celebrates its borderland location, whereby two separate wings stand for Narva and Ivangorod, the city in Russia, with the gutter representing the river Narva, which separates the two.[3]

The college not only is accessible to students, but hosts numerous public events, jazz nights, book clubs, and memory games in both Estonian and Russian languages. These events are attended by locals and international visitors alike. For example, the memory games, in which I also actively participated, take place at the café with a relaxing atmosphere, which encourages mingling and socializing between Estonian and Russian speakers and between the older and younger generations. Drinks are sold at the counter and the questions are always asked in two languages, with tables located close enough for communication to extend beyond one's own group. When, by the end of the evening, a man with an Estonian accent eagerly proclaimed, "*my pobedim*" ("we will win" in Russian) you could clearly sense the erasure of boundaries between the Russian- and Estonian-speaking worlds. The building and the people inside it became, even if for one night, an "open society"—a spatial counterpart to the forms of social exchange on the outside (Jašina-Schäfer 2020).

My interlocutors, of different ages and professions, often come to hang out at the college. To them, it is the only place in Narva where they can "immerse into Estonian" and where the feeling of being a foreigner disappears. As noted by Vera (see chapter 2):

When the new college was opened, I realized immediately that I want to study here even despite my age, which is not so good for education [laughs]. So, I fulfilled my dream and came here to study. [. . .] Narva College is the only place here in the city where I hear the Estonian language, and I am very happy about it. It is like an immersion in Estonian for me. (Vera, interview with the author, February 16, 2017)

The college is a place that offers an abundance of opportunities to generate new friendships. The structure and internal operation of the college make room for those whose opinions are marginal to the Estonian mainstream. They break down the ethno-hierarchy and enable Russian speakers to overcome the tacit exclusions grounded in the project of nation-building. Thus, the college and the people transgress the "normal" order of space and become architects of a new sociability in which both Russian and Estonian speakers, though in some ways different, are both still essential to the Estonian community. In certain ways, this place bears resemblance to Foucault's (1986, 24) idea of "heterotopias," which describes cultural, institutional, and discursive "counter-sites" that alter existing common spaces. At the same time, it is not only the material space of the building that shapes subjectivities and grants legitimacy to Russian speakers. Rather, it is the individual tactics of use—taking part in or organizing different events—that largely determine and unlock the meaning of the collage as a space of interiority that facilitates the building of new social networks based on common cultural preferences.

These examples highlight several ways in which my interlocutors stitch together pieces to "make" the city. They reconstruct Narva as a place that foregrounds the codependency and entanglement of past socialist materialities and memories, which have not yet been erased from the city landscape, with new architectural sites that enable interpretive freedom for individuals to work out their disagreements symbolically, politically, or personally. At the same time, the cityscape is exposed to externalities that shift the meanings of urban spaces, making certain everyday experiences more feasible. The

Figure 4.4   The River Promenade. *Source*: Author's photograph, July 2020.

localization of foreign patterns could be, for example, observed at the River Promenade. Recently revamped with the help of funding from the EU, it is now a favorite among the locals, and it is where they take their children to the playground, do outdoor sports, stroll, and attend open-air concerts and other events (figure 4.4). The Promenade is a long pedestrian street along the river embankment and, as such, represents "the basic unit of public life in the city" (Tonkiss 2005, 68). While it might seem to be less concerned with direct sociability and encounters between people, it too is subject to different uses and meanings.

Located in the immediate vicinity of the border with the Russian Federation, the Promenade represents the fusion of distinctive styles and cultures: Estonian, European, Russian, and "local." Each of these styles has been naturalized and cemented through everyday use and each intersects and reconfigures the other (Jašina-Schäfer 2020). On the one hand, the medieval ensemble of the Narva tower signifies to Russian speakers the long history of Narva in Estonia. In fact, having their own childhood memories of it and interacting with it helps to strengthen their own interiority within the larger Estonian collective:

> I will tell you now one of my school memories. We were travelling a lot with my class, we went to Moscow, to Saint Petersburg. I liked it everywhere. But

there is this turn to Narva, when our castle becomes visible. When the bus would turn, and you would see the Hermann Tower. I would immediately tear up—this is *rodnoe* (native space), this is my home. And I would say: I am finally home. (Nadezhda, interview with the author, February 16, 2017)

When you come back from Russia, there is this turn and then a straight way, the last 8.8 kilometers on the way to Narva. As I remember from childhood, this was an ideal place to see Narva Castle, this beauty. I remember how as a child I would jump around the bus, because I knew I would soon see it. It was such an aching feeling. I always loved coming back here. (Sveta, interview with the author, March 15, 2017)

On the other hand, the Promenade represents the symbol of European power layered upon other meanings: it is the place where the EU starts. Walking along the "European" alley, illuminated by twenty-eight lamps (each symbolizing a member of the EU), Dima pointed to me at the other side of the river, the small and (in comparison to Narva) rather unspectacular Promenade of Russia's Ivangorod and its semi-ruined castle. This striking material difference between two cities separated by the river helped Dima to demonstrate the cultural superiority of Narva over Russia and its clear belonging to the geocultural space of "Europe":

Life in Russia is *dikaya* (barbaric) [. . .]. You stand out there and see the Russian River Promenade and think, oh hell with it. Ours is much better, and this plays an important role. [. . .] Why should I go there? Should I look at their architecture that was built by their granddads? Well, the granddads were fine fellows and not the new generation of Russians that is uncultured. (Dima, personal conversation with the author February 2017)

Invoking this array of spatiotemporal narratives enables the dwellers to expose the limits of the "nationalizing state," which by its continuous emphasis on ancestry and Estonian language leaves the majority of Russian speakers outside of its public space. Instead, Narva is constructed as a multi-layered space both different to Estonia and the same, with Russian speakers being simultaneously "in" and "out" of the collective. Despite certain separations, numerous connecting paths which portray the area and the people as quintessentially Estonian and European are being built.

Petropavlovsk between Russia, Kazakhstan, and the Globe

Walking along the streets of Petropavlovsk, we are left with a clear impression of being in Kazakhstan (figure 4.5): traditional Kazakh ornaments with

Figure 4.5   The Central Street Konstitutsiya. *Source*: Author's photograph, August 2016.

a zoomorphic imitation of a ram's horns—*qoshqar müyiz*—are depicted on concrete fences, facades, and balcony panels; predominantly blue and yellow colors from the national flag can be found on the different material objects that dazzle the visitors to the city. However, exploring further we notice how all advertisements and street names are written in two languages and all bus stops are announced first in Kazakh and then in Russian. At the main pedestrian street, Konstitutsiya, we too are exposed to different cultures and times existing in symbiosis. The street greets us with the Soviet monument of Eternal Fire, honoring the victims of World War II. Next to it stands the monument erected in 1999 to honor Kazakh heroes from the sixteenth and seventeenth centuries, Karasai and Agyntai Batyrs. Halfway through the street we come across the brand new music fountain that plays songs in Russian, Kazakh, as well as in English. The ensemble of different temporalities in stone is completed by the monument to Pushkin and Abai that symbolizes the friendship of the people and the Stella of the Independence of Kazakhstan.

The plural cultural mosaics inscribed into the urban space by the state authorities and city planners is reverberated in the diverse practices and perceptions of Russian speakers, who co-construct the city as a "fragmented universe of meaning" (Berger 1967, 134). This unfinished fragmentation, in turn, largely complements and challenges the dominant representation of Petropavlovsk as a "Russian-speaking space," opening new potential ways for interiority to emerge. During our walking tours through the city, several of my interlocutors took me to Victory Park, which they regarded as an important site in Petropavlovsk, especially for visitors. The park, located at the outskirts of the city, was built in 1967 to honor the fallen soldiers of World War II who gave their lives protecting the homeland. Renovated in 2010, it now represents a materialized memory of the Soviet past, which, unlike in Estonia, has a uniting narrative for Russians and ethnic Kazakhs alike and serves to blur the boundaries between different members of Kazakhstani society.

The Pushkin-Abai monument is another spot in the city that highlights the unity and entanglement of cultures across time. It was erected only recently in the central park but became very dear to many. This is a place, as I was told, where lovers meet for a date, where newlyweds give their promises of eternal fidelity, where the guests of the city are taken. In addition to the personal memories associated with the monument, it also carries a broader symbolic meaning for the local inhabitants. It is a valued symbol to all those residents of the city who consider Pushkin a part of their cultural legacy: Russians, other Slavs, and Russophone Kazakhs. Not without purpose is Abai, a famous nineteenth-century Kazakh poet and philosopher, the second character of the composition. Over 100 years ago, Abai repeatedly highlighted the importance of the Russian language, considering it as a connecting point with the rest of the world. He urged his folk to get closer to Russians, whose culture, he believed, was more advanced. Thus, this monument is perceived by many as a symbol of unity of Kazakh and Russian cultures, which bears a particular importance to one of the most ethnically diverse cities in Kazakhstan.

Apart from more localized elements, the built environment of Petropavlovsk also became a space that accommodates the so-called global condition of cosmopolitanism by both absorbing and reworking foreign models. Cosmopolitanism, however, is not defined here in relation to cultural orientation towards the "West." Following Ferguson (1999, 212–17), it is less concerned with the "West" specifically and more with "the world out there," the place where hit songs and action films come from." Put another way, cosmopolitanism denotes the experiences of being integrated into global processes and phenomena locally, structured by people's consumption practices: what kind of clothes one wears, what kind of hairstyle one has, where and what kind of beer one drinks. In my sample of Russian-speaking residents, similar lifestyles, dispositions, interests, and tastes experienced within spaces of intensive leisure and consumption were indeed considered far more important for social relationships and belonging than traditional links to nation and homeland.

Following the collapse of the Soviet Union, the landscape development in Petropavlovsk has been accelerated exponentially under the influence of global mass culture and globalization. The vanishing of old socialist architecture, the process of privatization, and the entry of private investors all dramatically restructured the cityscape of Petropavlovsk, increasing the significance of land value surfaces such as shopping malls, restaurants, and cafés in the

central parts of the city (Darieva and Kaschuba 2011). As part of a growing trend among the local businessmen to create a new urbanized lifestyle in
Petropavlovsk, recently the inhabitants of the city have witnessed the opening of numerous fitness studios that promote healthy lifestyles, of cafés that
disseminate the idea of coffee consumption as a style for a modern society,
as well as restaurants and bars with numerous references to designer styles
and architectural traditions from foreign countries. Most places carry English
names and have interior designs that would seem familiar to many Western
readers. A grill-bar Marinad, where some of my respondents took me during
my stay, represents one such place (figure 4.6). Marinad, the website claims,
seeks to break the stereotypes about the usual perception of a restaurant in
Petropavlovsk and its primary goal is to promote a new philosophy of eating:
"sharing is caring"[4] (the English phrase is used in the original Russian text).
As my interlocutor Arsen noted, this place is "*brendovoe* (branded), and cor-
responds to very high standards due to its uncommon but tasteful interior and
more expensive furnishing" (from a personal conversation with the author,
September 2016).

According to Laszczkowski (2011, 98), as part of a new urbanized lifestyle, places like malls, cafés, and restaurants become sites for negotiating
identities and hierarchies of value as well as for expressing personal desires

Figure 4.6   Young people at the "Marinad." *Source:* Author's photograph, August 2016.

for affluence and advancement. Indeed, throughout my conversations with Lena, mentioned earlier in chapter 3, she frequently initiated a topic about financial stability, highlighting the absolute necessity for her to visit places like Marinad:

> I love earning money, and I am not ashamed of telling you this. . . . For me to feel comfortable and calm at any place, I need money. Maybe I think this way, because for a very long time I had serious financial problems. Maybe because of this . . . I need a sufficient sum, so that I could visit any places I like or buy any presents I want. (Lena, interview with the author, September 15, 2016)

For Lena, Arsen, and several other interlocutors, cafés and bars often offer spaces to demonstrate their self-realization as people who made it in the global economy (Jašina-Schäfer 2019, 50). By spending time in the bars and local shopping centers, and demonstrating their awareness of brands, local residents associate themselves with "transnational" places and express their ambitions for a better life. Such a socially situated practice of self-making comes with the alignment with people who share similar signifiers of modernity and a "cosmopolitan" lifestyle (clothes, consumables, music) in opposition to others who represent more traditional ways of life. By coming together as people who can afford the new aspirational lifestyle, Russians and Kazakhs alike reevaluate the meaning of traditional boundaries between nations and cultures. However, while seemingly overcoming the old divisions between "Russianness" and "Kazakhness," places like Marinad also create new hierarchies and exclude some from the joys of aspirational Petropavlovsk, thereby serving simultaneously as places of interiority for some and exteriority for others.

IN SEARCH OF NATURAL BELONGING

In the same way as concrete material places, natural landscapes also represent settings where complex social relations are acted out, within or against which one's own belonging is negotiated. These settings reflect the ongoing sociality, conditions, and processes of adaptation and integration. Historically, the social and the natural were often torn apart and dichotomized, with "nature" coming to be defined as the passive, non-agent world "out there"—the physical environment which exists separately from humanity.[5] In the past decades, however, scholarly accounts have clearly recognized that the ideas of nature are fundamentally intertwined with the dominant ideas of society. What we understand as the natural world today, Cronon (1995, 25) writes, is closely entangled with our own values and assumptions, so that the word "nature" often reflects both the things we label as that word—trees, rivers, lakes—and ourselves situated in those things. In other words, the objects and landscapes we label as "natural" are far from inhabiting a separate realm from humanity. They are deeply entangled with our human worlds; not only is nature consti-tuted through a variety of sociopolitical process, but so is the social life vali-dated and legitimated through appeals to nature and the natural (Machaghten and Urry 1998, 15). Thereby, landscapes that on their surface seem to be uncontaminated by humanity are often turned into human symbols and cul-tural icons which we use as repositories for values and meaning as well as conceptions of national identity and belonging.

In my research, I was particularly interested in the ways the ideas of nation and homeland in Estonia and Kazakhstan are legitimized through the appeals to nature but also how individual Russian speakers imbue nature with their own meanings to reposition themselves within the larger social fabric. Previous studies have increasingly depicted nature both as a container and the essential producer of national belonging. For example, for Elias Canetti (1973, 75) it is neither the language nor territory, written literature, history, form of government, or national feeling that lie at the heart of the conception of national belonging. Instead, he is convinced that what turns individuals into members of a particular nation is a natural "crowd symbol," the "collective unit which do[es] not consist of men, but which [is] still felt to be crowds." Corn, forest, rain, wind, sand, and the sea are such units that become the essential attributes of any nation through myths, dreams, speeches, and songs.

The perceived symbiosis between a community and "crowd symbols" rooted in landscapes is indeed central for the phenomenon of nationhood (Smith 1999). In his book, *Myths and Memories of the Nation*, Anthony Smith wages a critique on the current views of the rise of nations which emphasize the role of the political domain while overlooking the properties of territory and the role of ancestral homelands. To him, the question at the heart of nationalism—"Who are we?"—is always closely connected with the questions of "Where we are?" and "What is our place?" Official narratives of national identity seek not only to define the nation's character but also to delineate a special place for the nation to inhabit, a land of "their own," or what Smith (1999, 16) calls an "ethnoscape." It is not any land, but "a historic land, a homeland, an ancestral land" which is felt to "influence events and contribute to the experiences and memories that molded the community" (Ibid. 149–150). Ethnoscapes are endowed with poetic and ethnic meaning through the "historiadization of nature" and the "territorialization of ethnic memories" (Ibid.) and help bring about a sense of belonging to a specific territory and a territory to particular people: "The ethnoscape becomes an intrinsic part of the character, history and destiny of the culture community, to be commemorated regularly and defended at all costs lest the 'personality' of the ethnic or regional community be impugned" (Smith 1999, 151).

To foster the ferocious enchantment of national belonging, national entrepreneurs pay significant attention to inculcating love for particular natural features of a territory and lavish a lot of praise on a particular landscape tradition. Through a wide range of practices, leaders and educators of the community endow a distinct landscape with ethno-historical significance. Oliver Zimmer (1998, 638) calls these processes the "nationalization of nature," or infusing landscapes with authentically national meaning, and the "naturalization of nation," or shaping the understanding of nation through references to natural landscapes. Both processes are intertwined and reinforce the authenticity and distinctiveness of national culture, allowing a community to project a positive understanding of itself (Schwartz 2006). At the same time, however, an overeager emphasis on an authentic ethnoscape for a nation can serve as an exclusionary function towards those who are not considered "authentic" enough within a particular terrain (Feldman 2001). It might reinforce the differences between the so-called indigenous populations and recent immigrants, who have allegedly less right to claim the new landscape as their home, creating further potential for exclusions. It is on these aspects, on the role of the natural landscape and landscape myths in mapping the margins of homeland in Estonia and Kazakhstan but also on the meanings that nature carries for my interlocutors, that the next sections concentrate, seeking to further our understanding of the link between narratives and practices of exteriority and interiority.

On the Symbolic Meaning of Nature in Narva

On one sunny but chilly morning, Raisa, a sixty-six-year-old pensioner, and I decided to go for a walk. Reminiscing about her childhood, her parents, and her favorite places in the city, Raisa spontaneously cited an excerpt from a poem by Igor Severyanin, a Russian poet who moved to Estonia in 1918 and fell irreversibly in love with its beautiful landscapes:

В пресветлой Эстляндии, у моря Балтийского,	In the brightest Estonia, by the *lilitnyi,*
Лилитного, блёклого и неуловимого,	faded and elusive Baltic Sea,
Где вьются кузнечики скользяще-налимово,	Where the gliding grasshoppers are winding up,
Для сердца усталого—так много любимого,	There is so much beloved, holy, cherished, near and dear—for the
Святого, желанного, родного и близкого![. . .]	weary heart! [. . .]

(Excerpt from the poem 'Baltiiskie Kenzeli' (1914), author's translation)

For Raisa, this excerpt contains a wide spectrum of feelings she herself associates with Narva and Estonia in general. At the core of her feelings are memories of a nearby river, where she spent most of her childhood years, playing with her friends, catching butterflies, collecting flowers in summer and acorns in autumn. This place of her childhood, Raisa grew convinced, became her home, her *malaya rodina* (see chapter 6), considerably affecting her personality and her love for nature, not just any nature, but Estonian nature: "the fresh Estonian breeze, the cold but beautiful Estonian sea."

However, these personal memories that Raisa was so kind to share with me, of her own belonging rooted in particular natural places, often uneasily coexist with the state interpretations of belonging to a nation that draw on characteristics of nature in rather exclusionary ways. National entrepreneurs often portray Estonia's borderland geography as a crossroads, as a periphery of the periphery where not only different cultural influences met, making the Estonian language so peculiar, but also different natures: the sea in the west and the mires and bogs in the east. In the eyes of Valdur Mikita (2013, 9), who published a series of books on the relationship between nature and Estonian culture, Estonia represents simultaneously an open bridge between cultures (*asub tõlkepiiril*) and an exclusionary space. Both narratives define Estonian identity through territorial terms, reinforcing binary oppositions (inside versus outside, indigenous versus immigrant) as well as dramatizing or minimizing some of the boundaries (Feldman 2001, 15).

The outward-looking narratives of "Europeanness"[6] pursued since the collapse of the Soviet Union and the efforts towards multiculturalism and international integration are uneasily juxtaposed with inward-looking "homeland" narratives.[7] Europeanness is more inclusive and welcoming towards minorities and newcomers and it values Estonian multiculturalism and multiplicity of identities, presenting Estonia as a bridge between different cultures: Finno-Ugric, Russian, German. The homeland narrative, on the other hand, in the words of Feldman (2001), defines Estonian identity as sharply distinguished from the rest of the world. The narrative opposes both European and Russian influence, positing that "ethnic Estonians possess a unique relationship with the Estonian territory that gives them a primordial moral right to that space" (Feldman 2001, 13). This ancient and close relationship of Estonians with nature distinguishes them from other folks in a modern and alienated Europe:

> No one in Europe can imagine a family where father takes a bike after work and goes fishing, while mother picks up berries, grandmother stocks herbal medicine and children go on their own to a nearby forest lake. Such a world has long been a fairy tale. (Mikita 2013, 87–88)

To emphasize Estonia's genealogical rootedness and exclusive connection to the Estonian space, political and cultural elites often invoke metaphors of Estonian soil and indigenous culture. In his accounts, Mikita (2013, 78–79), for example, connects Estonian cultural memory to the Finno-Ugric world, expanding Estonia's genealogy and geography both temporally and spatially on a scale of thousands of years and kilometres. Furthermore, images of the idyllic Estonian countryside with which the local population shares close links are reverberated in Estonian songs (e.g. through words like *jää vabaks, Eesti pind!*[8] or "stay free, soil of Estonia") and in the speeches of political actors (Unwin 1999, 159). As noted by the first president of independent Estonia, Lennart Meri (1996, 486), "The bones of 50 or 100 previous generations rest in this soil," highlighting the fundamental aspect of Estonian identity rooted in a particular ethnoscape.

The narratives of the peculiar connection between Estonian people and nature are by no means new. They emerged back in the time of the country's national awakening in the 1860s, when land reforms and cultural changes not only led to the emergence of the Estonian farmers as landowners but also generated the Estonian intelligentsia, who through poems and folk epics promoted Estonian national identity.[9] Up until the Soviet occupation in 1944, which initiated a land reform leading to collectivization, Estonia remained a fundamentally rural country filled with small-scale farming sectors. The Soviet collectivization process was met with resistance by many Estonian farmers, who often joined the forces of *metsavennad* (the Forest Brothers) to wage a guerrilla war against Soviet rule. Living a precarious existence and hiding out in the thick, dark woods became a way of life for many thousands of Estonian men. During this time, the heavily forested countryside, which served both as a natural refuge and as a base for armed anti-Soviet resistance, turned into another, in the words of Canetti (1973), "crowd symbol" of Estonian national identity. To this day, the forest plays a special role in the narratives of Estonians who continue to see themselves as "forest people" (Pilvre 2017): not only does it represent a "church-like" sanctuary but it also determines the specific character of ethnic Estonians. Oskar Loorits (1990), a famous twentieth-century Estonian folklorist, was, for example, convinced that the forest environment made Estonians alert, introverted, and melancholic, at the same time increasing their appreciation of difference, individuality, and democratic decision-making.

While the top-down accounts use nature in rather exclusive ways, as a bordering practice that creates an imagined geography of a distinct Estonian nation, nature evokes a multiplicity of meanings. In the same way as the built environment, the natural landscape can be layered with different interpretations through lived experiences and everyday use. It serves both as a "door" that follows the logics of division, difference, and separation, and as a "bridge" that serves to connect and unite (Simmel 1997). As a bridge, nature enables individuals to overcome seemingly entrenched divisions and differences, to build connections with national and local landscapes, and to establish the continuity, historic "nativism," and "authenticity" that they seemingly lack. In the account of Raisa, nature emerges precisely in these terms, as a unifying force, a seemingly borderless space that helps transgress the conceptualization of the Estonian ethnonation: "In nature there are no divisions, they are all artificially established. Nature—the river, the forest—unites and connects, whereas life embedded in sociopolitical contexts tries to divide" (from a personal conversation with the author, March 2017).

Several other Russian-speaking interlocutors used nature in very similar ways, to establish their interiority in and general unity with the national Estonian landscape. According to them, growing up alongside the natural landscapes, almost habitually going into the woods to collect mushrooms and berries or going for strolls, allowed them to develop a personal connection with Estonian nature, appropriating it as their "own":

Karina: For me, there is nothing closer and dearer than fresh Estonian air, the ripples of numerous Estonian bogs, the splash of waves of the cold Baltic Sea. Such a thrilling, albeit sometimes harsh, landscape cannot be compared with any tropical palm trees and southern sands. There is nothing more pleasant than strolling along in our pine forests or along the seashore. Why do I speak in such a poetic form? There is really no other way to talk about Estonian nature. It is unique.

Author: But what about Latvia, does not it have a similar landscape?

Karina: Yes, but Latvia is not my *rodina* (home). Landscapes familiar from childhood cannot be compared with anything else. (Karina, twenty-eight-year-old museum worker, interview with the author April 7, 2017)

I love going on holidays to Bulgaria. Everything is so sunny there, and I truly miss it. But then I come back here, and everything seems to . . . the Estonian forest, our sea. Although it is often very cold, but still it is somehow. . . . This is your country, and everything here is so dear. For example, I would not want to live in Russia. A female friend of mine met a guy and moved to Russia. She told me that, at first, she could not bear it at all, Russians in Russia are not like ours in Estonia. I think they are a completely *drugoi narod* (different folk). (Lilia, twenty-seven-year-old schoolteacher, interview with the author, March 11, 2017)

When I visit the Mediterranean Sea, it is warm and sunny. Here the sea is cold, but I still always tell my husband that I want to go to Ust' Narva (in Estonian: Narva Jõesuu). Well the sea is cold, but it is *svoyo* (one's own). Probably nostalgia. I cannot forget or throw away Estonia because of the politics; I cannot throw it out of my soul and say that I am going to live in Russia. Sure, I like Russia, I have many relatives there, but I know that I always come back here with big enthusiasm. My soul is filled with joy. It is *moyo* (mine). (Nadezhda, interview with the author, February 16, 2017)

These short excerpts clearly demonstrate how Russian speakers seek to claim rootedness in the Estonian soil, to which they do not see an equivalent. Sharing close links with the idyllic Estonian countryside, conveyed though such possessive pronouns as *moyo* and *svoyo* or through denoting these landscapes as *rodina*, they at the same time exteriorize spaces that they deem as "other," different or not theirs. Throughout several conversations, Narvans seemed to separate themselves from unfamiliar locations, strengthening their belonging to Estonia, especially in contrast to places like Russia. For example, as Marina, a thirty-year-old administrative worker, notes, the utter disorder in Russia cannot compete with the clean Estonian forest: "Our forests are all clean. In some places we even have *lõkkekohad* (Estonian for campfire) with wooden tables and places for tents. In Russia, you go out of the city into the forest and see nothing but dumps everywhere" (interview with the author, February 23, 2017). This conviction of the superiority of Estonian nature against disorderly Russia, as well as their own personal locatedness within these superior landscapes, was largely used to challenge the state-enacted vision of community belonging that marginalized Russian speakers. In essence, it was used to cultivate a particular vision of interiority where order was juxtaposed to disorder and the local and national to the foreign and distant.

The Accounts of Nature in Petropavlovsk

Seeking to identify how the Kazakh nation should be understood and remembered, the elites in Kazakhstan too increasingly draw on the imagined geographies of Kazakh land, as well as its natural terrain. The beginning of the twentieth century, Kendirbaeva writes (1999), marked the outset of the search for the national idea and authentic history among the Kazakhs. Since then, under the influence of the turbulent period of Soviet modernization, the discourses about nation and nationhood had been written and rewritten by local intellectual elites. Especially the 1960s–1970s marked the cultural and national renaissance, heightening the debates about "authentic" Kazakh national identity. In these debates, spatial metaphors of territory, geography, and land became essential points of departure to define local culture and the self. As Diana Kudaibergenova (2017, 66) notes, nomads and nomadic lifestyles, suppressed during the Stalinist years, became sources of nostalgic reminiscing in the 1960s, sources for criticizing cultural amnesia in the late 1980s, and central narratives of the Kazakh nation in the present day.

During Soviet times, Kazakh cultural elites contributed significantly to the spread of interest in the lost nomadic past, which in the context of Soviet modernization was often condemned as backward. Mukhtar Auezov, who became one of the most influential writers in the history of Kazakhstan, was the first to produce the Kazakh novel series *Abai Zholy* (*The Path of Abai*), which dwelled considerably on the nature of the Kazakh nation and the place of the nomadic narrative in it. Published between 1942 and 1956, the novel centers on the peculiar way of life and the imagined geography of traditional Kazakh society, reconceptualizing the relationship between nomads and space (Kudaibergenova 2017, 59–81). Importantly, Auezov demonstrates how the natural condition of constant movement generated not only practical skills utilizing the ecological environment but also a whole system of ethical norms, aesthetic concepts, and philosophical reasoning among ethnic Kazakhs.

Many other authors followed Auezov's spatiogeographical discussion. The importance of nomadic spatial imagination, pasture routes, and nomads' harmonious relationship with nature as defining principles of Kazakh national identity became the central themes in numerous other works. The trilogy of Essenberlin, *Koshpendiler* (*Nomads*, published in 1976), for example, helped to construct a united continuous vision of Kazakhs as a community with a long history rooted in the native steppes. His work, detailed with chronological historical data about the emergence and life of the Kazakh nation that fell under the rule of a stronger state, was particularly influential in rural areas, arguably creating feelings of pride and patriotism among ethnic Kazakhs (Kudaibergenova 2017, 92). Interestingly, many historical ethnosymbols and figures in *Koshpendiler* became important symbols and trademarks of post-Soviet Kazakhstan. The names of historical personages were used in street naming and the erection of monuments and most of the symbols of nature and animals (horse, golden eagle, sky, sun) are depicted nowadays in the symbols of Kazakhstan's nationhood: the flag and the coat of arms.

Although Soviet authorities waged "war" against local Kazakh nationalism, attempting to dilute or completely eradicate the "backward" and "uncivilized" narratives of the Kazakh nation related to nomadism and the land, such narratives found their continuity in the post-Soviet period. The ideas of "distinctiveness" of the Kazakh nation, which is eulogized in the chronicles and ballads or cemented at specific sites, are often incorporated into the growing ideas of Kazakh ethnonationalism today. Especially recently, when during the youth forum Seliger-2014 Russia's president Vladimir Putin awkwardly questioned the statehood of Kazakhstan, noting that former president Nursultan Nazarbayev did a unique thing—"He created a state on a territory that had never had a state before" (Kalikulov 2014)—the need to emphasize a distinct landscape endowed with ethnohistorical significance grew further. A few months later, Nazarbayev announced that in 2015 the country will celebrate the 550th anniversary of Kazakh statehood, which rests on the long history of the Kazakh Khanate established back in the fifteenth century:

> In 1465 Kerey and Janybek created the first Khanate, and the Kazakh statehood begins its history from that time. It may not have been a state in the modern sense of this word, neither did it occupy the present territory (of Kazakhstan), or enjoyed its fame and prestige in the world. But the same is true for all the other states of that era. What matters is that back then the foundation was laid, and we are the successors of the great deeds of our ancestors. (Nazarbayev cited in Urazova 2014)

Such authentication of national culture through the construction of continuity with a nation's alleged ethno-historical past (historicism through memories, myths, and traditions) and creation of naturalness (through sites of memory and poetic spaces) gives Kazakh ethnonationalism power over other more civic accounts of nation. This search for the "authentic" Kazakh nation is, however, often criticized by some cultural elites for bifurcating the population into those with nomadic ancestry and those without it. Indeed, according to the Russian-speaking inhabitants of Petropavlovsk, the overemphasis on the symbols of Kazakh ethnic heritage more often pushes them away rather than attracts them.

Feeling exposed to Kazakh national-cultural revival grounded in the narratives of authenticity and the policies of Kazakhization embedded in the urban landscape, my interlocutors often turned to nature and imbued it with rather distinct meanings. The idyllic natural landscape not only offered them some degree of stability and continuity that they otherwise felt deprived of, but was increasingly noted as a so-called place of refuge.[10] It was a place that allowed individuals to avoid Kazakhization policies and new sociocultural expectations which they cannot necessarily meet (e.g. learning the Kazakh language). In other words, nature and the natural landscape provided Russian speakers with a certain "normality," a daily reality within which their presence could be legitimized, within which they are able to feel themselves "in place" as opposed to being "out of place." Away from societal divisions, away from language requirements, away from the negotiation of statehood and national questions, Petr walked me to the city outskirts to show what freedom means to him. As we stood in the stifling sun listening to the sound of the far-away church bells and looking at the vast expanses of the Ishim Rriver, Petr exclaimed:

I love looking at the river from here. This place gives me a sense of freedom.
I can come here for a walk, leaving everything behind. This gives you a sense
of freedom from statehood, from political machinery. In the city there is no
possible way to feel yourself free. (Petr, personal conversation with the author,
August 31, 2016)

Here Petr highlights, of course, a further aspect of life in the city and the
country in general: a growing sense of authoritarianism. In this sense, nature
as a place of refuge does not only represent a site of stability and one's own
continuity, but more so as a get-away place from the elites' desires to legiti-
mize their power, which is becoming increasingly projected onto the daily
lives of Petropavlovsk dwellers. Indeed, according to Peyrouse (2007), in the
context of Kazakhstan both political life and the nationality question remain
intrinsically connected: the discrimination that Russian speakers might experience is strongly linked to political machinery that reduces any possibilities
to defend one's own interests. Another research participant also felt the need
to address this point:

Even here [in Petropavlovsk] I come across not very pleasant things. This is
related to the issues of statehood. For example, during the elections, they watch
over people, whether they have been to the elections or not. It does somehow
bring a feeling of restrictions on our freedoms. In other words, you experience
rather substantial control from the side of law enforcement agencies and state
authorities over the population. On the one hand, we speak about order, but on
the other . . . well . . . it brings some discomfort. For example, you don't want
to come across the police. We have the policeman everywhere in the city; they
walk around the streets . . . and you know they violate many rules. (Arsen, interview with the author, August 24, 2016)

Apart from being depicted as a safe space, nature and natural landscapes carried
a further symbolic meaning for Russian speakers, being largely connected
with their images of home. In a process, that Smith (1999, 151) considers
to be a "territorialization of memory," my Russian-speaking interlocutors
imbued landscapes with particular childhood memories and past experiences,
thereby establishing a sense of belonging to Petropavlovsk as a peculiar
location somewhat disentangled from the national space of Kazakhstan. Very
exemplary here is the account of Nastya, a nineteen-year-old nurse, who
claims a special connection only with a place depicted on the photograph that
she brought along to one of our meetings, while stressing the difficulties of
being a Russian speaker in nationalizing Kazakhstan (figure 4.7):

This place is important. I spent nineteen years of my life there. I think I will
never be able to forget it, to take it out from my heart. So many pleasant

Figure 4.7 At the Sunset. *Source*: Photograph provided by Nastya and reproduced with her permission, September 2016.

memories. My whole growing up happened there and it will continue. I will not leave this place any time soon. This place is so important and warm to me. If you go down from here, you will find yourself at the beach. Every single summer I spend there. So many funny moments with my friends. (Nastya, interview with the author, September 6, 2016)

Through memory and embodied experiences, the seemingly unfamiliar and vast nature acquired a further layer of meaning for people like Nastya, becoming their own and endemic place, a part of what Russian speakers regard as their *rodina* (I will return to this notion in detail in chapter 6).

Disparate Paths

By paying specific attention to the meanings of concrete places, this chapter provided an account of the ways in which the experiences of belonging in the borderlands change along with different material forms in the city, the symbolic connotations that natural and built sites generate for Russian speakers, and the individual uses of these spaces. Entangling the perceptions of my interlocutors with the agency of material objects and natural sites, I reconstructed a complex cartography of interiority and exteriority, depicting "inside" and "outside" as states of constant relation and synthesis. Through numerous examples of dwelling, the belonging of Russian speakers emerges as a state of exterior interiority, a state embedded in the process of boundary construction and transgression between different "cultural styles" which not only overlap but also evolve. Different histories and the current sociopolitical realities in Estonia and Kazakhstan produce different conditions for the expression of exterior interiority in Narva and Petropavlovsk. Although both cities are characterized by the entanglement of multiple spatialities and temporalities—Soviet, Russian, Estonian/ Kazakh, European, or global, these entities exist and condition each other in dramatically different ways, making claims or expectations about the uniform experiences of belonging of Russian speakers across post-Soviet spaces rather problematic. Instead, what emerges out of this research is the existence of multiple versions of exterior interiority and multiple belongings thereafter. This will become even more apparent in the next chapter, as we turn to the discussion of the complex relationship between Russian speakers and the external space of Russia.

NOTES

1. In this chapter, some of the materials are being reused and reproduced with the permission of rights' holders. The section "Re-assembling Narva as a Plural World" reuses interviews with Artur and Yuliya, the description and discussion of the Narva College as well as the interviews excerpts with Vera, Nadezhda, and Dima from: Jašina-Schäfer, Alina. 2020. "Of Homogenous 'Freaks' and Heterogenous Members: Cultural Minorities and their Belonging in the Estonian Borderland." *New Diversities* 22 (2). The section "Petropavlovsk between Russia, Kazakhstan, and the Globe" reuses interview excerpts with Lena and Arsen from: Alina. 2019. "Everyday Experiences of Place in the Kazakhstani Borderland," *Nationalities Papers* 4 / (1).

2. For more information on conflicting narratives (liberation versus occupation) of World War II, see Onken (2010).

3. During Soviet times, despite being located in different republics, Narva and Ivangorod had shared transportation, water, and power supply systems, as well as shared telephone communication.

4. As I never observed this principle in action nor could my interlocutors explain its meaning, I was left with the impression that the phrase was simply reappropriated from other English-speaking restaurants without connoting any particular meaning to be transferred into practice.

5. For a good overview of the meanings of "nature" across cultures and times, see Macnaghten and Urry (2000), Williams (1980), Gold (1984), Glacken (1992), and Ely (2002). These authors reconstruct nature not as a fixed entity, but as a setting that is historically, geographically, and socially constituted.

6. This narrative defines both where and what Estonia is but also where it is not. In other words, while proclaiming the European character of Estonia, this narrative also acknowledges the insurmountable barrier between Estonia and Russia, with the former being a frontier of Western civilization and the latter being neither European nor Western.

7. According to Unwin (1999, 151) the resultant tensions of these competing images of national identity are expressed both within the political arena through contrasting patterns of support for political parties in different parts of the country, and in the dramatic changes taking place within rural society.

8. A soldier's song written by Viktor Konstantin Oksvort in 1930.

9. Note that before the nineteenth century, the territory of Estonia and the majority of its people were under the control of different ruling elite, including Danish, German, Swedish, and Russian.

10. In chapter 2, I already scrutinized how Russian speakers in Petropavlovsk, while seeking to overcome the growing unease with administrative Kazakhization, have constructed their place as a "Russian-speaking space," a legitimate space where they had rights to belong. The section here adds a further layer to this representation, demonstrating how individuals negotiate the division between inside and outside by finding refuge in nature, which grants Russian speakers a sense of freedom and stability.

Chapter 5

Relationship with the External Space of Russia

RUSSIAN SPEAKERS: A DIASPORA PROJECT?

On the 18th of March 2014, the day when the Treaty on the Accession of Crimea to the Russian Federation was signed, Russia's president Vladimir Putin spoke to the Duma deputies and Federation Council members of the tragedy of millions of Russian speakers in the former Soviet Union republics. Being the rightful citizens of the Soviet Union—the country that they arguably regarded as their own—people had been transformed, practically overnight, into minorities with unequal power and status, into foreigners outside of the Russian territory. In the aftermath of the fall of the Soviet Union, as Putin noted further, "time and time again the attempts were made to deprive Russia's 'own people' abroad of their 'historical memory,' of their language and to subject them to forced assimilation" (President of Russia 2014a). Russia, in turn, saw it as crucial to present itself as a guarantor of rights to Russians and Russian-speaking citizens, which it promised to uphold at all costs. It is not the first time that the Russian state presented itself as being responsible for the lives of Russian speakers. However, a momentous shift in the diasporization of Russian speakers has been traced by scholars and political observers after Putin returned to the presidency in 2012. The issue of the political membership of the Russophone communities in the post-Soviet borderlands was then elevated into the realm of geopolitics, resulting in the 2014 annexation of Crimea and military incursions into Eastern Ukraine.

In this chapter, I analyse the ways in which post-Soviet Russia seeks to reconstruct itself as an inclusive space for the Russophone community outside of its territory, the ways it reconfigures its boundaries through the vast notion of the "Russian World," and how this process is concurrently enmeshed in the individual belonging and positionality of Russian speakers

between the "inside" and the "outside." In essence, I explore and problematize the complex relationship to the external space that Russian speakers
develop and negotiate in the process of dwelling in Estonia and Kazakhstan.

When looking into Russia's relationship with the *near abroad*[1] or the
so-called space of its geopolitical interest, it is important to start with the
term "diaspora," the use of which has proliferated dramatically since 1991.
Although during the Soviet times hardly anything written existed on the
Russian diasporas in the global political dimension, the break-up of the
USSR crystallized Russia's huge "politically and socially disturbing 'diasporic' heritage" (Kosmarskaya 2011, 56). The outburst of the elite interest
in expatriate communities in the near abroad brought along "a discursive
reconfiguration of the borders of post-Soviet Russia according to the geographical location of the Russian *ethnos*, rather than [its] current administrative borders" (Pilkington and Flynn 2006, 56, emphasis in original). Indeed,
as Kosmarskaya (2006, 475) points out, numerous public debates on the
expatriate communities in Russia have been extensively focused on ethnicity and groupism, turning millions of Russian and other Russian-speaking
residents of former Soviet republics into the object of diasporization. Within
those discourses, the "Russian diaspora" emerged as a strongly consolidated
and homogeneous entity of people, who share a common ancestry, a cultural
link to their historic homeland and are, therefore, an object of special responsibilities on the part of their "motherland" (Pilkington 1998; Pilkington and
Flynn 2001).

The active use of the term in Russia considerably enhanced research
into the "Russian-speaking diaspora" in the West (among the most cited
are Aasland 1996; Kolstø 1995, 1999; Melvin 1995; Zevelev 1996). This
research, however, quite problematically defined Russian speakers as a more
or less homogeneous community, ignoring the ambivalent character of the
concept that is very much dependent on the changing sociopolitical circumstances and transnational flows (for critique, see Clifford 1994). As a result,
we were left with either a lack of terminological precision or a superficial
understanding of the term "diaspora" as an object of governance that (1) is
dispersed from an original homeland and maintains a memory of it; (2) is not
fully accepted in their host country or at least believes this to be the case; (3)
might eventually seek to return to the ancestral home (Brubaker 2005).

The question of whether the links to the original home of Russia indeed
exist and whether the "Russian-speaking diaspora" is more than just a
political project have long been understudied. Seeking to avoid the so-called
virtual diasporization, to date, Kosmarskaya (2006) is among the few who
has scrutinized the validity of the term in the context of Russian-speaking
communities abroad. In her research, Kosmarskaya seeks to understand how
first-generation Russian speakers integrate into a nationalizing society and

what attachments they hold to their country of residence and to Russia. After a prolonged fieldwork in Kyrgyzstan, Kosmarskaya finds a lack of support for a diasporic identity among Russian speakers, highlighting their strong emotional attachments to the places where they live. Scholars like Pilkington and Flynn (2006) have too pointed towards the absence of a clearly defined diasporic identity among Russian speakers who do not necessarily perceive Russia as their true "home/land."

In this research, in line with Kosmarskaya (2006, 2011) and Pilkington and Flynn (2006), I do not assume the existence of "diasporic" features— or worse, identities—with which the Russophone communities are often ascribed by the Russian authorities. Yet I do not wish to go as far as to disregard the top-down bordering and diasporization practices of the Russian state altogether. According to Cheskin and Kachuyevski (2019), the discursive practices of the Russian state remain important, as they create a basis for people to potentially associate themselves with a bigger part of the "Russian World." More importantly, as Schulze (2017) notes, such policies have a potential to influence policymaking regarding Russian speakers in their states of residence, which could lead to even more exclusionary national visions that exteriorize the minorities. Both studies build their remarks increasingly on the relational triadic nexus described vividly by Brubaker (1996) in his famous book *Nationalism Reframed*. In this work, Brubaker argues that the national question in post-Communist Europe is largely characterized by a specific juxtaposition and interaction between three mutually antagonistic elements: nationalizing states, national minorities, and external national homelands.[2] The defining elements in this triadic configuration have been the complex interrelations between the nationalism of the nationalizing state and that of the external national homeland. As a legacy of continuously fostered discrimination under foreign control, the nationalizing states (after having attained independence), Brubaker argues, sought "remedial" action by using state power to promote the specific interests of the core nation, as well as to draw external and internal boundaries between "us" and "them." Thus, when the nationalizing states impose policies that favor their own majority group at the expense of minorities, the "external national homeland" can arise in opposition to those policies, seeking to protect the rights and interests of "its" ethno-national kin.

As noted earlier, for many Russian speakers living in the post-Soviet states, Russia is considered to be "natural external homeland," for it not only can play an important role in their identity formation but, at a certain point in time, it might also attempt to exert a stronger influence on the people it considers its own. Of course, labeling states as external homelands for dispersed groups certainly does not automatically make them so (King and Melvin 1999, 116). This notwithstanding, Russia's continuous codification of Russian speakers as its kin-folk can make us better placed to understand how belonging is constituted through diverse and unraveling bordering practices not only of the states where minorities reside but also potentially by the external spaces. Exploring the narratives of the Russophones about and their expectations of Russia, this chapter demonstrates how this external spatiality comes to play an important role in the constitution of their belonging. The images of it, as I argue, are used considerably differently depending on whether we view it from the position of Russian speakers in Narva or in Petropavlovsk. In what follows, the empirical sections juxtapose the visions of Russia as overwhelmingly a foreign backward place in Narva to the perception of Russia as a cultural-historical and economic resource in Petropavlovsk, which demonstrates the complex existence of multiple "Russias" differently layered and reconfigured by Russian speakers in the course of their everyday lives.

Before turning to the detailed analysis of the narratives of Russian speakers, we will commence with a deeper look into Russia's practice of "diasporization" and its attempts to unify Russian speakers beyond its borders, which foremost involves the development of a political concept of *sootechestvenniki* or compatriots. In other words, we will first examine the ways the Russian state has recognized and claimed its compatriots abroad as well as the main objectives behind such policies.

FORGING LINKS THROUGH RUSSIA'S COMPATRIOT POLICY

From 1991 onward, millions of Russians and Russian speakers residing in the post-Soviet republics became the focus of the evolving set of policies by Russia, the self-proclaimed successor of the USSR. Seeking to conceptualize approximately 25 million ethnic Russians and a further eleven million culturally Russified former Soviet citizens as its own people, as a part of the Russian nation, a very loose concept of "compatriots" was created. It was, however, not an easy task to lump Russian speakers together, as they differ in their degree of integration, their economic well-being, future aims, and political rights. This became particularly visible through a broad and mutable usage of the term "employed" by the Kremlin at various points in time. To date, almost any Russian speaker or anyone born in the Soviet Union, regardless of their ethnicity or language, has been at some point defined as a Russian compatriot. While in the English language the term "compatriot" usually refers to "fellow countryman or countrywoman," the Russian word *sootechestvennik* encompasses ethnic, cultural, linguistic, political, and even spiritual connotations (Grigas 2016, 58).

Despite the absence of a clear conceptual definition, the harsh social realities and, in some cases, deprivation of civic and political rights experienced by Russian speakers in the neighboring states turned the issue of the Russian-speaking population into a prevalent debate inside Russia (Nozhenko 2006). The domestic political and economic difficulties that in the early 1990s prevented Russia from implementing policies that would assist compatriots abroad were seemingly left behind, when during the 1997 address to the Federal Assembly, Russian former president Boris Yeltsin (1997) officially stated that "the utmost priority of the Russian foreign policy was and would be the protection of the rights of our compatriots living abroad." Following the announcement, the basic legal framework for and a proper definition of the concept of "compatriots" was approved in 1999 by the Federal Law. The law defined compatriots as those who are "citizens of the Russian Federation living abroad," those who "were born in one state and are living or lived in it," those who "share common language, history, culture, customs and traditions," as well as their direct descendants, except for "descendants of persons who belong to titular nations of foreign states" (Federal Law 1999, Article 1). Thereby, the term "compatriots" moved from encompassing a civic core to a broader group of people who are culturally or spiritually oriented towards Russia.

The development of a fuzzy definition of compatriots, which became even more confusing following the amendments of 2010, should be seen in the broader context of Russia's bordering practices and nation-building dilemma. According to Kosmarskaya (2005), the broad perceptions of the make-up of compatriots fit perfectly into the overall political attempts to bridge two competing versions of the Russian nation: an ethnic one (*russkii*) and a civic one (*rossiiskii*). Like any other newly independent post-Soviet state, Russia's nation-building project faced serious problems in reconciling civic identities based on inclusive citizenship with exclusive ethnic identities defined by common characteristics such as culture, religion, language, and a common ancestor of the dominant nationality. The nation-building was further complicated by the overall disagreements among politicians, intellectuals, and ordinary people about the "just borders" of the Russian Federation, which since the collapse of the Soviet Union, has been struggling to define the symbolic as well as physical boundaries of Russianness and that of the Russian nation (Tolz 1998, 993). Such disagreement gave rise to the neoimperial nation-statehood project that seeks to build a strong multiethnic state that is able to protect its influence abroad (see, for example, Kolstø 2016). Inspired by the "Russian question" (*russkii vopros*), the term coined by Solzhenitsyn in 1995 in his famous book *The Russian Question at the End of the Twentieth Century*, the *impertsy* (champions of the empire) support Russia's reconnection with its pre-Soviet past, which implies including the historically defined

"Russian zone" into the newly formed Russian Federation. In this process, compatriots come to play a significant role. As Marlene Laruelle (2015a, 92) observes, in the early and mid-1990s President Yeltsin attempted to promote a civic identity, asserting that Russian speakers abroad are "sufficiently protected by international legislation on the protection of national minorities." However, due to pressure from radical national groups, he had to abandon the civic Russian idea and take up the topic of the protection of the Russian diaspora. This symbolized, as Ammon Cheskin and Angela Kachuyevski (2019) note, a clear shift in the understanding of symbolic boundaries of the Russian Federation, with the historical, ethnocultural boundary going beyond the actual physical border of the state.

While the seeds of Russian compatriot policy were planted under Yeltsin, it was only when Putin took office in 2000 that the strategy towards compatriots changed significantly, becoming central to the country's political rhetoric. In his first annual address to the Federal Assembly in 2001, Putin stressed the priority to defend "the rights and interests of Russians abroad, our compatriots in other countries" (cf. Hedenskog and Larsson 2007, 33). The necessity to protect compatriots abroad was consequently declared a natural priority of Russian foreign policy objectives. It first entered the Foreign Policy Concept of the Russian Federation in 2008 and then reappeared in 2013. The latter document insists on the need to ensure comprehensive protection of the "rights and legitimate interests of Russian citizens and compatriots residing abroad" (The Ministry of Foreign Affairs of the RF 2013a). Another important change involved Russia's Compatriot Law itself. The amended law of 2010 was equally if not more ambiguous than that of 1999, facilitating a wide range of cultural, historical, and ethnic axes for individuals to claim compatriot status (Cheskin and Kachuyevski 2019). Indeed, the law not only focused on claiming compatriots as an organic part of the Russian nation, but it included new groups of people thereby redefining the history-bound understanding of Russianness, Russian identity, and Russian culture (Kozin 2015, 288). As a result, to date, any person who feels a spiritual or cultural connection with Russia and is descended from any of 185 nationalities inhabiting the Russian Federation currently or other nationalities that used to inhabit Imperial Russia could be called a compatriot (Grigas 2016, 90). In her research, Oxana Shevel (2011) usefully outlines the functionality of such ambiguity in the law, arguing that it effectively helps the government to solve Russia's nation-building dilemma: with the ambiguous law the policymakers can, on the one hand, avoid emotionally charged debates on the questions of the nation's boundaries, while being in a position to pursue a broad range of policies in the name of compatriots, on the other hand.

Compared to Yeltsin's regime, the rhetoric under Putin became more focused on blurring the previously established borders of Russian identities and that of the Russian space. This can be particularly discerned in two of Russia's central tools of compatriot policy: the repatriation program and the legitimization of the concept of *Russkii Mir* (Russian World). While the inward centered repatriation program (launched in 2007) seeks to encourage the return and a general orientation of compatriots towards the so-called historic homeland, *Russkii Mir* is an outward project used for the promotion of a common ideational and civilizational space of Russia. The latter has also been actively employed in several foreign policy domains and used to literally expand the borders of the Russian state beyond the politically manifested geographies. For example, in 2014, following the annexation of Crimea, Putin drew particular attention in his speech to the notion of Russia as a "divided nation," emphasizing the gap between Russia's territorial body and its cultural body, with Russian speakers abroad appearing as boundary markers of the Russian nation (Laruelle 2015a, 95). In this sense, the reunification with the peninsula symbolized the reunification of the nation (Cheskin and Kachuyevski 2019), which has been uneasily observed, even feared, by other states that are home to a large number of Russian speakers.

THE BORDERLESS SPACE OF THE RUSSIAN WORLD

The theme of a unique inclusive "Russian World" that extends beyond Russia's borders has clearly become an important symbolic appeal to Russia and could be attractive to many Russian speakers who feel increasingly marginalized in their states of residence. The concept had been discussed by Russian philosophers, sociologists, and political scientists long before it entered Russia's mainstream political vocabulary in 2001. According to Laruelle (2015b, 3), in many aspects, the "Russian World" resembles the ancient perception of a shared civilizational space, such as the ancient Greek World or Roman World. The notion of "world" comprises broad territories dominated by a singular center that share the center's cultural values, display political loyalty to it, and are integrated into its economic space. Analyzing the origins and trajectories of the post-Soviet Russian World concept, Laruelle (2015b) highlights Petr Shchedrovitskii and Gleb Pavlovskii as its key creators. In 1996, Pavlovskii, for example, founded the Russian Institute, with a declared mission to promote the institutionalization of Russian cultural identity and *vossozdanie russkogo kak novogo* (recreation of the Russian as the new) through the "re-birth and resurrection of the Russian soil under the new Russian sky" (Chernyshev and Pavlovskii 1997). In the manifesto, Pavlovskii and Chernyshev criticize the long unsuccessful attempts to understand *russkoe samosoznanie* (Russian national consciousness) that arguably leads to a desperate "denial of the existence of the Russian as such" (Chernyshev 1996).

During this time, Petr Shchedrovitskii, who worked under Pavlovskii's main consulting firm—the Foundation for Effective Policy, made further efforts to develop the idea of *mir Rossii* (Russia's World). Along with his colleagues, Shchedrovitskii described *mir Rossii* as a peaceful reestablishment of Russia's identity that reconnects with its diasporas and with its past (cited in Laruelle 2015b, 4). It was, however, only in 1997 that the term "Russian World" emerged in its current form. In the article entitled "Russia: The Country That Did Not Exist," Shchedrovitskii and Ostrovskii elaborated on their definition of the Russian World further:

> During the twentieth century, under the influence of tectonic historical shifts, world wars and revolutions, the 'Russian World' was created on Earth—a network of large and small communities that think and speak in Russian. It is known that the territory of the Russian Federation contains hardly half of this Russian World population. The state form that arose on the territory of the Russian Federation at the turn of the 1990s did not turn out to be an adequate means to incorporate Russian society into the world historical process. [. . .] This process of modern social degradation has been compensated by the process of formation, over the course of the twentieth century, of a large Russian diaspora in the world (Ostrovskii and Shchedrovitskii 1997).

While the term *russkii* (ethnically Russian) lay at the center of their Russian World project, the designers of the concept sought to depict Russia's identity as encompassing, as standing in a dialogue with the world. The Russian World as such was to be understood as a progressive *Russkii Mir v Mire Mirov* (Russian World in a peaceful World), not seeking territorial expansion or aggression. Under the presidency of Putin, however, the term acquired a particular interpretation as a space that extends "far from Russia's geographical borders and even far beyond the borders of the Russian ethnicity" (Putin 2001). The Russian World was, thus, imagined broadly "as a naturally existing civilizational community" defined through the Russian language, spiritual and religious values, as well as a common historical past (Feklyunina 2016, 783). The Russian World Foundation, founded in 2007, drew an even blurrier picture of the Russian World as a world consisting "not only of Russians, Russian citizens, Russian compatriots in the countries of near and far abroad, emigrants, natives of Russia and their descendants," but also "foreign citizens, who speak the Russian language, who have chosen to learn or teach the Russian language and those who developed sincere appreciation for Russia and are interested in its future" (Russkii Mir n.d.).

Such fuzzy geopolitical imagination of the space of the Russian World offers to Moscow a particularly powerful repertoire, whereby different regions in the world and their links to Russia can be articulated in very fluid terms (Larulle 2015b). On the one hand, it can be used as a justification for Russia to oversee and interfere with the development of its neighbors or as means to reconcile with its diaspora abroad; on the other hand, it can serve as a crucial instrument to position itself on the international stage. As a "common civilizational space" (Chepurin 2009) the concept of *Russkii Mir* goes hand in hand with the compatriot policy discussed earlier. As the director of the Department for Compatriots Abroad, Anatolii Makarov, stated:

> In order to achieve its main goals, the multifaceted Russian World beyond Russia is based firmly on compatriots. The goals include, first of all, strengthening the ties with the historical homeland and preserving Russian civilizational space (language, culture, national customs and traditions). (Ministry of Foreign Affairs 2013b)

By promoting Russian language, culture, and specific spiritual and moral values (the latter often advocated through the Russian Orthodox Church), the Russian World hopes to reinforce the ideational identification of compatriots with the Russian state (Cheskin and Kachuyevski 2019). There are numerous ways in which Russia seeks to cultivate a sense of what Russia stands for and to forge stronger links to its "imagined diaspora" abroad. Enshrined as a key component of Russia's cultural diplomacy, the cultural and value-related narratives of the Russian state are advanced through cultural centers, exchange programs, historical commemorations, as well as through the media. According to Kolstø (2011), Russian media, which continues to enjoy a strong position in most of the Soviet successor states, exerts a considerable pull on Russian speakers in post-Soviet republics. In countries like Estonia, Latvia, and Lithuania, it reinforces the divisions between the titular populations and the Russian-speaking minorities, who inhabit different information spaces. By consuming Russian newspapers, online news portals, watching Russian soap operas, reality TV, and talk shows they all become part of a Russian virtual space. Of course, pinpointing exactly the source of this appeal is rather problematic, as the reasons might include the Russian speakers' identification with Russia, the limited media offerings by their states of residence, or something else entirely (Grigas 2016, 87). This notwithstanding, the multifaceted efforts to unify Russian speakers into the greater space of the Russian World cannot be ignored.

However, neither can we ignore the attempts of the Russian state to draw a clear boundary between the imagined community of *Russkii Mir* that is based on the civilizational values of Russianness and the non-Russian "other" (Cheskin 2016, 179; Torbakov 2017). Keeping, on the one hand, the boundaries between Russia's geobody and cultural body intentionally blurred while, on the other hand, emphasizing its distinctiveness from the "others," gives the

Russian government much room to manoeuver between observational policy and direct interventionism. Speaking on behalf of its so-called diaspora, Russia has, for example, criticized exclusionary nation-building policies and their discriminatory effects on the lives of Russian speakers, especially in the Baltic states. Already in the early 1990s, Russia accused Estonia and Latvia of ethnic cleansing, internationalized the issue of Russian speakers by placing it into the agenda of all major regional and international institutions, and passed a law in 1992 allowing all former Soviet citizens to register for Russian citizenship. Various cultural initiatives and media sources are also used to project more assertive signals to Russian speakers abroad; to bolster Russian cultural, linguistic, and spiritual values, and to forge stronger ties with Russia on a state-based level (Cheskin 2016, 174–181; Gromyko 2010).

Taking into account these complex bordering practices by the Russian state and its attempts at creating an inclusive civilizational space under the banner of *Russkii Mir*, the rest of this chapter aims to understand different ways in which Russian speakers negotiate their relationship with Russia and how Russia feeds into their meanings of belonging.

FROM A HISTORICAL HOMELAND TO A FOREIGN PLACE: VIEWING RUSSIA FROM NARVA

Writing about Russian-speaking diasporas and their place in the world, Russia's famous ethnologist and the former Chairman of the State Committee on Nationalities, Valerii Tishkov (2003) once argued that the concept of homeland represents individuals' rational choice and less so their historical connection to a country or a region. Had Estonia not turned to such an exclusionary citizenship policy, a more favorable economic environment, Tishkov is certain, would have broken down the links to present Russia. Should Russia, however, get the impression of satiety and well-being, Russian-speaking Narvans could significantly change their orientation, especially if the obstacles to their integration into the dominant society prevail. Then, Tishkov continues, it is not only the manifestation of a solid diasporic group which becomes possible but also irredentism (i.e. movement for reunification with Russia).

While the rational choice argument is significant, and reappears in several other studies (see, for example, Laitin 1998), during my stay in Narva the individual understanding of belonging or not belonging, inclusion or exclusion, did not rest upon economic considerations alone. Equally important were the symbolic meanings places convey, defined through memories, behavior, as well as cultural and linguistic practices. In fact, many Narvans confessed that they adhere to the Russian culturescape (derived from Appadurai's multiple scapes, Appadurai 1996), understood in broad terms as related to the Russian language, traditions, and common memories of historical events. Exemplary here is the way one of my interlocutors, Yuliya, a student in her twenties, refers to Russia as her *istoricheskaia rodina* (historical homeland):

> To me, Russia remains a historical homeland, which we cannot reject entirely. Because of the language, because of traditions, I am not ready to give my child to an Estonian kindergarten, to let it dive into Estonianness. I want it to preserve the traditions of Russia. And since our countries do not get along well, we are forced to give up on our traditions, on the holidays that we are so used to celebrating. (Yuliya, interview with the author, February 17, 2017)

Reading these lines, we are left with the impression that Yuliya has an affinity with Russia as a container of history and culture—the exact response that the Russian government would have hoped for in pursuing the consolidated inclusive Russian World. However, the scarcity of such accounts among my interlocutors is noteworthy. The majority, as Yuliya herself admits, "do not associate themselves with Russia," at least not as a political entity. Having spent decades among the peoples of Estonia, Russian speakers remain clearly aware of their differences from the residents of Russia. The dividing line runs, in fact, as deep as the vision of Russian culture itself, whereby *russkaia kul'tura* (Russian culture) has been divorced from *rossiiskaia kul'tura* as represented by the Russian Federation. Contrary to the previous scholarly observations that highlight Russia's high cultural attraction for Russian-speaking populations in the Baltic states (Cheskin 2015; Kallas 2016), Yura, a salesman in his thirties, claimed the following:

> What is Russian? If someone told me that it means belonging *k velikoi derzhave* (to a great power), then I don't have that. To begin with, I don't even have relatives in Russia. No relatives, nothing. I don't feel my belonging to that country. I only have my native language that we happen to share, that's it. (Yura, interview with the author, February 27, 2017)

The excerpt serves as an example of how, following the collapse of the Soviet Union, the Russian culturescape in Narva, or *Russkokul'turnost'*, in the words of Kosmarskaya (2011), took on a life of its own without staying necessarily connected to the self-proclaimed core representative of this culture—the Russian state. This is not to argue that Russia has lost any connection to Russian speakers in Estonia. Rather, the statement captures well the complex emotional relationship that has been lost to Russia in the process of long-term dwelling in Soviet and, later, independent Estonia. The formation of cultural differences between Russian speakers living in Narva and

Russia was not only true for the younger people but ran across generations, who also perceived the departure from the Soviet past in a positive light. To that end, the boundary with Russia, as I dissect in the coming paragraphs, is not only physical or political (Cheskin 2016, 110) but also increasingly symbolic, which refers to differences in behavior, life modes, everyday "cultural styles," and even culinary preferences.

In numerous conversations, my interlocutors highlighted their clear orientation towards and belonging to the space of Estonia. The symbols of such attachment vary from positive experiences in particular places in Estonia (see chapter 4), through narratives of one's own continuity in place, to memories of unforgettable Estonian landscapes. On several occasions, my respondents were indeed quick to portray Russia as a foreign place, once again refuting the "teleology of original return" (Clifford 1994, 306):

> Russia is something different. We have lived here long. Before we had some friends in Ivangorod, visited the cinema, regularly crossed the bridge. And now it is a foreign place to me. Simply overnight. . . . I recently got myself a visa, haven't been to Russia in a few years. I came there and thought 'Oh, God'. Nothing has changed, nothing at all. It is like everything froze there. (Vika, interview with the author March 6, 2017)

Artur: Before it used to be one infrastructure. Everyone visited each other. We bought things there [in Ivangorod], and they bought them here [in Narva]. It was one united city. But when the separation started, we understood that [Ivangorod] is no longer ours.
Author: What about now?
Artur: Now it is like heaven and earth. I was there not so long ago, and you know, I think the city [Ivangorod] used to be better, cleaner back then [in the Soviet Union]. Of course, Narva is well cared for, I would even say better than Tallinn. But the difference between Russia and Narva is tremendous. (Artur, interview with the author, February 21, 2017)

Drawing upon emerging local differences between two sides was a common practice among Narvans. By comparing Estonia and Russia, Narva and Ivangorod, to "heaven" and "earth," Artur seeks to distinguish between two countries. In his eyes, Estonia represents development and progress, whereas Russia remains down at the bottom—on earth. Such symbolic boundaries are not new and already existed in the Soviet times. Through mostly "tourist" observations in other parts of the Soviet Union, my Russian-speaking interlocutors often claimed Russia to be "wild," "alien," and backward not only in terms of living standards but also its political freedoms. Previous impressions were strengthened in independent Estonia, which after 1991 chose a clear trajectory towards Europe. The "return to Europe" narrative marked Estonia's historical belonging to a "superior" cultural space and was readily adopted locally by people seeking to make sense of life in the borderland.

What is more, Estonia's high economic performance and consumerist orientation has created "an image of urban renewal" (Pfoser 2017, 34) and enlightenment in Narva: several streets have been refurbished, and new cafés, restaurants, a cinema, and shopping malls have been opened. On the other side of the river, in Russian Ivangorod, these changes remained clearly missing. Seeking to lead a "decent life," many Narvans embraced their lives in Estonia even despite the state's exclusionary citizenship policies, which to many signified a rejection of their legitimate membership in Estonian society. Socioeconomic differences between Narva and Ivangorod represented a common trope in the narratives of the Russian speakers, but the divide was further strengthened through perceived sociocultural differences.

Earlier, some have argued that Russia holds a strong cultural appeal for Russian speakers abroad (Vihalemm and Masso 2003). Whether through Russian historical narratives, consumption of Russian media, or through the commonly shared Russian language, cultural interests, and lifestyles, Russia remains an attractive location (Cheskin 2015). However, the extent of Russia's symbolic appeal should not be overestimated. As already briefly mentioned in the previous chapters, describing the individual daily experiences during the Soviet as well as post-Soviet periods, Russian speakers often highlighted the civilized and cultured Estonian and European character of the Narvan space:

> For me Narva is Estonia. I cannot even imagine it being a part of Russia and I can say why. When I was a child, we would often go to Russia. Now I still go to Russia, we have a house there on the Lake Peipus, about 80 kilometers away. People are different there. Our mentality is completely different. Of course, Russian stays Russian, this we cannot deny, but. . . . (Sveta, interview with the author, March 15, 2017)

For my interlocutors, belonging to a specific place and a specific cultural community is based on a clear awareness that they are different from residents of Russia. Rooted in the experience of life in Estonia, described as superior and more civilized, my respondents made a clear-cut division between "us" and "them" in terms of living modes, behaviour, and everyday culture. The narratives of being different Russians or "the other Russians" (see Kosmarskaya 2005) speaks to the development of a separate space of "Russianness" and Russian culturescape. Already in the 1990s, Kolstø (1996, 618) suggested that Russian speakers of the near abroad see themselves as "Russians of a special kind" who have adopted new habits, customs, and ways of life prevalent in the region. The growing differences between Estonian Russophones and

Russians in Russia represent, in fact, a longer process. What Kazlas (1997, 241) terms the "Balticization" of Russian settlers in the area was already detected in the 1970s. The intense appreciation of the high standards of living in the Baltic states and the perception of the indigenous culture as equal or even superior to Russians' own gave a strong incentive to emulate the "Baltic way of life" during the Soviet times (Kolstø 1996, 628).

Indeed, many of my respondents believed that dwelling in Estonia had profoundly impacted them. In this process, they acquired the admirable characteristics of ethnic Estonians (e.g. sensibility, calmness) as well as adapted to enlightenment and modernity. Russia, in this regard, remained an exterior space, "backward," "noisy," and "disorderly." Artur, for example, claims the following:

> You know, being in some foreign country I would feel very comfortable to hear Russian speech and to know that these are *rossiyane* (citizens of Russia). And then I would hear Estonian. Whom do you think I would choose? Of course, an Estonian. After all, we are from Estonia, which is *moya zemlya* (my land). Despite my Russian language I can tell you right away that Russians in Russia are entirely different, their way of life . . . . Even the ads in the Estonian language warm my heart more than those in Russian. This astonishes me sometimes. A person who comes from my country is more important to me—*moi zemlyak* (my fellow countryman). (Artur, interview with the author, February 21, 2017)

Taken together, the interview narratives indicate how physical, political, and economic boundaries drawn against Russia expand to the symbolic realm. For people like Artur, the transformation of the Russian-speaking population in Estonia was so profound that it would be hard to bridge the boundary that arose between Estonian Russians and Russian Russians. As another respondent points out, he was born in Estonia, and therefore is *ne russkii* (no longer Russian) and definitely ne *rossiyanin* (not a citizen of Russia):

> I am a Russian speaker. My mother tongue [here he uses the Estonian word '*emakeel*'] is Russian because my parents are Russian. But I am Estonian. I am a kind of hybrid produced by Soviet times that appeared here on the territory of Estonia. (Dima, interview with the author, February 15, 2017)

Despite the negative developments in Narva, manifested through the socioeconomic peripheralization and sociopolitical marginalization of the Russophone inhabitants, many claimed that their local roots embedded in the country where their parents grew up, where their children were born. In this case, being a "hybrid," as Dima calls himself, does not refer to a liminal experience of being "in-between the host country [Estonia] and their parents' country of origin [Russia]" (Nimmerfeldt 2011, 206). "Hybridity" emerges here as a performative symbiosis of fractal but overlapping cultural forms cultivated by Narvans, often unconsciously, over time. It refers to their ability to identify simultaneously as "the other Russians" and to claim their belonging to a greater space of Estonia and Europe by exteriorizing Russia.

WHAT IS RUSSIA IN PETROPAVLOVSK?

The longstanding academic discourse claims that Northern Kazakhstan is politically, economically, and culturally geared towards Russia (Kolstø 1996). This could be showcased well through the persistent migratory flows that connect the two countries today. When the Soviet Union collapsed, the fog of uncertainty considerably hastened the migration of Russian speakers to Russia's territory. Altogether, about two million Russophones left Kazakhstan between 1989 and 1999 (including about half a million Germans who left for Germany). In 2000, migration from Kazakhstan to Russia alone constituted more than 28 per cent of the internal migration in the former Soviet Union (Peyrouse 2008). To compare briefly with Estonia, the population outflow there towards Russia reached around 20,000 people in 1992 but dropped very quickly (Tishkov 1993). Estonia's higher quality of life and entanglements with everyday Estonian social and cultural practices all strengthened the reluctance of Estonian Russians to follow the call of the so-called historical homeland for repatriation. For example, during 2008–2012, 1,355 persons emigrated from Estonia to Russia while a total of 4,378 moved from Russia to Estonia (Kallas 2016). Although in Kazakhstan the migratory tendency has also dropped from 2004 onward, numerous Russian speakers still leave for Russia. According to statistics, 104,407 Russians have left Kazakhstan over the last five years (Simakova 2016, 105).

The lure of Russia remains strong particularly when it comes to socioeconomic opportunities. According to Simakova (2016, 107), dissatisfaction with the current quality of life and scarce prospects for self-realization motivate the emigration of Russian speakers. This is especially evident in the Northern Kazakhstan Region, which since 2012 has persistently constituted the lowest regional gross product in the country (Kazakhstan National Agency for Statistics 2016). In 2016, the growth of tariffs for utilities in this region outpaced the growth of salaries, which represent countrywide the lowest average of 101,814 Tenge (roughly 260 EUR) (Novikov 2017b). Furthermore, Kazakhstan loses out to Russia in terms of development of social support and provisions. The established opinion that the representatives of a nontitular ethnicity lose out to ethnic Kazakhs, have difficulties in achieving success, and building a career in the government sector also damages Kazakhstan's image. For example, a young twenty-five-year-old resident of Petropavlovsk, Anya, notes that Russia offers not only jobs and higher salaries but also more equal opportunities for employment:

> Many of my friends left. My best friend went to Novosibirsk, got married, found a job, and has a perfect life now. Another friend is in Ekaterinburg and life there treats him well. He works in an oil company, all is good. In comparison to Petropavlovsk, there is more work, better salaries, more opportunities. And here people commonly say that if a Russian and a Kazakh apply for the same position, chances are higher for Kazakhs to get employed. (Anya, interview with the author, September 15, 2016)

Economic conditions in Kazakhstan visibly deteriorated since 2014–2015; despite the assumption of at least 5 per cent annual growth promoted by the Kazakhstan-2015 vision, the overall growth slowed to an estimated 1.5 per cent per year (Laruelle 2015c). International sanctions against Kazakhstan's primary trading partner, Russia, falling oil prices, technical problems at the giant Kashagan oil field, and the overnight devaluation of the national currency have rattled the Kazakhstani population (International Crisis Group 2015). In light of the economic decline, the lack of social change and the underdevelopment in a city like Petropavlovsk became particularly visible, aggravating a sense of marginality among the inhabitants. These problems led one journalist to describe Petropavlovsk as a "beautiful city that does not exist" (Novikov 2017a). Poetically, Novikov writes about memorable old-time buildings and streets that are now filled up with a "dense veil of architectural debris: billboards, poles, wires," aggravated by a lack of governmental incentive to heal the "warts on the beautiful face" of the city. To people like Novikov, all these ruined landscapes serve as real non-human reminders or "phantomic spaces" (Navaro-Yashin 2012) of the past that were laid to waste by current political projects.

The seeming lack of modernization in Petropavlovsk can be linked to the prevailing elite's focus on the capital of Nur-Sultan as "a central site for inscribing the desired vision of the future in Kazakhstan" (Koch 2010, 774), a "showcase for the achievements" to give citizens a sense of positive social change and order, to reaffirm the goals of development and progress (Bissenova 2014, 133). For the Petropavlovsk inhabitants, however, Nur-Sultan is too distant to identify with the designed progress and change. Instead, they associate themselves with the immediate built environment of their city and the "devastation" surrounding it. Consider, for example, the reasons Lev, an NGO worker in his thirties, provides for leaving for Russia:

> As I was saying, our region is in depression. Almost every month around 2,000 people leave. Here we have no town-forming production centers, no factories.

When people come here from Russia, they don't understand how people live. We say, 'well, how we live . . . well, business, sell and buy, you know. That's it.' In truth, we have a lot of teachers, doctors, but no big factories. So, when young people finish schools, university, they have no idea where to go next. It's then easier to leave. (Lev, interview with the author, September 9, 2016)

Another respondent, Igor, who just graduated from university, confirmed that Petropavlovsk lacks offers in the job market: "Here there is no opportunity to live, no means for a good life" (from a personal conversation with the author, August 2016). Russia, in this context, often acts as an important socioeconomic resource, as a place to do business and find jobs, a place that offers a large variety of consumer goods, and a place to acquire prestigious higher education in a convenient Russian-speaking environment. This convenient environment is often forged through the presence of friends and relatives on the territory of Russia who not only provide emotional support to the newcomers but also amplify the negative image of Kazakhstan:

What is really important is the presence of friends, relatives and acquaintances in Russia, those who moved a long time ago. I also have relatives in Tyumen' and no one wants to return. By now, they all have negative stereotypes about our country—that Kazakhstan is destitute, poor, and highly corrupt, that everything here is done *po blatu* (through connections). If you have a relative, you will make it [in Russia]. If not, then you won't. (Lev, interview with the author, September 9, 2016)

Scholars who have conducted research in Northern Kazakhstan convincingly argue that for Russian speakers a trip to Russia does not necessarily represent a stressful journey into a foreign country (Kosmarskaya and Savin 2018). It is instead a daily routine through which the borderland is constituted as an extension of a Russian common space, the so-called Russian-speaking space (see also chapters 2 and 3). Such extension helps to bring a sense of "worldliness" (Ferguson 1999, 212) to Petropavlovsk, a sense of being integrated into global processes locally. As such, the trips to more economically advanced Russia represent spatializing everyday practices "that creatively imagine and shape alternative social visions and configurations" of Petropavlovsk as a "worlding city" (Ong 2011, 12).

An image of Petropavlovsk as a "worlding" location is reconstructed further through a narrative of a cultural-historical commonality with Russia. Memories of the Soviet past and the domination of the Russian language reinforce a sense of a common Russian space and dilute interest in traditionally Kazakh "culture" or Kazakhstan altogether:

I am Russian and live in Kazakhstan. I don't want it to be like this. Here, only ethnic Kazakhs can achieve something higher, something better. Russians are no longer accounted for. You know, I am listening to the radio here. . . . It is the radio of our country, and I don't understand it. You watch TV channels of your country, but don't understand them. When you go to Russia, on the other hand, you feel you belong. You don't have to translate, you don't have to wait 'til the weather forecast is announced in Russian [. . .] Of course, I probably have too little contact with Kazakh culture, too little. Their holidays are foreign to me, yes, foreign. But holidays in Russia, it's a different thing. I do appreciate Kazakhstan; it has beautiful nature. Well OK, it's a good country. But I love Russia more. (Nastya, interview with the author, September 6, 2017)

How did such a profound divide and alienation from Kazakhstan emerge? How did Russian language and culture come to play such a peculiar role? The answers go back in time as far as Imperial Russia and the Soviet Union. While in countries like Estonia Russian speakers tended to see the indigenous civilization as equal or even superior to their own, in Kazakhstan Russians were cast in role of social *Kulturträger* (culture carrier) on a mission to "civilize" the titular population (Fein 2005). Seeking to socially advance the Central Asian region, both the Russian Imperial and later Soviet rule created an Orientalist geopolitical hierarchy of people that designated the indigenous populations as "backward" (Grant 2009). On a *kul'turnaya missiia* (cultural mission), seen as noblesse oblige—a duty to those under domination—the Russian language came to represent modern social life and access to high culture. With time, ethnic Kazakhs who lacked access to education came to associate knowledge of Russian with being *kul'turnyi* (cultured) and belonging to a larger "European civilization" (Dave 2007, 68). While, for example, in Estonia an elite assumption of Estonia's cultural and economic superiority vis-à-vis Russia prevailed, in Kazakhstan it was the Russian language that was unequivocally linked with modernity and mobility. Its diffusion to all echelons of the society, as Dave (2007) notes, enabled the Russian language to attain hegemony and to be accepted as "normality." Those who joined "the civilization" and modern social life had to pay a significant price: their distinctive national customs, language, and traditions. As a consequence, during the "cultural mission" the new modernized Russophone urban clusters formed on Kazakh lands with few, if any, socio-cultural contacts with the indigenous population residing in the surrounding villages. By the time the Soviet Union collapsed, the cultural gap between the urban Russified residents of big centers like Almaty and Kazakh rural inhabitants was strongly palpable.

The hierarchy of cultures that designated ethnic Kazakhs as backward and Russophones as culturally superior has also carried over into the post-Soviet period. Russian speakers' unequivocal sense of cultural and civilizational superiority in Kazakhstan is firmly grounded in the belief in their decisive contribution to the transformation of tribal Kazakhs into a modern Kazakh nation state (Dave 2007; Grant 2009). In times when their cultural superiority was seemingly challenged, many of my research interlocutors imbued Russia with a positive image, as a "safe haven" for the Russian language, history, and culture. Consider, for example, the words of the nineteen-year-old Lera, who feels uneasy about the growing influx of titular nationalities from southern rural areas:

> I think Petropavlovsk will soon too . . . I think it [normal life] soon will be over. Because slowly, slowly they all come here. They fill our Russian lands. I would be happy if Petropavlovsk joined Russia. Many people are waiting for it. (Lera, interview with the author, September 5, 2016)

The arrival of rural migrants, as I discussed elsewhere, aggravates concerns among the long-standing Russophone dwellers about the urban composition of their cities. It also heightens the feeling of commonality with Russia; this is, however, not ethnically conditioned. Kosmarskaya and Savin (2018), who conducted research on the perception of Russia among Kazakhstani citizens, argue that both Russians and Russophone ethnic Kazakhs view the vicinity to the Russian Federation similarly. They no longer see Russia as simply a neighboring foreign country but as an economic resource and a container of history and culture. As a result, the social divisions in Kazakhstani society continue to grow (Karaulova 2018). The gap between different groups is particularly visible in values and everyday outlooks: the Russian-speaking part of the population increasingly consumes Russian media, with its own heroes and role models, whereas other groups prefer Kazakh-language content.

Although the symbolic cultural-historical importance of Russia could not be denied, it should not be overstated either. My numerous conversations with Russian speakers provide evidence for the simultaneous development of a Russian culturescape independent of the Russian Federation, whereby Russianness gains new meanings in the process of close contact with ethnic Kazakh culture and people. Although some express contempt for the Kazakh culture, depicting it as "foreign," in chapter 3 I extensively discussed how the distance form Kazakh culture always goes hand in hand with "cultural intimacy" (Herzfeld 2005) with it. Through repetition of cultural practices alongside ethnic Kazakhs—and often unconscious incorporation of certain Kazakh cultural traits—the boundaries of Russianness become eroded. It is only through confrontation with other cultural codes that this gap is revealed.

Many émigrés to Russia recount numerous negative stories of life in their destination country. Following Russia's resettlement program, Russian speakers are often confronted with a lack of acceptance of their "Russianness" by the local population in Russia. The reality of being in the Russian Federation often utterly differs from the official state discourse that promotes Russian language and historical ties as the main determinants of one's belonging to the Russian World (Jašina-Schäfer 2018, 14). Many newcomers experience hostile attitudes from the local population, which often leads to their exclusion from the everyday Russian ethnic and civic community (Pilkington and Flynn 2006). The direct interaction with the compatriot policy does not always serve Russia either, creating the image that the country is indifferent to their plight. For example, Potap, a journalist in his mid-twenties, told me how *bezperspektivnost'* (futility) combined with a desire for a better life brought him to Russia: "I couldn't breathe here anymore. It is hard to live in a city with limited opportunities. People already have a very negative picture of the city and so did I." However, although some manage to move to Russia successfully, there are also people like Potap who return: "Well, it's a good program, but you are treated like a pig, like a second-class person. This was so humiliating" (personal conversation with the author, October 1, 2016). Before the resettlement attempt, Petropavlovsk seemed to Potap grey, monotonous, and shabby. Coming back, however, gave him a second wind and strengthened the idea that Petropavlovsk—not Russia—is his home.

AN OUTSIDE-INSIDE SPACE

Seeking to draw a more comprehensive picture of everyday belonging among Russian speakers, this chapter focused on the relationship the borderland dwellers hold to the external space of Russia. The detailed analysis of the ways in which Russia's authorities conceptualize the Russian-speaking population abroad as well as the individual attitudes towards Russia, helped us crystallize the different meanings that Russianness carries across post-Soviet countries. These divergent visions and incarnations of Russia as both an exterior and interior space feed significantly into the ways belonging is constituted and negotiated in different local contexts.

In Narva, while links to Russia prevail in terms of common language and memory of historical events, Russianness took on a life independent from the self-proclaimed core representative of this culture: the Russian Federation. Drawing a boundary between *rossiiskaia kul'tura* and *russkaia kul'tura*, the latter is tightly linked to a discourse of becoming European; *rossiiskaia kul'tura* (culture of the Russian state) is, in turn, used as a negative reference point to reinscribe oneself into the national space of Estonia and to strengthen the claim of inherent interiority within the larger space of Europe. For the Russian-speaking residents of Petropavlovsk, Russia carries a different meaning: it represents both a significant economic resource in the context of the declining Kazakhstani economy and a long-standing cultural-historical reference point against the seemingly inferior culturescape of Kazakhstan. However, even in a context of predominantly positive image of Russia, the boundaries of Russianness were also often eroded. In the process of dwelling alongside ethnic Kazakhs, Russian speakers came to position themselves as "different Russians" and claim their local roots and links to their place of birth.

As such, Russia represents different spaces at once. As an "outside" space of difference and an "inside" space of commonalities and aspirations, Russia is actively used in the process of demarcation and negotiation of boundaries and spatial belonging of Russian speakers.

NOTES

1. The conception of the near abroad (*blizhnee zarubezh'e*) as a specific region of interest was formed by Russian authorities following the immediate collapse of the Soviet Union. For a detailed discussion of this term that refers to the geopolitical space of the former Soviet Union, see Laruelle (2015b).

2. David Smith (2002) later expands this framework into a "quadratic nexus," considering how the global European and Euro-Atlantic intergovernmental organizations shape the dynamics of post-Soviet state- and nation-building.

Chapter 6

Defining *Rodina* for Russian Speakers

IN ENGLISH "HOME" AND "HOMELAND,"
IN RUSSIAN *RODINA*

What is the meaning of home and where do Russian speakers feel at home in light of their complex experiences of inclusion and exclusion, of constant movement between inside and outside? Feeling "at home" is an essential element in people's daily lives (Dixon and Durrheim 2004; Yuval-Davis et al. 2018). Some may relate this concept to the physical structure of their house and how it affects their attachments; some may refer to spatial connections to their cities, nations, and countries; others might talk in more abstract terms of their childhood memories, present experiences of safety and comfort, as well as future aspirations. The widespread usage of the notion of home not only in everyday life, but also in popular culture and in political discourses makes it one of the "key characteristics of the world" today, mirroring multiple individual practices and social relations (Blunt and Dowling 2006, 2). As such, the ways "home" is being deployed in different contexts can tell us much about people's values, attitudes, and their ways of thinking about the world and life in it.

In this chapter, I seek to understand the meanings that home carries for the Russian-speaking residents of Narva and Petropavlovsk, as well as how these meanings are used to reflect upon their own exteriority or interiority. Despite the prominence of political discourses that attempt to define or redefine home for Russian speakers (remember, for example, the conceptualizations of *Russkii Mir*), very little attention has been devoted to the specific ways individuals negotiate their own visions of the notion. The overwhelming focus on the politically constructed space could have been induced by the problematic equation of the Russian everyday concept of *rodina*, both personal

119

and sociopolitical, with a category of homeland as a communal sociospatial marker that largely lacks the personal intimate connotations commonly associated with home.

The interest of the Anglophone literature in the term *rodina* grew exponentially after Brubaker (1993, 1996), whom I already mentioned in the previous chapter, famously introduced the notion of "external homeland" while referring to Russia. According to Brubaker, an external national homeland represents a top-down political construct to which minorities within a different state hold a sense of ethnocultural affinity (Brubaker 1993, 7). Following these assertions, other scholars have at first replaced *rodina* with the notion of homeland bound up with the politics of place, identity, and collective memory. At this time, research focused primarily on homelands as political entities, scrutinizing how through political discourses countries like Russia seek to inscribe a geography of inclusion for Russian-speaking compatriots abroad (see, for example, Kaiser 2004).

Later studies, however, began to also consider the micro-level perspectives, focusing more and more on people's personal feelings, which led to the emergence of several new conceptualizations, such as "internal homeland" and "mixed homeland" (Barrington et al. 2003; Nimmerfeldt 2011).[1] At the same time, these informative perspectives remain overwhelmingly concentrated on a national space, still determined by the use of the English term "homeland," which simply cannot be stretched to the expanses of *rodina*. Indeed, as Anna Wierzbicka (1997) notes, the meanings of the words from different languages often do not correspond, despite being artificially matched by dictionaries. These words are culture-specific and reflect the ways of living and thinking in a particular society. In this sense, "homeland" or "home" separately do not carry the dense connotational baggage of *rodina*. When my Russian-speaking interlocutors spoke to me about *rodina* they spoke about both spatial imaginaries generated through individual familiar practices as well as political boundary discourses. In what follows, I preserve this duality of the term *rodina* and emphatically intertwine with it the Anglophone ideas of home and homeland.

As a spatially "elastic" concept full of internal conflicts and differences (Wiles 2008, 121), throughout my research *rodina* was often used by Russian speakers to position themselves and move between different meanings of exteriority and interiority. In order to facilitate a better understanding of belonging in the post-Soviet borderlands, I will now dissect spatialities that are regarded as *rodina* and the ways through which my interlocutors redraw the boundaries of home. The multiplicity of places that this chapter considers as *rodina*, whereby not only the nation represents home but also the city, a village nearby, or a symbolic imaginary location that does not exist on the map, stands in stark contrast to previous sociological studies. These studies either argue for the complete obliteration of the notion of *rodina* for many Russian speakers following the collapse of the Soviet Union (Vitkovskaya 1999) or are convinced that Russian speakers still hold strong emotional bonds to Russia and identify with it as their only true home (Lebedeva 1995). My analysis reveals, however, the dynamic and often open-ended process of constructing *rodina* among Petropavlovsk and Narva dwellers. It is a process in which "new and renovated cultural symbols, activities, and materials are continually being added to and removed" in order to transgress one's own exteriority (Nagel 1994, 162).

RODINA: ETYMOLOGY AND SEMANTIC MEANING

Every society, Wierzbicka (1997, 195) writes, has its own keywords. On the one hand, such keywords represent the collective spiritual, cultural, and material heritage of a given society, while, on the other hand, they can depict a certain "mental reality" in place. Often sought to be matched with analogues in other languages, such keywords are idiomatic and are not entirely translatable (Vorkachaev 2006). While they do overlap with other social concepts, experience breaks, and take detours, they are nevertheless always linked with the specific social and historical circumstances of their space of production and reception (Bachmann-Medick 2016). As such, these keywords are not free-floating and unchangeable, but are always spatially and temporally anchored. In the Russian language, Wierzbicka (1997, 191) notes, *rodina* is a type of concept that reflects a society's past experience of doing and thinking about things in certain ways.

How can we then define *rodina*? Deduced from numerous interview narratives, in this research *rodina* represents a term that invokes the vast and intractable web of memories and personal feelings that people associate with a place. Stemming from the root word *rod* (origin, species), it simultaneously connotes familiarity, proximity, and a sense of ownership, designated through words such as *rodnoi* (loosely translated as one's own, familiar, close to one's own heart), the most common derivate of *rod*. *Rodnoi*, first of all, refers to an "inner circle," directly linked with one's body and, thus, inherently one's "own," inherently close: *rodnaya* family, *rodnoi* father, *rodnye* eyes. The circle of *rodnoi* is then inhabited by familiar people, friends, and family members and is linked to places of personal dwelling: *rodnoi* house, *rodnaya* village, *rodnye* places. The geographical boundaries of *rodnoi* have a further tendency to include into its spectrum a city, a country, and the world, demonstrating the capacity of the concept for spatial expansion from personal and familiar to a form of communal identification (Sandomirskaya 2004).

Being semantically connected with the word *rodnoi, rodina* is equally inclined to be spatially elastic. Scholars like Veronika Teliya (2001, 410–415), for example, dissect two closely interlinked meanings of the term: *rodina* 1 or *malaya* (small) *rodina* and *rodina* 2 or *bol'shaya* (big) *rodina*. In this sense, *malaya rodina*, according to Teliya (Ibid., 414), is a familiar microcosm, a highly personal understanding of spatiality as one's own place, where a person was born, dwelled for an extensive period of time, and has relatives and close friends. *Malaya rodina* is often viewed as an integral part in the process by which individuals make sense of the self and belonging (Terkenli 1995). *Bolshaya rodina*, in turn, is a socially, politically, histori- cally, and culturally established collective niche, often used in the language of power. It is a continuation of *malaya rodina*, whereby the boundaries between the two remain always blurred.

Roughly speaking, *rodina* exists simultaneously on different spatial scales: as a house where one's family is, one's neighbourhood, city, nation, or region. As a notion, it is also highly temporal and can be produced through habits repetitively unfolding in certain contexts (Wiles 2008); numerous behavioral and affective routines help individuals to develop over time their own sense of home and may contribute to the creation of a collective home in the form of a common imagined homeland (Terkenli 1995). *Rodina* is, furthermore, a social phenomenon, established through social relations that reconfigure boundaries, excluding or including an individual, as well as his or her belonging, in a broader collectivity. Not being necessarily a fixed place or even a node, *rodina*, as such, could be defined as a relationship between people and things in place shaped by sociopolitical and economic settings in which this relationship unfolds. Put like this, the notion certainly intersects with the Anglophone concept of "home" that too is seen as a space that "traverse[s] scales from the domestic to the global in both material and symbolic ways" while located on "thresholds between memory and nostalgia for the past, everyday life in the present, and future dreams and fears" (Blunt and Varley 2004, 3). At the same time, while "home" is politically, culturally, and socially constituted, it does not necessarily include the broader meaning of *bolshaya rodina* as a reflection of a state-based socioterritorial locus of ethnicity, people, and the nation.

This brief analysis highlights the limits of a straightforward "cultural trans- lation"[2] of the term *rodina*, which would lead inevitably to the changes and shifts of its meaning in the process of recontextualization and reception. The terms "native country" or "native land," as stressed by Pilkington and Flynn (2001), are too limited in that they preclude the possibility of an adopted *rodina*; yet a person does not have to be born in a particular place to feel that he or she belongs. Other words like "native country" or "homeland" are also too political, whereby "country" or "land" refers to the nation and the state, overlapping with the Russian word *otechestvo* (fatherland). Encompassing the archetype of mother and origin, concepts like "motherland" or "mother country" could coincide with the value of *rodina*, which in Russian represents the image of a female progenitor (Esmurzaeva 2008). Still, at the same time, *rodina* is not only associated with a country, but, as stressed earlier, has a narrower, more localized, and more intimate meaning that emerged and became rooted as time passed.

Historically speaking, the formation of *rodina* as an ideological construct (in Teliya's sense, *bolshaya rodina*) has undergone several transformative stages. While I argued repeatedly that *rodina* represents a so-called cult of particular locality (Sandomirskaya 2001, 17), we should not overlook the incorporation of several discursive elements from other cultural contexts that first defined the understanding of *otechestvo* and later formulated the concept of *rodina* itself. Indeed, the Russian phraseology of *rodina* had initially borrowed a lot of patriotic rhetoric from Napoleonic France and even more so from the discourse of German national romanticism (Sandomirskaya 2004). According to Juri Lotman and Boris Uspenskii (1996), the design of patriotic *otechestvo/bolshaya rodina* has in many ways proved to be a kind of utopia of the European nation state, which promotes the idea of national exclusivity. The term *otechestvo*, borrowed from the Western discourses of statehood, was first introduced by Peter the Great as a political ideology of the state, whereby the state represented a supreme being that should be loved, that awaits service and can claim sacrifice, devotion, and full surrender. Subsequently, in the process of the search for cultural self-identification, the phraseology of *otechestvo* transformed under the influence of social thinkers and literature of the late eighteenth and nineteenth centuries.

Seeking to understand the meaning of Russianness beyond statehood, poets and thinkers started using the concept of *rodina* as a sign of the domestic, a sign of identity and sacrality particular to *iskonno russkomu* (something inherently Russian) (Wierzbicka 1997). For example, in his poem "*Rodina*," Mikhail Lermontov, a famous nineteenth-century Russian Romantic writer, clearly counterpoised his own patriotism and love for the country to official state patriotism and political ideology. He claimed to have a close relationship with Russian nature and the Russian people, but opposed himself to the Russian state as an autocratic serfdom. Framed in the literary language of the nineteenth century, this new angle on *rodina* began to prioritize localism and local experiences of the inhabitants in place over the state discourses. By the time the Russian Empire collapsed, the personal and intimate meaning of *rodina* became entrenched in opposition to the impersonal *otechestvo*.

During Soviet times, a visible shift occurred in the mid-1930s when the official state rhetoric began to promote the patriotic discourses on *rodina*, projecting it as a *mat'* (mother) that had to be defended from foreign invaders. Admittedly, phrases such as *rodina zovet* (motherland is calling) had often been employed in the Soviet public discourse as state propaganda to emphasize the importance of one's own native country (Wierzbicka 1997, 192). Even then, while often used in conjunction with such verbs as "to serve," "to defend," or "to die for," *rodina* never came to embody an impersonal sociopolitical and militaristic character. Instead, it continued to develop as a highly personal and local understanding of spatiality, as a place of familiarity, security, and comfort, diluting its close association with a country. Over time, *rodina* has, therefore, accumulated multiple connotations that have turned the concept into a rich reservoir ripe for exploration by scholars and policymakers.

How is *rodina* understood by people today? The break-up of the Soviet Union, followed by the transformation of political and economic systems, has in many ways corroded the previous (often publicly entrenched) images of *rodina*, especially for Russian speakers. Although there was no actual physical movement of people, upon the collapse of the Soviet Union Russian-speaking communities experienced "a form of stationary or figurative displacement," whereby political borders demarcating their homelands "moved over them" (Flynn 2007, 267). Their marginal position and lack of incentive to learn the state languages and integrate with the so-called "host" communities have, in turn, generated numerous communal myths of their desire to cherish their links to Russia as the "external homeland." As a result, academics, politicians, and media representatives alike have primarily viewed *rodina* in sociopolitical terms, as necessarily a country or a nation of their parents' origin, avoiding the search for diverse meanings that the notion might invoke.

To provide a more nuanced picture of Russian speakers' understanding of *rodina*, it is essential to go beyond the national confines, seeing the notion not as a fixed center from which the world can be perceived, but as a mobile location with multiple simultaneously attached meanings across different sociopolitical realities. In my personal conversations with my interlocutors about life in the city, about their favorite places, about marginalization and belonging, *rodina* emerged as a place that reflects the heterogeneity of their retrospective views regarding the bordering process of their states of residence, of Russia, and their own ways of challenging these processes. The excerpts from the interviews to which I turn later all point to a certain dualism in the understanding of home. It is both a concrete place of origin and an abstract space, "not a location, but an entity in becoming," a symbolic reference point that moves beyond territorial boundaries (Nowicka 2007, 77). It is a notion that complexly entangles the narratives of exteriority and interiority and will be sketched out as follows: I begin by investigating the significance of origins, of a birthplace, for determining one's own belonging; I then scrutinize how feelings of exclusion might create obstacles to define *rodina* as a concrete location on a map. Acceptance becomes in itself a key defining aspect of *rodina*, whereas a lack of it pushes Russian speakers to search for other alternative symbolic attachments—expressed, for example, through the notion of imaginary *rodina* (see also Jašina-Schäfer 2019). Finally, caused by certain discomfort in the present, *rodina* can signal the desire of the Russophone population for new forms of interiority defined not only through social and cultural but also economic circumstances. Emphasizing individual internal conflicts to perpetually negotiate between different meanings of *rodina*, the concluding section highlights how and why the meanings of seemingly the same Russian-speaking keywords vary in Narva and Petropavlovsk.

DOES A BIRTHPLACE DETERMINE A WALK OF LIFE?

"*Gde rodilsya, tam i prigodilsya*": this famous Russian saying claims that people should not seek other places to feel comfortable and useful. Instead, a birthplace—where one grew up, of which one has memories and experiences—is the only place where you will be truly valued and cherished. It is, I should say, not an empty phrase, as its underlying message reappears in numerous academic studies (see, for example, Dixon and Durrheim 2004; Wiles 2008). For hooks (2009), a black feminist writer, it is only in the place of her birth—the Kentucky hills filled with personal childhood memories—where she feels she can truly belong. While the racist exploitation and oppression of people of color, the disenfranchisement of poor and "hillbilly" people, and the resurgence of white supremacy have profoundly affected her emotional life, hooks nevertheless decided to return to the place where her life began. After spending more than thirty years across different states, hooks writes, she did not naively believe that she would return to the uncorrupted innocent world of her native place. Rather, she sought to find the living remnants of the world in which she grew up, the essential remnants for a sense of her belonging: "During my time away, I would return to Kentucky and feel again a sense of belonging that I never felt elsewhere, experiencing unbroken ties to the land, to homefolk, to our vernacular speech" (hooks 2009, 24).

The inclusionary sense of belonging that a birthplace can offer to individuals has been equally highlighted by my research interlocutors. In Narva, several Russian speakers described *rodina* as a focal point of departure and a reference point to which one can always return. Through the acts of dwelling and numerous childhood memories, Narva and its diverse parts have acquired a symbolic importance. Consider, for example, how Raisa, a sixty-six-year-old pensioner (see also chapter 4), associates *rodina* with the vivid memory of her parents:

Of course, it is linked with the memory of my parents. Even when I simply go for a walk and cross Gerasimov Park, I immediately remember my father and mother. These are my native places, and places connected with my dearest and beloved parents. When I cross the railway bridge, I remember that my father used to work here. Now I look at this railway with love, because by dearest father used to work there. When I walk in the direction of Krenholm, my dearest mother used to work at the factory there. I now look at it also with love. So, when I walk through the city, I feel that these places became through my parents not only familiar but very dear to me. (Raisa, interview with the author, March 5, 2017)

In our almost two-hour conversation and a walk through the city, Raisa spoke a lot of her childhood memories, showing me photographs from her family album and then guiding me to the places where they were captured almost sixty years ago. For her, *rodina* emerges clearly as a place of birth within which the emotionally dense relations with her parents, her own history, and past experiences are anchored. Such autobiographical and relational factors also constitute the integral aspects of feeling "at home" for many other Narvans:

I think my *rodina* is my native city. I am a kind of a person who follows the idea '*gde rodilsia, tam i prigodilsia*'. I cannot say that I am attracted by politics, or certain social privileges here or an opportunity for self-fulfillment. Not really. It is, I think, simply 'naked' patriotism, not backed by anything. My home is Narva. Not a particular street, or a house, but the whole city. In this city I know all the streets, all the corners, all the places. I care for Narva. I will never litter or spit on the streets. I always have a need to come back here. Here live my family, my friends, my relatives, my colleagues whom I love. I love people in general [laughs]. (Vera, interview with the author, February 16, 2017)

For me, *rodina* is first of all my native home. My *rodina* is Krenholm. This is my home, where I was born, where my friends live, where my relatives are buried. *Rodina* begins from your childhood, and my childhood was here in Estonia. Even if life is not smooth here, it is still your *rodina*, where you want to return. So, I came back to Estonia. Yes, my life here is not easy, I have a small Russian pension, but I still came back here. (Vladimir, interview with the author, February 28, 2016)

My ancestors lived here for quite some time, about 200 years, even longer. Therefore, I consider this place to be my home in any case. I know that I have no other home and, therefore, I love the place where I am at. *Rodina* is defined for me by my family and friends, and the places where I dwelled. Narva, I think, is my *rodina*. Besides, I admire other parts of Estonia. So, my home is not limited to Narva but runs across Estonian territory. Estonia as a whole is my home. (Vadim, interview with the author, March 15, 2017)

The foregoing excerpts highlight the importance of one's continuity in a place and familiarity with different corners to feel as a part of it, to feel belonging. What is particularly interesting, however, is the multiplicity of scales through which *rodina* has been depicted: while for some it was clearly the city itself, others redrew the boundaries of home from the local to the national within a frame of a short conversation. As such, the spatial perception of *rodina* expanded particularly for those who spent a considerable amount of time abroad. Vladimir, who got Russian citizenship, moved to Russia, but later returned to Estonia, felt the necessity to challenge his marginality by emphasizing not only a concrete place in Krenholm but the whole country to be his *rodina*, which he remembers in exceptionally positive terms. In this process, he drew comparisons to his life in Russia, which he described as a less modern and less developed space (see also chapter 5).

While in Narva, numerous respondents could relate to the whole country, regardless of their intentions to stay or to leave, in Petropavlovsk just a few associated *rodina* with Kazakhstan. As such, it rather carried a more localized meanings with my interlocutors expressing belonging to the concrete birthplace, be it a town, village, or even a particular courtyard:

A person who was born in a village would love it more than Astana or Moscow, because this place is *rodnoe*, regardless of how beautiful it is in comparison to other places. Here you grew up, received your education. So, *ne plyui v kolodets—prigoditsya vody napitsya* (do not cast dirt into the well that gives you water). (Kim, thirty-one years old, construction worker, interview with the author, September 17, 2016)

This is my *rodnoi* city. Despite the devastation that it endures, despite the fact that the damned hagglers along with our local authorities turned the industrial town into a big market with cheap backlighting and snotty small architectural structures that are not capable of surviving even one season. Despite the abundance of the *derevenskoe bydlo* (uncultured rural mob) and urban ghouls. Despite the fact that this city is the most destitute in the country, I want to return here. To walk along the places that still hold history, to hide from the sun under the tree canopies that haven't been felled yet. To meet friends and old acquaintances, and to lament together what the damned creative minds are doing with the city. (Potap, interview with the author, September 24, 2016)

Rodnye places . . . this is not an empty phrase. Once I read in a book that to understand the self we should begin from the final point—our funeral. Who is going to attend it, where is it held, what do people say about you? Remembering this, I wish to be buried in Sergeevka [a small town nearby Petropavlovsk], where I lived, where I worked, where people know and love me. Our lifepath is defined by our childhood, school, university. Our youth, our memories of it are eternal. (Taras, interview with the author, August 31, 2016)

According to Taras, *rodina* as a localized place of birth becomes a center of human existence, an "irreplaceable center of significance" (Relph 1976, 39). Difficulty to associate oneself with the whole country, however, could have emerged through the profound differences that in the words of Russian speakers exist between the north and the south of Kazakhstan (see also chapters 2 and 3). Whereas the north has been depicted as more accommodating towards Russian speakers, as an inclusive Russian-speaking space, the south was imagined as more nationalistic and backward. The keyword is here "imagined," as many of my interlocutors have never been further down south than the capital Nur-Sultan and could only speculate about the interaction with the locals in other places. The localized meaning of *rodina* is, therefore, linked closely to an imagined distinction between insiders and outsiders, our space and alien space, the unknown and foreign that constitute a part of what is not home. Accordingly, however dismal it might sound, an integral part of feeling "at home" for Petropavlovsk inhabitants may derive not so much from the determination of it as a birthplace, but from either a disidentification with places of others where they do not feel accepted or from the comforting realization that the others are absent from their place of dwelling (Cresswell 1996). The contested politics of belonging in Kazakhstan, which I discussed throughout previous chapters, unsettle even further ideas about the nation as home. Through the erection of boundaries—be it through language laws or resettlement policies—Kazakhstani elites construct the social collectivities in particular ways, often causing discomfort and detachment among the Russophones in Petropavlovsk.

AN UNMAPPED PLACE OF ACCEPTANCE

In order to feel included, Antonsich (2010) writes, people should feel recognized as an integral part of the community where they live. Political entitlement, equal rights, and equal treatment at the state level do not always succeed in responding to the individual need of being accepted. It is not only the political institutions but also the people that "grant" recognition and accept individuals into the club of 'insiders'. The uncanny experiences of exclusion can, in turn, undermine the capacity of places to act as "comfort zone" (Dixon and Durrheim 2004, 459), leading to the experience of being in place and "out of place" simultaneously. These experiences are often followed by the search for alternative ways to belong. In the case of my Russian-speaking interlocutors, the alternative inclusions were sought in particular through the narrative representation of *rodina* as an imaginary symbolic place of acceptance that does not necessarily exist on a map.

After finishing school in Estonia, Platon, a 26-year-old marketing manager, moved to study at a Russian university in Saint Petersburg. In an online conversation, Platon defines home as a feeling of importance, belonging and, most importantly, of acceptance in the society—the kind of feelings that remained absent for him in Estonia:

Of course, Estonia is my *rodina* in a sense of being born here. But at the same time, there I don't feel that I am important to the state, to the people, that I can influence something or that I have equal opportunities as ethnic Estonians. Every society has the notion of the privileged nation, meaning that the representatives of this nation occupy the leading positions both in the state apparatus and in business. In Estonia, such privileged positions are relegated to ethnic Estonians. It doesn't mean that Russian speakers cannot become a part of the political elite. Yet it does mean that in order to belong to a solid middle class or higher one has to in many ways abandon one's own Russianness. This is one of the reasons that actually pushed me to leave and move to Russia. I cannot say that Russia is my *rodina*, my home. But, at the moment, I live here and feel good, fulfilled. Who knows what's next. I don't plan to go back to Estonia, I still have this grievance that to be accepted in your own *rodnoi* country you have to invest so much power to prove your devotion. . . . It's really strange. (Platon, interview with the author, July 14, 2017)

The idea of being taken for granted was also shared by other Narvans. Vera, for example, notes that many of her friends do not feel comfortable in their birthplace:

Many people say that no one needs us here. Half of them, who are by the way no longer young, want to leave or have already left. They don't feel comfortable here and live in Narva only because they were born here, studied here, met each other and founded families. It is their habit. For them leaving everything behind is a huge stress and I understand them. Many people dream of leaving or already plan to. They go to England, Sweden, Finland, where there is no such pressure with the language. (Vera, interview with the author, February 16, 2017)

In the context of Estonia, there still appears to be a widespread lack of national acceptance of Russian speakers as fully fledged members of the Estonian national community. For one thing, the integration model promoted by the state revolves around the essentialized discourses of a core ethnically Estonian nation (Kruusvall et al. 2009). This implies the integration of non-Estonians into the hegemonic core while, as Platon notes, requiring them to abandon their Russianness. In this regard, many Russian speakers feel an increasing sense of alienation, often reinforced through political institutions that contest the status of Russian speakers and question their legitimate membership in Estonian society (Jašina-Schäfer and Cheskin 2020). Dima, a stateless person (see more on him in chapters 2 and 3) sums up his prevailing mood:

> I remember when I just got my grey [non-citizen's] passport. I was standing at the German border and felt ashamed for being 'alien'. While politicians sit and decide whether there is Russian question or not, people's lives pass by. It's so weird—a person without citizenship devotes more of his free time for this country than one with citizenship. Out of spite I don't want Russian citizenship, because my *rodina* is Estonia. A *rodina* that doesn't accept me. (Dima, interview with the author, February 15, 2017)

The alienation of many Russian speakers in Estonia, a recurrent theme from the extant literature, clearly cannot be ignored. Feeling ashamed and not accepted significantly shapes the daily meanings of *rodina* for Narvans and their longing for alternative attachments. Some, like Platon, fulfil this through migration; others, like Vera, through the strengthening of local identification or through speaking about *rodina* in very abstract terms: *rodina* is where "everything is closer to your heart, where your native language and a particular Russian mentality is present" (Vladimir, interview with the author, February 28, 2017). In essence then, pressures to assimilate, which would require relinquishing Russianness, made some of my interlocutors project their feelings of being at home onto the language, friendships, and memories of childhood—a kind of home that does not have tangible geographical borders.

In Kazakhstan, Russian speakers also often feel disadvantaged on ethnic grounds, losing out to ethnic Kazakhs and not having a firm standing in their country of birth (Laruelle and Payrouse 2007). Petr, a worker in a philharmonic society, expressed concerns for not being treated as an equal citizen in all parts of the country, claiming that in the southern Kazakhstan he is viewed as an "outsider":

> You know, if they would treat me everywhere here in Kazakhstan as an equal citizen, then I would feel I belong here. When people accept you and treat you well then you see this place as your *rodnoi*. So, if I had been treated well everywhere in Kazakhstan, I would even call Shemkent [city in the south of Kazakhstan, used here in a sense of 'some far-off place'] my *rodina*.

The idea of *rodina* is associated with a yearning for connectedness and social relationships that would enable my interlocutors to feel accepted as equal members of society. Thus, not feeling included in the country or city where one was born creates difficulties in calling any geographical place *rodina*. That being said, not feeling accepted in the context of the whole of Kazakhstan did not necessarily motivate Russian speakers to reconstruct Russia as their *rodina*. The reasons for the narratives of distance from Russia as a physical entity were thoroughly discussed in chapter 5, including a lack of acceptance of their "Russianness" by the local population in Russia as well as a lack of experience of life on the territory of Russia in general. As a result, many Russian speakers were eager to speak of a Russian-speaking space as a cradle of *Russkokul'turnost'*, as an imaginary *rodina* that does not exist on the map but provides them nevertheless with a sense of comfort, security, and inclusion.

ANY PLACE OF FINANCIAL SECURITY

Throughout these conversations not every understanding of *rodina* was linked to social or cultural circumstances. According to Morley (2000, 44), the idea of home may equally vary with economic circumstances: home is where you have a job, where you can feel worthy. Economic and pragmatic interests contribute to "safe and stable material conditions for the individual and her/his family" and therefore often play a necessary role in the process of generating a sense of spatial belonging (Antonsich 2010, 648). Several Russian-speaking interlocutors indeed highlighted the importance of self-fulfilment for their meanings of *rodina*, whereby *rodina* emerged as anyplace of comfort and economic security.

Although considerably less frequently than Petropavlovsk inhabitants, Narvans pointed towards certain material discomforts in their present life in the city. While Estonia offers an overall higher quality of life than Kazakhstan, some commentators see socioeconomic factors as the primary dividing line between ethnic Estonians and Russian speakers (Solska 2011). Magdalena Solska (2011, 1001), for example, notes that many Russian speakers feel that ethnic Estonians have "better opportunities for jobs and education as well as participation in political and community life because of their belonging to the core nation." Some economic studies focusing on the average wage earnings even suggest that non-Estonians face an "ethnic wage gap," whereby the mean wage of ethnic Estonian workers is 10–15 per cent higher (Leping and Toomet 2008, 614). Several of my interlocutors have indeed expressed socio-economic concerns during our conversations. Yet these concerns were mostly related to the economic depression (limited flow of investments, high unemployment rates, poverty) and peripheralization of the north-eastern region rather than to "ethnicity" as a factor that can explain income inequalities. Consider, for example, Bogdan, a forty-year-old who was in-between jobs when I met him:

> People run away from here, because . . . I have myself quite a high qualification and understand a lot. I go to different interviews. My goal is to find a job here, because I don't want to leave everything behind and go someplace else for work. To go to Tallinn, drag my whole family there, get a flat . . . . It would be stupid at my age. This is one thing. The other thing—here I have everything, my whole life scheme. I don't want to go someplace else and start from scratch. Here you come to different companies for interviews, they offer you a respectful position with minimum wage. This is so pitiful. But that's not the worst. In all honesty, everything significant is ruined here. Even when the press writes about new companies, factories. I went there once for fun. In truth, it was interesting. But they needed 100 engineers who would also work on the weekends. *Nafig ono nuzhno* (why the heck would I need that)? [. . .] The majority of people leave for Tallinn or abroad. People here have nothing to do. (Bogdan, interview with the author, March 2, 2017)

In a similar vein, although Vera claims to be a patriot of Narva, she confessed to me that she too has been having thoughts of leaving, especially when she learned how low her pension in Estonia is going be:

> When I went to get advice on a pension question and was told that my pension will be something around 217 Euros, I realized that I won't be able to survive here. I called my husband and shouted for about ten minutes that *valit' otsyuda nado* (we have to get out of here). This was about three or four years ago. Before that I always told my friends and everyone else that I love my city, that I wished to stay here forever and that here everything is *rodnoe*—every stone, even every unfamiliar face on a street. Before that, when I went somewhere else, I always missed the city and came back with a great pleasure. (Vera, interview with the author, February 16, 2017)

The accounts of Bogdan and Vera as well as several other Narvans demonstrate the slow process of reevaluation of the *rodnoe* place, the place of their childhood, the place of their memories, in light of declining job prospects. In this process, *rodina* defined as a place of birth where one is automatically needed (*gde rodilsya, tam i prigodilsya*) is often redefined as any place of self-worth (*gde prigodilsya, tam i rodina*). Home is, thus, not a singular physical entity fixed in a particular place, but precisely as David Morley (2000, 47) defines it, a "mobile, symbolic habitat, a performative way of life and of doing things in which one makes one's home while in movement."

In Petropavlovsk, several interlocutors were also quick to question the birth-place as necessarily one's *rodina*. For example, Arsen, a thirty-year-old student, argues that *rodina* to him is clearly not a fixed place, but rather a setting or an environment which is more beneficial, which allows to secure a job and enjoy certain material comforts: "You know, if I think of a place where I was born, I wouldn't now want to live there, to get attached to a place where one was born and think of it as your *rodina*" (Arsen, personal conversation with the author September 2016). While speaking of his life, another interlocutor, Daniil, a man in his thirties working as a religious analyst in Petropavlovsk, similarly stresses comfort and material security as defining aspects of home:

> I don't think home is where you were born. As I already told you, although I like it in Bishkul' [the nearby village where the respondent came from], I don't want to live there ever again. At first, I experienced yarning, when I left Bishkul'. But after spending time in the city, in comfort, where you don't have to heat the stove or bring water. . . . And if I end up in a more comfortable environment, where life is better. . . . Like in those American films. You walk on clean, beautiful grass, sit down on it. If I had this comfort, I would never come back. I would even leave now, if only I had the chance.

In our conversation, Daniil frequently mentioned the role of infrastructure in enabling him to feel good in a place. The presence of amenities and facilities in Petropavlovsk in contrast to the village of his birth made the city more attractive and generated a feeling of security and comfort. The United States, in turn, represented in his imagination an even better place to be. In the previous chapter, I already highlighted that the inhabitants of Petropavlovsk were increasingly dissatisfied with the current quality of life and the scarce prospects for the future. Many described Petropavlovsk as a small and quiet city, but one that fails to provide people with sufficient opportunities for employment. Marina, a woman in her forties, while participating in a public discussion of migration in the group *Tipichnyi Petropavlovsk* (Typical Petropavlovsk on vk.ru) writes the following:

> I love my *rodina*, because I was born here, because my mother is buried in this land. Well, there are numerous other reasons why. . . . But I don't like how life in my *rodina* gets worse. The salaries in the Northern Kazakhstan Region are the lowest, medicine is bad. Why has the state that some people praise so much withdrawn money from the pension fund to sponsor EXPO? The state must ensure that the citizens have a decent life instead of ripping off their savings. (Commentary translated by the author, January 23, 2017)

In her narrative, Marina expresses growing frustration with the uneven income distribution across Kazakhstan, which contributes to prosperity only of certain regions in the country and only of certain societal layers. As most of my interlocutors belong to the so-called basic (economic) layer, able to meet basic nutritional needs or buy clothing but lacking possibilities of bigger purchases, such as cars, housing, or electrical devices (Nastyukova 2018, see also Introduction), deterioration of the life standards seems to dramatically affect their desire to stay in Petropavlovsk. Many seek other places that offer better material conditions and express disenchantment associated with a lack of positive social and aesthetic change in the city:

> I hope that one day I will be able to love this city. Not for the moments or emotions, not for the warm memories connected to people who were once here and a few who stayed. I want the banal things, which do not necessarily depend in an ordinary person. For example, that the roads stay put for longer than just one season and don't thaw together with the snow. Or for the pavement stone not to be replaced on the same spot every year. That after the rain, the water would flow away, and you wouldn't have to make complex mathematical calculations on how to get over the puddle. [. . .] For the city to be cleaned not only on the eve of celebrations or international forums but also the rest of the time. [. . .] I want to walk around the city in white sneakers and not to collect with them all the dirt in the world. Come on, the spring is over, it's the second month of the summer and what we see is the rebellion of debris and dirt. I really want some parts of the city not to resemble *Silent Hill* [referring to the US American horror movie]. You can love Petropavlovsk, but you cannot admire it. No way. (Potap, interview with the author, October 1, 2016)

Thus, for most of the respondents, dissatisfaction with the current quality of life and scarce prospects for self-fulfilment served as a primary incentive to leave the country, mostly in the direction of Russia. Although since 1999 the overall migratory tendency in Kazakhstan has been declining (the number of citizens leaving the country dropped almost tenfold), Russian speakers represent the group most likely to migrate (Simakova 2016). In the past five years, ethnic Russians alone constituted 44.5 per cent of the total external migration. According to the polls conducted by Simakova in April 2015, 36 per cent of Russian participants ($N = 572$) expressed a desire to change their place of residence. In turn, having thoughts to migrate, to leave the nest, often leads to the redefinition of *rodina* in particularly blurry terms as a situational place of comfort.

MULTISCALAR *RODINA*

Home, as Hamid Naficy (1999, 6) explains, is "temporary, and it is moveable; it can be built, rebuilt, and carried in memory and by acts of imagination."

As such, it does not simply exist but is produced through complex social and emotional relationships as well as power geometry. People are differently positioned in relation to home and experience it differently depending on the political, economic, and cultural circumstances surrounding them. My Russian-speaking respondents both in Narva and Petropavlovsk illustrate well Naficy's notion of temporarily constructed homes and challenge the traditional interpretations that favor rootedness and essentialism. By analyzing the meanings of *rodina*, this chapter continued our discussion on the process of belonging among Russian speakers in the post-Soviet borderlands and their complex relationships with different places and people in them. Throughout the interviews, *rodina* emerged as a spatial marker for understanding people's spatial belonging on multiple scales, from the domestic to the global (Blunt and Varley 2004). Despite numerous top-down attempts to define a concrete place to call or not to call home for Russian speakers, the multiple, often divergent, examples of *rodina* highlight the conflicting images of belonging that individuals are developing in the process of constant movement and negotiation between inclusion and exclusion.

Time and time again, *rodina* was reconstructed in a slippery variety of ways: as an emotional place of origin and a place that symbolizes the lived experience of a concrete locality, as a "mythic" place of acceptance, and as any place of financial security and material comfort. Russian speakers not only spoke of *rodina* from the viewpoint of their ideals and desires as a "state of their mind" (Blunt and Dowling 2006, 13), but also as tangible everyday realities, practices, and social interactions. Some of these narratives reflected the challenges Russian speakers experience in not being accepted, recognized, or treated equally in their states residence. The challenges of belonging to a society on their own terms as well as economic pressures often led to the reinvention of *rodina* and a search for new alternative places to belong. As a spatially elastic concept, *rodina* thus contained numerous different spaces and times simultaneously.

Implicitly and sometimes more explicitly, this chapter sketched out several connections and certain disconnections that run between the perceptions of *rodina* in Petropavlovsk and Narva. Although Russian speakers refer to seemingly the same keyword, the meanings within the three main narrative frames outlined here vary considerably. As such, we could say that *rodina* is not only entirely untranslatable into other languages but also cannot be easily transferred into other cultural contexts with their own ways of life, ideas, values, and modes of behavior. The stories of exclusion that we observed here as well as in previous chapters were overcome in different ways, whereby Narvans more readily than Petropavlovsk inhabitants embraced the idea of the geographical space of a whole nation being their home. In Petropavlovsk, in turn, people subscribed to more localized meanings, trying to preserve the familiar Russian-speaking space as a space of normality. A further vivid point of departure lies in the more pronounced readiness of Petropavlovsk inhabitants to embrace *rodina* as anyplace of material comfort, determined by the dissatisfaction with the current quality of life and the scarce prospects for their self-fulfilment. Although it might sound somewhat rude, some Petropavlovsk inhabitants abruptly concluded that home is a place where "your bottom feels warm," meaning literally any place where you are economically better off.

NOTES

1. According to Barrington et al. (2003), "internal homeland" refers to a particular part within the state of residence of minorities. The authors argue that situations in which a minority group considers a region to be national homeland could fuel secessionist drives and are at the heart of many ethnic conflicts around the world. "Mixed homeland," in turn, refers to a situation in which members of a minority in one state see the homeland as comprising both a part of the state of residence and an external region or state.

2. "Cultural translation" widens the understanding of translation as that from one language to another to characterize the transfer of ideas and values, of patterns of thought and behavior between different cultural contexts (see Lutter 2016, 156).

Chapter 7

Conclusion

Today belonging represents one of the most important yet difficult issues confronting all of us. The questions of who a stranger is and who does not belong to the political and cultural community are continuously being raised, modified, and contested. Of fundamental importance to people's lives, belonging can be ambiguous and exclusionary, reductionist and open, "in place, with place, [and] as a place" (Wright 2015, 404). Its use proliferates equally in the academic realm, where the notion has come to connote a range of different meanings, from more abstract to more concrete definitions. In this book, I did not attempt to solve the puzzle of what belonging means, as a straightforward answer would shut down its many uses, contradictions, and inconsistencies. Rather, by looking at the everyday lives of Russian speakers in the post-Soviet borderlands, I attended more deeply to the ways it is narrated, felt, and practiced.

I started this book by describing the peculiar situation of the politically displaced Russian-speaking minorities, whom scholars often describe as being in-between their countries of residence and the external homeland of Russia. When the Soviet borders receded, Martinez (2018, 158) writes, Russian speakers "were divorced from a previous family without finding a new one" and emerged as a distinct milieu with their own visions of normality, surroundings, and community. Seeking to understand what the essence of this "in-betweenness" is and how it is embedded within the so-called politics of belonging (Yuval-Davis 2006), boundary work, and difference, this research followed a space-sensitive theorization of belonging. It reconstructed belonging as an ambiguous, complex, and plural practice, a spiral movement between "inclusion" and "exclusion" that emerges spatially at the intersection between power settings and individual positionings. In the case of Russian speakers, as the empirical chapters demonstrated, exclusion first materialized through the dislocation and rescaling of the borderland cities and their inhabitants under the influence of state nationalization policies. Despite the marginalizing consequences, the destabilization of social codes and previous daily routines also led to the production of new forms of sociality and meanings of inclusivity that move between different spatial and temporal scales of the global, national, and local, between Soviet and post-Soviet.

In this final chapter, I summarize the key empirical and conceptual contributions of this monograph but also go beyond them to explore and underscore their broader implications for understanding belonging. Furthermore, I elaborate on the considerable divergences in the ways time and space are ordered in Narva and Petropavlovsk. By engaging critically with the current scholarly debates on the concepts of "postsocialism" and "post-Soviet," I discuss the peculiarities of conducting a comparative research across countries like Estonia and Kazakhstan.

BELONGING AS A PRACTICE OF
EXTERIOR INTERIORITY

Previous studies have usefully noted how the sudden retraction of the Soviet borders pushed the Russophone populations into an area of ambiguity, of being neither here nor there, no longer entirely "other" but not yet part of the new independent nation states. They became, in the words of Victor Turner (2008, 95), liminal subjects or "threshold people" that occupy a transitory phase in a path leading to new statuses and positionalities. Following the initial experience of detachment and marginality that the sociopolitical displacement had produced, some Russian speakers are believed to have entered a path leading to their integration into a new group, with the potential for full incorporation. For others, the transitory stage became an arguably perennial condition of existential outsidedness defined by continuous identification difficulties, feelings of nonbelonging, or being in-between. More recent grounded observations of empirical realities, however, offered a third perspective that goes beyond the binary representation of inclusion and exclusion as opposite sides and demonstrates instead the paradoxical complexities in the identification of Russian speakers (Makarychev and Sazonov 2019). On the one hand, they position themselves as inalienable parts of their sociopolitical communities; on the other hand, their narratives also transmit a certain detachment from the larger collective. Such in-betweenness represents a possibility for a "cultural hybridity" that "entertains difference without an assumed or imposed hierarchy" (Thomassen 2012, 27).

Being driven by similar questions of how belonging or not belonging manifests itself among the Russophones, this book took a rather different turn from the previous perspectives. I am in general sympathetic to the critical aims of the concept of hybridity, through which scholars seek to destabilize fixed categories and counter unproductive dichotomies that have long dominated the studies on Russian speakers. However, I also believe that dissolving the internal hierarchies between different affiliations of hybridity in its current state underplays the essential role of background structures and boundary work which, in turn, became essential for understanding belonging in my own research (for critique, see also Bachmann-Medick 2016, 123–28). Across the pages of this book, which draws extensively on the everyday narratives and performances of Russian speakers in Narva and Petropavlovsk, belonging came to represent a practice of exterior interiority that depicts a complex movement between foreign and domestic worlds separated by certain boundaries. What counts as foreign or exterior and what signifies domestic and interior are subjects of constant reflexivity and are, therefore, temporally unstable.

The movement between exteriority and interiority could be better imagined as passing through a door (Thomassen 2014; van Gennep 1960). To cross the threshold, Thomassen (2014, 13) writes, is to unite oneself with another world. Such incorporation into the new world simultaneously entails a certain separation from a previous world but does not preclude return. Hence, to think with the lens of exterior interiority has to do with a thorough understanding of a spiral experience that implies the constant crossing and recrossing of boundaries, challenging old ones, and drawing new ones. To summarize the process of transition from one position to another, it would be useful to turn one last time to my Russian-speaking interlocutors, in particular to the narratives of Yuliya, a young student in her twenties from Narva. The short excerpt below is representative of the many different worlds that Yuliya simultaneously inhabits and moves between:

Very little attention is paid to us. Neither politicians nor people know much about us. This is not to say that we are a separate world. No. We pay taxes and everything that happens in Estonia affects us in the same way. Narvans want to be accepted. It's like *v semye ne bez urodov i etim urodom okazalis' my* (every family has a freak and it turned out that this freak is us). This is upsetting. And when Estonians say, like, we are not Estonia . . . How come? At least geographically. Yes, we are Estonians, Estonia . . . not Estonians, but Estonia. And a lot of Narva dwellers, simple workers, working in factories or in shops, they value Estonia and love living here. (Yuliya, interview with the author, February 17, 2017)

The feeling of being physically and symbolically marginalized alongside other Russian speakers as "freaks" is followed by the narratives of incorporation or desires for inclusion back into Estonian society. To cross a threshold from an outsider into a world in which she represents an essential part of Estonia and Europe, Yuliya detaches herself from the space of Russia as a foreign world of carelessness and chaos:

> When I went to visit my relatives in Bryansk [a city in Russia], I understood how different we are. They are so . . . The guys there are like the Russian fairy-tale figure Ivan the Fool. They don't buckle up, don't wear light reflectors, don't look around before crossing the roads. I think it is my Europeanness that speaks now. Careless, this word describes Russians well. It permeates everything—the driving, their attitude, relationship to family. In Europe we began to appreciate that parents spend time with children and pay attention to teenagers. In Russia, they are far from there. [. . .] You come back to Narva and think, 'Lord, where was I . . . in some wilderness or something.'

Yet the distancing from Russia and "their" Russian culture does not necessarily strip Yuliya of her Russianness. Later on, she comes back to that point to highlight how the continuity of certain traditions, routines, and, most importantly, the ability to practice the Russian language also constitute an important part of what interiority means to her: "To me Russia is a historical *rodina*, and I can't abandon it entirely. Because of the language, because of traditions, I am not ready to send my child to the Estonian kindergarten, into a complete immersion. I want him to keep the traditions of Russia."

The way Yuliya moves between these multilayered narratives of interiority and exteriority is not representative of all experiences among Russian speakers in Narva, less so across Estonia, and even less across different countries. But it should illustrate the gist of the complex spiral play that lies at the essence of people's belonging, as a process always situated within broader background structures that determine how "various agents maneuver and how they encounter each other" (Björkdahl and Buckley-Zistel 2016, 1).

In the empirical sections, I thoroughly demonstrated how under the influence of state nationalization policies cities like Narva and Petropavlovsk suffered, albeit in different ways, a dramatic rescaling into borderland spaces of potential separatism. Through the erasure of the undesirable Soviet/Russian representations of the past and the introduction of new cultural symbols into the urban landscapes, a creation of new spatiotemporal ordering has occurred that in many ways exteriorized Russian speakers. For the Russophone dwellers in Narva, who came to represent the internal "other" in Estonia, exteriority came to connote a negative experience of often self-induced Orientalization and alienation. In Petropavlovsk, due to considerably different nation-building policies and different historical experiences, exteriority has rather emerged as a positive experience of normality, of a known superior cultural order and security against the socially-coded (rural) Kazakh "other."

However, the destabilization of social codes and everyday experiences also meant the emergence of numerous alternative heterogeneous representations of the self and the meanings of one's own belonging. As such, the worlds of Narva and Petropavlovsk continue to be built anew as spaces that bridge different histories, cultural styles, scales, and versions of Estonianness/ Kazakhness, Europeanness/Cosmopolitanness, and Russianness. In this process, Russian speakers do not simply integrate in a one-way direction, living as existential outsiders or finding themselves as "people of in-between" in no man's land. Rather, through memories, performative activities, and narratives about natural and built spaces, Russian speakers differently position themselves in their everyday lives, reconstructing their belonging multilocally. How precisely this positioning occurs is increasingly a matter of the spatial order, the sociopolitical and economic structures around them, and of their different social locations, to which future studies should be more attentive.

At the same time, multilocal narratives of belonging in many ways emerge in response to a researcher herself. Through the course of my fieldwork and subsequent reflexivity, I became aware that my own positionalities—a Tallinner in Narva and an Estonian in Petropavlovsk—differently resonated with my interlocutors, functioning as further elements in relation to which Russian speakers articulated their everyday representations of belonging. In Narva most of the interlocutors tended to balance out between the urban and national articulations of belonging, claiming persistently that "Narva is Estonia, it is you who forgot about it." Most commonly, the word "you" referred not only to the state institutions or ethnic Estonians but to other Russian speakers from Tallinn (including myself). Living in the same country, the Russophone population experiences substantially different realities of the everyday life, depending which location we are speaking from. The further east we go from Tallinn, the stronger the perception becomes of one's own segregation and Russifiedness of the surrounding landscapes. In this process, a desire increases to reconnect with Estonia on a national scale. My interlocutor Natalya (chapter 2), a former Tallinner, precisely highlighted this point—her own Russianness in Tallinn and an inherent desire to be more Estonian in Narva.

In stark contrast, a transnational scale and comparisons were more prominently articulated in Petropavlovsk. My exposure to these narratives (e.g. "global Petropavlovsk" or "Russian-speaking space") may have been to a substantial extent induced by my Estonian nationality and a Russian-speaking heritage, which to my interlocutors carried an implicit value of "civilization." Indeed, my "internationalism" was a focal point of many discussions—I was often asked to share my impressions of Petropavlovsk and to draw comparisons between the city and other places in Estonia and Germany, where I am professionally based in. My interlocutors, in turn, sought to reassure me of their own cultural superiority against "the uncivilized/nomadic other" (chapters 2 and 3) and the ability to *idti v nogu so vremenem* (get with the times).

Although these different scales through which Russian speakers articulate their belonging problematize the attempts to draw the straightforward comparisons between Narva and Petropavlovsk, juxtaposing different social realities is not a surrealist project. Future comparative ethnographic revisits should therefore consider more the situatedness of the narratives in a scholar's own self and how our multiple selves are involved in the coconstruction of the concepts in question.

POST-SOVIET BORDERLANDS: ON DIFFERENT WAYS OF ORDERING SPACE AND TIME

The aim of this book was not to develop a synthetic typology of belonging across countries that, as I demonstrated throughout, diverged greatly in political and cultural practices, transnational orientations, and economic situations. Rather, I uncovered how and why complex practical and cultural relations are alternatively imagined and lived in these two diverse contexts; how and why a transnational space like Russia is differently understood and enmeshed into the relational spatial constitution of localities; how natural landscapes are imbued with different symbolic meanings; or why the spatial placement of *rodina* diverged greatly from more localized meanings in Petropavlovsk to the bounded area of the whole country in Narva.

Engaging critically with these two cases has hopefully offered new empirical and conceptual insights into the complex manifestations of belonging among national minorities, reconfiguring it as a collage of relations alternatively imagined, an assemblage of diverse individual practices located at the discursive boundaries of selective pasts and contested presents. The contribution the regional approaches can make is, however, not limited to the production of new case studies only. The perspectives from and juxtaposition of countries as different as Estonia and Kazakhstan can also offer new opportunities to rethink belonging as a "concept in translation" that does not circulate in a free-floating manner across borderless spaces but is very much anchored in regional and historical contexts as well as cultural formations (Bachmann-Medick 2016). Thus, whenever we speak about belonging, we "have to go through translation" that becomes a crucial practice for connecting seemingly universalizing concepts back to life-worlds and local histories (Mignolo 2012, 210).

In this sense, turning to local histories does not mean viewing countries like Estonia and Kazakhstan through the prism of their Soviet legacy, which obstructs our views of numerous ontological differences between the countries that emerged out of the ashes of the Soviet regime (Makarychev and Yatsyk 2016). Maria Todorova (2010, 182) furthermore importantly reminds us how any geographical entity, any region, is a "complex result of interplay of numerous historical periods, traditions, and legacies." The regions are not only changing but are also subject to different internal self-perceptions, as well as attempts at self-reinvention and repositioning at different times by different individuals or groups. Thus, when I used the terms "post-Soviet" or "postsocialist," I did not wish to reify socialism into the "uniform experience that it never was" (cf. Müller 2019, 541). Rather, as I attempted to illustrate throughout the book, not only did Estonia and Kazakhstan have different profiles prior to imposition of the Soviet rule and different experiences of the socialism that followed, but they are now attuned to a plurality of different forces and have extremely different relationships with their socialist periods. While Estonia puts a strong emphasis on the temporal break between the Soviet period and the present, which brought about integrations into the EU, the cultural and political practices in Kazakhstan are more often characterized by the seeming continuity between the periods. Both countries also engage differently with the meanings and the ideas of "Russianness." Today a "core" of a broader concept of Kazakhstan, in Estonia Russianness, still remains a symbol of the traumatic past and a potential threat in the present. Even more pronounced is Estonia's economic and political distance from Russia and its integrationist plans, whereas Kazakhstan cooperates closely with its northern neighbor, especially through such economic mechanisms as the Eurasian Economic Union.

The dissimilar paths that the countries took and are following consequently produce different conditions for the everyday life of the majority and minority populations. It is, however, precisely because the borderland regions are so different that they offered unique insights into the specific practices of belonging as well as the movement between scales and meanings of inclusion or exclusion. Eventually, this array of fragmented memories, lifestyles, cultural codes, and narrations exposed the limits of such homogenizing grids as "Russian diaspora" or "Russian-speaking nationality," to which it is perhaps time to say goodbye. Instead of trying to produce catchy pictures of the wholes entrapped in automatic and associative thought (such as the unbreakable or unproblematic bond between the Russophones and Russia), more focus should be devoted to the interrelated but distinct facets of Russian speakers' lives—that of their positioning along socioeconomic nets of power, their experiences and practices of belonging, as well as their normative value systems. Only this way it will be possible to conduct a research that is truly reconnected with life-worlds and local histories, as Walter Mignolo calls for.

Only this way it will be possible to trace how the ongoing spatial changes and sociopolitical orientations continuously reconfigure the lives of individuals and how, for example, the recent attempts of the Estonian government to make Narva "cool rather than alien" (Makarychev 2018, 9) open new potential doors for the people to pass through.

References

Aasland, Aadne. 1996. "Russians Outside Russia: The New Russian Diaspora." In *the Nationalities Question in the Post-Soviet States*, edited by Graham Smith, 477–97. London, New York: Longman.

Aboim, Sofia, Paulo Granjo, and Alice Ramos, eds. 2018. *Changing Societies: Legacies and Challenges. Ambiguous Inclusions: Inside Out, Outside in.* Lissabon: Imprensa de Ciências Sociais de Universidade de Lisboa.

Agarin, Timofey. 2010. *A Cat's Lick: Democratization and Minority Communities in the Post-Soviet Baltic.* On the Boundary of Two Worlds Ser v. 22. Leiden: BRILL.

Akiner, Shirin. 1995. *The Formation of Kazakh Identity: From Tribe to Nation-State.* London: Royal Institute of International Affairs.

Alexander, Catherine, and Victor Buchli. 2007. "Introduction." In *Urban Life in Post-Soviet Asia*, edited by Catherine Alexander, Victor Buchli, and Caroline Humphrey, 1–39. London, New York: University College London Press.

Allan, Julie. 2008. *Rethinking Inclusive Education: The Philosophers of Difference in Practice.* Inclusive education: cross cultural perspectives v. 5. Dordrecht: Springer.

Amin, Ash, and N. J. Thrift. 2002. *Cities: Reimagining the Urban.* Cambridge: Polity.

Andrews, Hazel, and Les Roberts. 2012. "Introduction: Re-Mapping Liminality." In *Liminal Landscapes: Travel, Experience and Spaces in-Between*, edited by Hazel Andrews and Les Roberts, 1–18. London: Routledge.

Anthias, Floya. 2002. "Where Do I Belong?" *Ethnicities* 2 (4): 491–514. doi:10.117 7/14687968020020040301.

Anthias, Floya. 2006. "Belongings in a Globalizing and Unequal World: Rethinking Translocations." In *the Situated Politics of Belonging*, edited by Nira Yuval-Davis, Kalpana Kannabiran, and Ulrike Vieten, 17–31. London: SAGE Publications Ltd.

Anthias, Floya. 2008. "Thinking Through the Lens of Translocational Positionality: An Intersectionality Frame for Understanding Identity and Belonging." *Translocations: Migration and Social Change* 4 (1): 5–20.

Anthias, Floya. 2013. *Identity and Belonging: Conceptualizations and Political Framings.* KLA working paper series no. 8, 2013. Köln, Germany: Kompetenzwerk Lateinamerika.

Antonsich, Marco. 2010. "Searching for Belonging—An Analytical Framework." *Geography Compass* 4 (6): 644–59. doi:10.1111/j.1749-8198.2009.00317.x.

Appadurai, Arjun. 1995. "The Production of Locality." In *Counterworks: Managing the Diversity of Knowledge*, edited by Richard Fardon, 204–25. London: Routledge.

Appadurai, Arjun. 1996. *Modernity at Large: Cultural Dimensions of Globalization.* Public worlds v. 1. Minneapolis, London: University of Minnesota Press.

Assmann, Aleida. 2008. "Transformations between History and Memory." *Social Research* 75 (1): 49–72.

Bachelard, Gaston. 1994. *The Poetics of Space.* Boston: Beacon Press.

Bachmann-Medick, Doris. 2016. "From Hybridity to Translation: Reflections on Travelling Concepts." In *the Trans/National Study of Culture*, edited by Doris Bachmann-Medick, 119–36. Berlin, Boston: De Gruyter.

Bakhtin, Mikhail. 1981. "Forms of Time and of the Chronotope in the Novel." In *the Dialogic Imaginations: Fours Essays by M. M. Bakhtin*, edited by Michael Holquist, 84–259. Austin: University of Texas Press.

Barrington, Lowell W., Erik S. Herron, and Brian D. Silver. 2003. "The Motherland Is Calling: Views of Homeland among Russians in the Near Abroad." *World Politics* 55: 290–313.

Bell, Duncan. 2008. "Agonistic Democracy and the Politics of Memory." *Constellations* 15 (1): 148–66. doi:10.1111/j.1467-8675.2008.00478.x.

Bennett, Julia. 2014. "Gifted Places: The Inalienable Nature of Belonging in Place." *Environmental Planning* 32 (4): 658–71. doi:10.1068/d4913p.

Berger, Peter L. 1967. *The Sacred Canopy: Elements of Sociological Theory of Religion.* New York: Doubleday.

Bhabha, Homi K. 1994. *The Location of Culture.* London, New York: Routledge.

Bhabha, Jacqueline. 1999. "Belonging in Europe: Citizenship and Post-National Rights." *Int Social Science J* 51 (159): 11–23. doi:10.1111/1468-2451.00173.

Bissenova, Alima. 2014. "The Master Plan of Astana: Between the "Art of Government" and the "Art of Being Global"." In *Ethnographies of the State in Central Asia: Performing Politics*, edited by Madeleine Reeves, Johan Rasanayagam, and Judith Beyer, 127–49. Indiana: Indiana University Press.

Bissenova, Alima. 2017. "The Fortress and the Frontier: Mobility, Culture, and Class in Almaty and Astana." *Europe-Asia Studies* 69 (4): 642–67. doi:10.1080/09668136.2017.1325445.

Björkdahl, Annika, and Susanne Buckley-Zistel. 2016. "Spatializing Peace and Conflict: An Introduction." In *Spatializing Peace and Conflict: Mapping the Production of Places, Sites and Scales of Violence*, edited by Annika Björkdahl and Susanne Buckley-Zistel, 1–24. New York: Palgrave Macmillan.

Blunt, Alison, and Robyn M. Dowling. 2006. *Home.* Key ideas in geography. London: Routledge.

Blunt, Alison, and Ann Varley. 2004. "Geographies of Home." *Cultural Geographies* 11 (1): 3–6. doi:10.1191/1474474004eu289xx.

Bohle, Dorothee, and Bela Greskovits. 2007. *Capitalist Diversity on Europe's Periphery*. Cornell studies in political economy. Ithaca: Cornell University Press.

Boldyrev, Oleg. 2015. "Baltiiskii Put'. Estonia—Rodina, Putin—Prezident." *BBC News Russkaya Sluzhba*, July 4. Accessed March 06, 2020. https://www.bbc.com/russian/international/2015/04/150407_baltic_special_estonia.

Bond, Ross. 2006. "Belonging and Becoming: National Identity and Exclusion." *Sociology* 40 (4): 609–26. doi:10.1177/0038038506065149.

Bös, Mathias, and Kerstin Zimmer. 2006. "Wenn Grenzen Wandern: Zur Dynamik Von Grenzverschiebungen Im Osten Europas." In *Grenzsoziologie: Die Politische Strukturierung Des Raumes*, edited by Monika Eigmüller and Georg Vobruba, 157–84. Wiesbaden: Verlag für Sozialwissenschaften.

Bourdieu, Pierre. 1977. *Outline of a Theory of Practice*. Cambridge studies in social anthropology 16. Cambridge: Cambridge University Press.

Boym, Svetlana. 1994. *Common Places: Mythologies of Everyday Life in Russia*. Cambridge, London: Harvard University Press.

Braun, Aksana, and Monika Wingender. 2015. "Kazakhstan and Tatarstan—Building Identities in Russian-Turkic Speech Communities." In *Kazakh in Post-Soviet Kazakhstan*, edited by Raihan Muhamedowa, 69–94. Wiesbaden: Harrasowitz.

Braun, Virginia, and Victoria Clarke. 2008. "Using Thematic Analysis in Psychology." *Qualitative Research in Psychology* 3 (2): 77–101.

Brednikova, Olga. 2008. "'Windows' Project Ad Marginem or a 'Divided History' of Divided Cities? A Case Study of the Russian-Estonian Borderland." In *Representations of the Margins of Europe: Politics and Identities in the Baltic and South Caucasian States*, edited by Tsypylma Darieva and Kaschuba Wolfgang, 43–64. Frankfurt, New York: Campus Verlag.

Brezhnaya, Elena. 2016. "Vokzal Dlya Dvoikh: Pochemu Stantsiya Petropavlovska Otnositsya K Rossii." *Sputnik*, September 20. Accessed April 07, 2018. https://ru.sputniknews.kz/analytics/20160920/197025.html.

Brubaker, Rogers. 1993. "National Minorities, Nationalizing States, and External National Homelands in the New Europe. Notes toward a Relational Analysis." *IHS Reihe Politikwissenschaft* 11: 1–21.

Brubaker, Rogers. 1996. *Nationalism Reframed: Nationhood and the National Question in the New Europe*. Cambridge: Cambridge University Press.

Brubaker, Rogers. 2005. "The 'Diaspora' Diaspora." *Ethnic and Racial Studies* 28 (1): 1–19. doi:10.1080/0141987042000289997.

Brubaker, Rogers. 2006. *Ethnicity without Groups*. 1. Harvard Univ. Pr. paperback ed. Cambridge: Harvard University Press.

Brubaker, Rogers. 2013. "Categories of Analysis and Categories of Practice: A Note on the Study of Muslims in European Countries of Immigration." *Ethnic and Racial Studies* 36 (1): 1–8. doi:10.1080/01419870.2012.729674.

Brubaker, Rogers, and Frederick Cooper. 2000. "Beyond 'Identity'." *Theory and Society* 29 (1): 1–47.

Brüggemann, Karsten, and Andres Kasekamp. 2008. "The Politics of History and the 'War of Monuments' in Estonia." *Nationalities Papers* 36 (3): 425–48. doi:10.1080/00905990802080646.

Buchli, Victor. 1999. *An Archaeology of Socialism*. Materializing culture. Oxford: Berg.

Burch, Stuart, and David J. Smith. 2007. "Empty Spaces and the Value of Symbols: Estonia's 'War of Monuments' from Another Angle." *Europe-Asia Studies* 59 (6): 913–36. doi:10.1080/09668130701489139.

Butler, Judith. 1990. *Gender Trouble: Feminism and the Subversion of Identity*. Thinking gender. New York, London: Routledge.

Butler, Judith. 1993. *Bodies That Matter: On the Discursive Limits of "Sex"*. New York, London: Routledge.

Canetti, Elias. 1973. *Crowds and Power*. [Revised ed.]. Harmondsworth: Penguin.

Casey, Edward S. 1987. *Remembering: A Phenomenological Study*. A Midland book MB 409. Bloomington: Indiana University Press.

Certeau, Michel d. 1984. *The Practice of Everyday Life*. Berkley: University of California Press.

Chepurin, Aleksandr. 2009. "Kongress Sootechestvennikov: Itogi I Perspektivy Rossiiskoi Politiki." Accessed March 09, 2020. http://www.russkie.org/index.php ?module=fullitem&id=15889.

Chernyshev, Sergei. 1996. "Iz Vystupleniya S. Chernysheva V Sobranii Russkogo Instituta." *Russkii Institut*. http://old.russ.ru/ri/. Accessed May 12, 2018.

Chernyshev, Sergei, and Gleb Pavlovskii. 1997. "K Vozobnovleniyu Russkogo." *Russkii Zhurnal*. http://old.russ.ru/journal/dsp/97-07-14/pav-che.htm. Accessed May 12, 2018.

Cheskin, Ammon. 2012. "History, Conflicting Collective Memories, and National Identities: How Latvia's Russian-Speakers Are Learning to Remember." *Nationalities Papers* 40 (04): 561–84. doi:10.1080/00905992.2012.685062.

Cheskin, Ammon. 2015. "Identity and Integration of Russian Speakers in the Baltic States: A Framework for Analysis." *Ethnopolitics* 14 (1): 72–93. doi:10.1080/174 49057.2014.933051.

Cheskin, Ammon. 2016. *Russian Speakers in Post-Soviet Latvia: Discursive Identity Strategies*. Russian language and society. Edinburg: Edinburgh University Press.

Cheskin Ammon, and Angela Kachuyevski. 2019. "The Russian-Speaking Populations in the Post-Soviet Space: Language, Politics and Identity." *Europe-Asia Studies* 71 (1): 1–23. doi:10.1080/09668136.2018.1529467.

Clifford, James. 1994. "Diasporas." *Cultural Anthropology* 9 (3): 302–38.

Coalson, Robert. 2014. "Is Putin 'Rebuilding Russia' According to Solzhenitsyn's Design?" *Radio Free Europe / Radio Liberty*, January 9. Accessed March 06, 2020. https://www.rferl.org/a/russia-putin-solzhenitsyn-1990-essay/26561244.html.

Coffey, Luke. 2015. "Why Narva Is Probably Not Next on Russia's List." *Al Jazeera*. Accessed March 06, 2020. https://www.aljazeera.com/indepth/opinion/2015/04/ narva-russia-list-150414121342078.html.

Cohen, Anthony. 2000. "Introduction: Discriminating Relations: Identity, Boundary and Authenticity." In *Signifying Identities: Anthropological Perspectives on Boundaries and Contested Values*, edited by Anthony Cohen, 1–15. London, New York: Routledge.

Colebrook, Claire. 2002. "The Politics and Potential of Everyday Life." *New Literary History* 33 (4): 687–706.

Commercio, Michele E. 2004. "The 'Pugachev Rebellion' in the Context of Post-Soviet Kazakh Nationalization." *Nationalities Papers* 32 (1): 87–113. doi:10.1080/0090599042000186205.

Connerton, Paul. 1989. *How Societies Remember.* Cambridge: Cambridge University Press.

Cresswell, Tim. 1996. *In Place/out of Place: Geography, Ideology, and Transgression.* Minneapolis: University of Minnesota Press.

Cresswell, Tim. 2011. "Place—Part I." In *the Wiley-Blackwell Companion to Human Geography*, edited by John Agnew and James Duncan, 235–45. West Sussex: Blackwell Publishing.

Cresswell, Tim. 2015. *Place: An Introduction.* 2. ed. Chester: Wiley Blackwell.

Cronon, William. 1995. "Introduction: In Search of Nature." In *Uncommon Ground: Rethinking the Human Place in Nature*, edited by William Cronon, 23–58. New York, London: W. W. Norton & Company.

Csordas, Thomas. 1994. *Embodiment and Experience.* Cambridge: Cambridge University Press.

Cummings, Sally N. 2005. *Kazakhstan: Power and the Elite.* London, New York: I.B. Tauris; New York: Distributed in the US by Palgrave Macmillan.

Cummings, Sally N. 2010. *Symbolism and Power in Central Asia: Politics of the Spectacular.* London: Routledge.

Daly, John C. K. 2008. *Kazakhstan's Emerging Middle Class.* Silk Road paper. Washington, DC: Central Asia-Caucasus Institute & Silk Road Studies Program.

Darieva, Tsypylma, and Kaschuba Wolfgang. 2011. "Sights and Signs of Postsocialist Urbanism in Eurasia: An Introduction." In *Urban Spaces After Socialism: Ethnographies of Public Spaces in Eurasian Cities*, edited by Tsypylma Darieva, Kaschuba Wolfgang, and Melanie Krebs, 9–32. Frankfurt, New York: Campus Verlag.

Datta, Ayona. 2012. "'Where Is the Global City?' Visual Narratives of London among East European Migrants." *Urban Studies* 49 (8): 1725–40. doi:10.1177/0042098011417906.

Dave, Bhavna. 2007. *Kazakhstan: Ethnicity, Language and Power.* London, New York: Routledge.

Devine-Wright, Patrick. 2013. "Think Global, Act Local? The Relevance of Place Attachments and Place Identities in a Climate Changed World." *Global Environmental Change* 23 (1): 61–69. doi:10.1016/j.gloenvcha.2012.08.003.

Diener, Alexander C. 2016a. "Assessing Potential Russian Irredentism and Separatism in Kazakhstan's Northern Oblasts." *Eurasian Geography and Economics* 56 (5): 469–92. doi:10.1080/15387216.2015.1103660.

Diener, Alexander C. 2016b. "Imagining Kazakhstani-Stan: Negotiations of Homeland and Titular-Nationality." In *Kazakhstan in the Making: Legitimacy, Symbols, and Social Changes*, edited by Marlene Laruelle, 131–55. Maryland: Lexington Books.

Diener, Alexander C., and Joshua Hagen. 2013. "From Socialist to Post-Socialist Cities: Narrating the Nation Through Urban Space." *Nationalities Papers* 41 (4): 487–514. doi:10.1080/00905992.2013.768217.

Dixon, John, and Kevin Durrheim. 2004. "Dislocating Identity: Desegregation and the Transformation of Place." *Journal of Environmental Psychology* 24 (4): 455–73. doi:10.1016/j.jenvp.2004.09.004.

Durkheim, Émile, and Karen E. Fields. 1995. *The Elementary Forms of Religious Life.* New York, London: The Free press.

Duvold, Kjetil. 2006. *If Push Comes to Shove. Territorial Identification Amongst the Baltic Russians.* Proceedings of International Conference Uncertain Transformations—New Domestic and International Challenges, Riga: LU Akademiskais Apgads: 293–304.

Dyusenov, Serik. 2017. "Ekspo 2017 S Astane I Turizm V Petropavlovske." *Elektronnaya Biblioteka.* Accessed March 06, 2020. at:

Ehala, Martin. 2009. "The Bronze Soldier: Identity Threat and Maintenance in Estonia." *Journal of Baltic Studies* 40 (1): 139–58. doi:10.1080/01629770902722294.

Ely, Christopher D. 2002. *This Meager Nature: Landscape and National Identity in Imperial Russia.* DeKalb: Northern Illinois University Press.

Esmurzaeva, Zhanbota. 2008. "Kontsept "Rodina" (V Russkom I Angkliiskom Yazykakh) V Sisteme Tsennostnykh Kontseptov Yazykovoi Kartiny Mira." *Gramota* 8 (15): 169–88.

Federal Law, No. 9.-F. 1999. "On State Policy of the Russian Federation with Regard to Compatriots Abroad." Accessed May 12, 2018. www.carim-east.eu /2963/2963/.

Fein, Lisa. 2005. "Symbolic Boundaries and National Borders: The Construction of an Estonian Russian Identity." *Nationalities Papers* 33 (3): 333–44.

Feklyunina, Valentina. 2016. "Soft Power and Identity: Russia, Ukraine and the 'Russian World(S)'." *European Journal of International Relations* 22 (4): 773–96. doi:10.1177/1354066115601200.

Feldman, Merje. 2001. "European Integration and the Discourse of National Identity in Estonia." *National Identities* 3 (1): 5–21. doi:10.1080/14608940020028466.

Ferguson, James. 1999. *Expectations of Modernity: Myths and Meanings of Urban Life on the Zambian Copperbelt.* Berleley: University of California Press.

Feyerabend, Paul. 1993. *Against Method.* 3rd ed. London, New York: Verso.

Florin, Moritz. 2011. "Elity, Russkii Yazik I Sovetskaya Identichnost' V Postsovetskoi Kirgizii." *Intelros* 6. http://www.intelros.ru/readroom/nz/neprikosnovennyy-zapas -80-2011/12777-elity-russkiy-yazyk-i-sovetskaya-identichnost-v-postsovetskoy-k irgizii.html. Accessed March 30, 2018.

Flynn, Moya. 2007. "Renegotiating Stability, Security and Identity in the Post-Soviet Borderlands: The Experience of Russian Communities in Uzbekistan." *Nationalities Papers* 35 (2): 267–88. doi:10.1080/00905990701254359.

Fortier, Anne-Marie. 2000. *Migrant Belongings: Memory, Space and Identity.* Oxford: Berg.

Foucault, Michel. 1977. *Language, Counter-Memory, Practice: Selected Essays and Interviews.* Edited by Donald F. Bouchard. Ithaca: Cornell University Press.

Foucault, Michel. 1995. *Discipline and Punish: The Birth of the Prison.* 2nd Vintage Books ed. New York: Vintage Books. http://www.loc.gov/catdir/description/random048/95203580.html.

Fuller, Martin G., and Martina Löw. 2017. "Introduction: An Invitation to Spatial Sociology." *Current Sociology* 65 (4): 469–91. doi:10.1177/0011392117697461.

Gali, A. 2004. "Kazakhisatsia, Kak Etnosotsial'naya Mobilizatsiya Dlya Sozdaniya Postetnicheskogo Kazakhstana." *Tsentr Aziya*, 2004. Accessed March 06, 2020. https://openrussia.org/post/view/11690/.

Glacken, Clarence. 1992. "Reflections on the History of Western Attitudes to Nature." *GeoJournal* 26 (2): 103–11. doi:10.1007/BF00241203.

Gold, Mick. 1984. "A History of Nature." In *Geography Matters! A Reader*, edited by Doreen Massey and John Allen, 12–34. Cambridge, New York: Cambridge University Press.

Grant, Bruce. 2009. *The Captive and the Gift: Cultural Histories of Sovereignty in Russia and the Caucasus.* Culture and society after socialism. Ithaca: Cornell University Press.

Grigas, Agnia. 2016. *Beyond Crimea: The New Russian Empire.* New Haven, London: Yale University Press.

Grigorichev, Konstantin. 2007. "Granici Kazakhstana: Scenarii Razvitiya." In *Migranty I Diaspory Na Vostoke Rossii: Praktiki Vzaimodejstviya S Obschestvom I Gosudarstvom.* Moscow, Irkutsk: Natalis.

Gromyko, Andrei. 2010. "Russkii Mir: Ponyatie, Printsipy, Tsennosti, Struktura." In *Smysly I Tsennosti Russkogo Mira*, edited by Vecheslav Nikonov, 20–24. Moscow: Fond Russkogo Mira.

Hallik, Klara, and L. M. Drobizneva. 2001. *Neestonci Na Rynke Truda V Novoi Estonii.* Moscow: Kanon-Press-C.

Halse, Christine. 2018. "Theories and Theorizing of Belonging." In *Interrogating Belonging for Young People in Schools*, edited by Christine Halse, 1–28. Basingstoke, Hampshire: Palgrave Macmillan.

Haraway, Donna. 1991. "Situated Knowledges: The Science Question in Feminism and the Privilege of Partial Perspective." In *Simians, Cyborgs and Women: The Reinvention of Nature*, edited by Donna Haraway, 183–201. London: Free Association Books.

Hartley, John. 2003. *A Short History of Cultural Studies.* London, Thousand Oaks: Sage.

Hedenskog, Jakob, and Robert Larrson. 2007. *Russian Leverage on the CIS and the Baltic States.* Stockholm: Swedish Defence Research Agency FOI, Defence Analysis.

Heidegger, Martin. 1962. *Being and Time.* London: SCM Press.

Herzfeld, Michael. 2005. *Cultural Intimacy: Social Poetics in the Nation-State.* New York: Routledge.

Hirsch, Eric. 1995. "Landscape: Between Place and Space." In *the Anthropology of Landscape: Perspectives on Place and Space*, edited by Eric Hirsch and Michael O'Hanlon, 1–30. Oxford: Clarendon Press.

hooks, bell. 1984. *Feminist Theory from Margin to Center.* Boston: South End Press.

hooks, bell. 2009. *Belonging: A Culture of Place*. New York, London: Routledge.

Ingold, Tim. 2000. *The Perception of the Environment: Essays on Livelihood, Dwelling and Skill*. London, New York: Routledge.

Ingold, Tim. 2004. "Culture on the Ground." *Journal of Material Culture* 9 (3): 315–40. doi:10.1177/1359183504046896.

International Crisis Group. 2015. "Stress Tests for Kazakhstan." Accessed March 09, 2020. https://www.crisisgroup.org/europe-central-asia/central-asia/kazakhstan/str ess-tests-kazakhstan.

Isaacs, Rico, and Abel Polese. 2015. "Between 'Imagined' and 'Real' Nation-Building: Identities and Nationhood in Post-Soviet Central Asia." *Nationalities Papers* 43 (3): 371–82. doi:10.1080/00905992.2015.1029044.

Isin, Engin. 2002. *Being Political: Genealogies of Citizenship*. Minneapolis: University of Minnesota Press.

Jackson, Lucy. 2016. "Intimate Citizenship? Rethinking the Politics and Experience of Citizenship as Emotional in Wales and Singapore." *Gender, Place & Culture* 23 (6): 817–33. doi:10.1080/0966369X.2015.1073695.

Jašina-Schäfer, Alina. 2019. "Where Do I Belong? Narratives of Rodina among Russian-Speaking Youth in Kazakhstan." *Europe-Asia Studies* 71 (1): 97–116. do i:10.1080/09668136.2018.1508645.

Jašina-Schäfer, Alina. 2019. "Everyday Experiences of Place in the Kazakhstani Borderland: Russian Speakers between Kazakhstan, Russia, and the Globe." *Nationalities Papers* 47 (1): 38–54.

Jašina-Schäfer, Alina, and Ammon Cheskin. 2020. "Horizontal Citizenship in Estonia: Russian Speakers in the Borderland City of Narva." *Citizenship Studies* 24 (1): 93–110. doi:10.1080/13621025.2019.1691150.

Jašina-Schäfer, Alina. 2020. "Of Homogenous 'Freaks' and Heterogenous Members: Cultural Minorities and theri Belon in the Estonian Borderland." *New Diversities*.

Kadyrzhanov, Rustem. 2014. *Ethnokul'turnyi Simvolizm I Natsionalnaya Identichnost' Kazahstana*. Almaty: Institut filosofii, politologii I religiovedeniya KN MON RK.

Kaiser, Robert, and Elena Nikiforova. 2008. "The Performativity of Scale: The Social Construction of Scale Effects in Narva, Estonia." *Environmental Planning D* 26 (3): 537–62. doi:10.1068/d3307.

Kalekin-Fishman, Devorah. 2013. "Sociology of Everyday Life." *Current Sociology* 61 (5–6): 714–32. doi:10.1177/0011392113482112.

Kalikulov, Dinmukhamed. 2014. "V Kazakhstane Ozadacheny Slovami Putina O Russkom Mire." *BBC News Russkaya Sluzhba*. Accessed March 09, 2020. https://www.bbc.com/russian/international/2014/09/140901_kazakhstan_putin.

Kallas, Kristina. 2016. "Claiming the Diaspora: Russia's Compatriot Policy and Its Reception by Estonian-Russian Population." *Journal of Ethnopolitics and Minority Issues in Europe* 15 (3): 1–25.

Kalvet, Tarmo. 2010. *Expert Evaluation Network Delivering Policy Analysis on the Performance of Cohesion Policy 2007–2013: Task 2: Country Report on Achievements of Cohesion Policy*. Tallinn: Tallinn University of Technology.

Karaulova, Asel. 2018. "Nel'zya Rabotat' Na Obschestvo I Byt' Svobodnym Ot Nego." Accessed March 09, 2020. http://www.exclusive.kz/expertiza/biznes/113513/.

Kasekamp, Andres. 2000. *The Radical Right in Interwar Estonia.* Studies in Russia and East Europe. Houndmills Basingstoke Hampshire, New York: Macmillan Press; St. Martin's Press.

Kazakhstan's National Agency for Statistics. 2016. Accessed May 12, 2018. http://stat.gov.kz/faces/homePage?_afrLoop=10519272158276520#%40%3F_afrLoop%3D10519272158276520%26_adf.ctrl-state%3De9j1omoaw_34.

Kazlas, Juozas. 1977. "Social Distance among Ethnic Groups." In *Nationality Group Survival in Multi-Ethnic States*, edited by Edward Allworth, 228–54. New York: Praeger.

Kendirbaeva, Gulnar. 1999. "'We are Children of Alash…' The Kazakh Intelligentsia at the Beginning of the 20th Century in Search of National Identity and Prospects of the Cultural Survival of the Kazakh People." *Central Asian Survey* 18 (1): 5–36.

Kesküla, Eeva. 2015. "Reverse, Restore, Repeat!" *Focaal* 2015 (72): 95–108. doi:10.3167/fcl.2015.720108.

Kikimov, T. 1998. "Koyandinskoi Yarmarke 150 Let." *Industrial'naya Karaganda*, 1998. http://catalog.karlib.kz/irbis64r_01/Kraeved/Istoriya_Karkaraly/Koyandinskooy_yarmarke_150_let.pdf.

King, Charles, and Neil. J. Melvin. 1999. "Diaspora Politics: Ethnic Linkages, Foreign Policy, and Security in Eurasia." *International Security* 24 (3): 108–138.

Koch, Natalie. 2010. "The Monumental and the Miniature: Imagining 'Modernity' in Astana." *Social & Cultural Geography* 11 (8): 769–87. doi:10.1080/14649365.2010.521854.

Koch, Natalie. 2012. "Urban 'Utopias': The Disney Stigma and Discourses of 'False Modernity'." *Environment and Planning A: Economy and Space* 44 (10): 2445–62. doi:10.1068/a44647.

Koch, Natalie. 2014. "Bordering on the Modern: Power, Practice and Exclusion in Astana." *Transactions of the Institute of British Geographers* 39 (3): 432–43. doi:10.1111/tran.12031.

Koch, Natalie. 2015. "'Spatial Socialization': Understanding the State Effect Geographically." *Norida Geographical Publications* 44 (4): 29–35.

Kolstø, Pål. 1995. *Russians in the Former Soviet Republics.* Bloomington: Indiana University Press.

Kolstø, Pål. 1996. "The New Russian Diaspora—An Identity of Its Own? Possible Identity Trajectories for Russians in the Former Soviet Republics." *Ethnic and Racial Studies* 9 (3): 609–39.

Kolstø, Pål. 1998. "Anticipating Demographic Superiority: Kazakh Thinking on Integration and Nation Building." *Europe-Asia Studies* 50 (1): 51–69. doi:10.1080/09668139808412523.

Kolstø, Pål. 1999. "Territorializing Diasporas. The Case of Russians in the Former Soviet Republics." *Millennium: Journal of International Studies* 28 (3): 607–31.

Kolstø, Pål. 2011. "Beyond Russia, Becoming Local: Trajectories of Adaption to the Fall of the Soviet Union Among Ethnic Russians in the Former Soviet Republics." *Journal of Eurasian Studies* 2 (2): 153–63. doi:10.1016/j.euras.2011.03.006.

Kolstø, Pål. 2016. "Introduction: Russian Nationalism Is Back—But Precisely What Does That Mean?" In *the New Russian Nationalism: Imperialism, Ethnicity and Authoritarianism 2000–2015*, edited by Pål Kolstø and Helge Blakkisrud. 1st ed., 1–17. Imperialism, ethnicity and authoritarianism 2000–2015. Edinburgh: Edinburgh University Press.

Komarova, Milena, and Liam O'Dowd. 2016. "Belfast, 'The Shared City'? Spatial Narratives of Conflict Transformation." In *Spatializing Peace and Conflict: Mapping the Production of Places, Sites and Scales of Violence*, edited by Annika Björkdahl and Susanne Buckley-Zistel, 265–85. New York: Palgrave Macmillan.

Kõresaar, Ene. 2004. "The Notion of Rupture in Estonian Narrative Memory: On the Construction of Meaning in Autobiographical Texts on the Stalinist Experience." *Ab Imperio* 2004 (4): 313–39. doi:10.1353/imp.2004.0088.

Korts, Külliki. 2008. "Contacts between Ethnic Estonians and Estonian Russians." In *Estonian Human Development Report 2007*, edited by Mati Heidmets, 72–77. Tallinn: Eesti Koostöö kogu.

Kosmarskaya, Natalya. 2005. "Post-Soviet Russian Diaspora." In *Encyclopedia of Diasporas: Immigrant and Refugee Cultures Around the World* Vol. 124, edited by Melvin Ember, Carol R. Ember, and Ian A. Skoggard, 264–72. New York: Springer.

Kosmarskaya, Natalya. 2006. *Deti Imperii' V Postsovetskoi Tsentralnoi Azii: Adaptivnye Praktiki I Mental'nye Sdvigi*. Moscow: Natalis.

Kosmarskaya, Natalya. 2011. "Russia and Post-Soviet "Russian Diaspora": Contrasting Visions, Conflicting Projects." *Nationalism and Ethnic Politics* 17 (1): 54–74. doi:10.1080/13537113.2011.550247.

Kosmarskaya, Natalya. 2014. "Russians in Post-Soviet Central Asia: More 'Cold' Than the Others? Exploring (Ethnic) Identity under Different Sociopolitical Settings." *Journal of Multilingual and Multicultural Development* 35 (1): 9–26. doi:10.1080/01434632.2013.845195.

Kosmarskaya, Natalya, and Artyom Kosmarski. 2019. "'Russian Culture' in Central Asia as a Transethnic Phenomenon." In *Global Russian Cultures*, edited by Kevin M. F. Platt, 69–93. Madison: University of Wisconsin Press.

Kosmarskaya, Natalya, and Igor Savin. 2018. "Chto Dumayut Kazakhstanci Ob Otnosheniyakh S 'Severnim Sosedom'." *Tsentral'naya Evraziya* 1: 175–95.

Kozin, Alexander. 2015. "'The Law of Compatriot': Toward a New Russian National Identity." *Russian Journal of Communication* 7 (3): 286–99. doi:10.1080/194094 19.2015.1082439.

Kruusvall, Jüri, Raivo Vetik, and John W. Berry. 2009. "The Strategies of Inter-Ethnic Adaptation of Estonian Russians." *Studies of Transition States and Societies* 1 (1): 3–24.

Kucera, Joshua. 2014. "North Kazakhstan Isn't the Next Crimea—Yet." *Al Jazeera America*, June 19. Accessed March 06, 2020. http://america.aljazeera.com/articles /2014/6/19/north-kazakhstanisntthenextcrimeaayet.html.

Kudaibergenova, Diana. 2012. "Post Socialist Culture in Latvia and Kazakhstan: An Introduction to Reasons, Criticisms, and Perspectives." In *National Identity: Time, Place, and People*, edited by Evija Zaca, 40–51. Riga: University of Latvia Press.

Kudaibergenova, Diana T. 2017. *Rewriting the Nation in Modern Kazakh Literature: Elites and Narratives.* Contemporary Central Asia. Lanham: Lexington Books.

Kudaibergenova, Diana T. 2018. "Punk Shamanism, Revolt and Break-up of Traditional Linkage: The Waves of Cultural Production in Post-Soviet Kazakhstan." *European Journal of Cultural Studies* 21 (4): 435–51. doi:10.1177/1367549416682962.

Kultuuriministeerium. 2017. "Kultuurministeerium on 'Teeme Ära' Talgutel Narvas." Accessed April 15, 2018. https://www.kul.ee/et/uudised/kultuuriministeerium -teeme-ara-talgutel-narvas.

Lähdesmäki, Tuuli, Tuija Saresma, Kaisa Hiltunen, Saara Jäntti, Nina Sääskilahti, Antti Vallius, and Kaisa Ahvenjärvi. 2016. "Fluidity and Flexibility of "Belonging"." *Acta Sociologica* 59 (3): 233–47. doi:10.1177/0001699316633099.

Laitin, David. 1998. *Identity in Formation: The Russian-Speaking Population in the Near Abroad.* London: Cornell University Press.

Laruelle, Marlene. 2015a. "Russia as a 'Divided Nation,' from Compatriots to Crimea: A Contribution to the Discussion on Nationalism and Foreign Policy." *Problems of Post-Communism* 62 (2): 88–97. doi:10.1080/10758216.2015.1010 902.

Laruelle, Marlene. 2015b. "The 'Russian World': Russia's Soft Power and Geopolitical Imaginations." *Center on Global Interests* (May 21), 1–29.

Laruelle, Marlene. 2015c. "The Power of Soft Power in Kazakhstan." Accessed March 09, 2020. http://www.ponarseurasia.org/article/power-soft-power-kazakh stan.

Laruelle, Marlene, and Sebastian Peyrouse. 2007. *Russkii Vopros V Nezavisimom Kazahstane: Istoriya, Politika, Identichnost.* Moscow: Natalis. (translated from French by Tat'yana Grigor'eva).

Laszczkowski, Mateusz. 2011. "Superplace: Global Connections and Local Politics at the Mega Mall, Astana." *Etnofoor* 23 (1): 85–104.

Laszczkowski, Mateusz. 2016. *"City of the Future": Built Space, Modernity and Urban Change in Astana.* New York: Berghahn Books.

Latour, Bruno. 2005. *Reassembling the Social: An Introduction to Actor-Network-Theory.* Clarendon lectures in management studies. Oxford, New York: Oxford University Press.

Lauristin, Marju, and Mati Heidmets. 2002. *The Challenge of the Russian Minority: Emerging Multicultural Democracy in Estonia.* Tartu: Tartu University Press.

Lauristin, Marju, and Peeter Vihalemm. 2009. "The Political Agenda during Different Periods of Estonian Transformation: External and Internal Factors." *Journal of Baltic Studies* 40 (1): 1–28. doi:10.1080/01629770902722237.

Law, John. 2004. *After Method: Mess in Social Science Research.* International library of sociology. London: Routledge.

Lawrence, Denise L., and Setha M. Low. 1990. "The Built Environment and Spatial Form." *Annual Review of Anthropology* 19: 453–505.

Lebedeva, Nadezhda. 1995. *Novaya Russkaya Diaspora: Sotsial'no-Psikhologicheskii Analiz.* Moscow: Institut etnologii I antropologii im. N.N. Miklukho-Maklaya.

Lefebvre, Henri. 1991. *The Production of Space.* Oxford: Basil Blackwell.

Leping, Kristian-Olari, and Ott Toomet. 2008. "Emerging Ethnic Wage Gap: Estonia during Political and Economic Transition." *Journal of Comparative Economics* 36 (4): 599–619.

Lewicka, Maria. 2014. "In Search of Roots: Memory as Enabler of Place Attachment." In *Place Attachment: Advances in Theory, Methods and Applications*, edited by Lynne Manzo and Patrick Devine-Wright, 49–61. London: Routledge.

Liebscher, Grit, and Jennifer Dailey-O'Cain. 2013. *Language, Space, and Identity in Migration*. Online-ausg. Language and globalization. New York: Palgrave Macmillan.

Linz, Juan J., and Alfred C. Stepan. 1996. *Problems of Democratic Transition and Consolidation: Southern Europe, South America, and Post-Communist Europe*. Baltimore: Johns Hopkins University Press.

Loorits, Oskar. 1990. *Eesti Rahvausundi Maailmavaade*. Tallinn: Perioodika.

Lotman, Juri, and Boris Uspenskii. 1996. "Otzvuki Kontseptsii 'Moskva—Tretii Rim' V Ideologii Petra Pervogo (K Probleme Srednevekovoi Traditsii V Kul'ture Barokko)." In *Semiotika Istorii. Semiotika Kul'turi, Izbrannye Trudy*, edited by Boris Uspenskii. 1st ed., 125–41. Moscow: Yazyki Russkoi Kulturi.

Low, Setha M. 2000. *On the Plaza: The Politics of Public Space and Culture*. 1st ed. Austin: University of Texas Press.

Low, Setha M. 2009. "Towards an Anthropological Theory of Space and Place." *Semiotica* 175: 46. doi:10.1515/semi.2009.041.

Low, Setha M. 2017. *Spatializing Culture: The Ethnography of Space and Place*. London: Routledge.

Low, Setha M., and Lawrence-Zúñiga Denise. 2003. "Locating Culture." In *the Anthropology of Space and Place: Locating Culture*, edited by Setha M. Low and Lawrence-Zúñiga Denise, 1–49. Oxford: Blackwell.

Löw, Martina. 2008. "The Constitution of Space." *European Journal of Social Theory* 11 (1): 25–49. doi:10.1177/1368431007085286.

Lutter, Christina. 2016. "What Do We Translate When We Translate? Context, Process, and Practice as Categories of Cultural Analysis." In *the Trans/National Study of Culture*, edited by Doris Bachmann-Medick, 155–67. Berlin, Boston: De Gruyter.

Lynn-Ee Ho, Elaine. 2006. "Negotiating Belonging and Perceptions of Citizenship in a Transnational World: Singapore, a Cosmopolis?" *Social & Cultural Geography* 7 (3): 385–401. doi:10.1080/14649360600715086.

Macnaghten, Phil, and John Urry. 1998. *Contested Natures*. Theory, culture & society. London: SAGE.

Macnaghten, Phil, and John Urry. 2000. "Bodies of Nature: Introduction." In *Body and Society*, edited by Phil Macnaghten and John Urry, 1–11. London, Thousand Oaks, New Delhi: SAGE Publications Ltd.

Makarychev, Andrey. 2018. "Narva as a Cultural Borderland: Estonian, European, Russophone." *Russian Analytical Digest* 228: 9–13.

Makarychev, Andrey, and Vladimir Sazonov. 2019. "Populisms, Popular Geopolitics and the Politics of Belonging in Estonia." *European Politics and Society* 20 (4): 450–69. doi:10.1080/23745118.2019.1569341.

Makarychev, Andrey, and Aleksandra Yatsyk. 2016. *Celebrating Borderlands in a Wider Europe: 'Nations and Identities in Ukraine, Georgia and Estonia.* Baden-Baden: Nomos.

Malloy, Tove H. 2009. "Social Cohesion Estonian Style: Minority Integration Through Constitutionalized Hegemony and Fictive Pluralism." In *Minority Integration in Central Eastern Europe: Between Ethnic Diversity and Equality,* edited by Timofey Agarin and Malte Brosig. On the boundary of two worlds 18. Amsterdam, New York, NY: Rodopi.

Manzo, Lynne C. 2003. "Beyond House and Haven: Toward a Revisioning of Emotional Relationships with Places." *Journal of Environmental Psychology* 23 (1): 47–61. doi:10.1016/S0272-4944(02)00074-9.

Manzo, Lynne C., and Douglas D. Perkins. 2006. "Finding Common Ground: The Importance of Place Attachment to Community Participation and Planning." *Journal of Planning Literature* 20 (4): 335–50. doi:10.1177/0885412205286160.

Marotta, Vince P. 2008. "The Hybrid Self and the Ambivalence of Boundaries." *Social Identities* 14 (3): 295–312. doi:10.1080/13504630802088052.

Martinez, Francisco. 2018. *Remains of the Soviet Past in Estonia:An Anthropology of Forgetting, Repair and Urban Traces.* London: UCL Press.

Massey, Doreen. 1984. "Introduction: Geography Matters." In *Geography Matters! A Reader,* edited by Doreen Massey and John Allen, 1–11. Cambridge: Cambridge University Press.

Massey, Doreen. 1991. "The Political Place of Locality Studies." *Environ Plan A* 23 (2): 267–81. doi:10.1068/a230267.

Massey, Doreen. 1994. *Space, Place and Gender.* Cambridge: Polity.

Massey, Doreen B. 2005. *For Space.* London, Thousand Oaks: SAGE.

Massumi, Brian. 2002. *Parables for the Virtual: Movement, Affect, Sensation.* Post-contemporary interventions. Durham: Duke University Press.

May, Vanessa. 2011. "Self, Belonging and Social Change." *Sociology* 45 (3): 363–78. doi:10.1177/0038038511399624.

Meinhof, Ulrike H., and Dariusz Galasiński. 2005. *The Language of Belonging.* Language and globalization. Basingstoke: Palgrave Macmillan.

Melly, Caroline. 2010. "Inside-Out Houses: Urban Belonging and Imagined Futures in Dakar, Senegal." *Comparative Studies in Society and History* 52 (1): 37–65. doi:10.1017/S0010417509990326.

Melvin, Neil. 1995. *Russians beyond Russia: The Politics of National Identity.* Chatham House papers. London: Pinter.

Meri, Lennart. 1999. *Presidendikõned.* Tartu: Ilmamaa.

Mignolo, Walter. 2000. *Local Histories/global Designs: Coloniality, Subaltern Knowledges, and Border Thinking.* Princeton, Oxford: Princeton University Press.

Miller, Linn. 2003. "Belonging to Country—A Philosophical Anthropology." *Journal of Australian Studies* 27 (76): 215–23. doi:10.1080/14443050309387839.

Mol, Annemarie. 2002. *The Body Multiple: Ontology in Medical Practice.* Reproduction available: electronic resource, 2014. Science and cultural theory. Durham, London: Duke University Press.

Moran, Joe. 2005. *Reading the Everyday.* London: Routledge.

Morley, David. 2000. *Home Territories: Media, Mobility and Identity*. London: Routledge.

Müller, Martin. 2019. "Goodbye, Postsocialism!" *Europe-Asia Studies* 71 (4): 533–50. doi:10.1080/09668136.2019.1578337.

Naficy, Hamid. 1999. "Framing Exile: From Homeland to Homepage." In *Home, Exile, Homeland: Film, Media and the Politics of Place*, edited by Hamid Naficy, 1–17. London, New York: Routledge.

Nagel, Joane. 1994. "Constructing Ethnicity: Creating and Recreating Ethnic Identity and Culture." *Social Problems* 41 (1): 152–76. doi:10.2307/3096847.

Narva City Government. 2013. "Narva in Figures." Accessed March 06, 2017. http://www.narva.ee/files/7095.pdf.

Nastyukova, Olga. 2018. "Srednii klass v Kazakhstane: legche uehat', chem chto-to menyat'." *Forbes Kazakhstan*. Accessed July 23, 2020. https://forbes.kz/process/expertise/intervyu_ileuova/

Navaro-Yashin, Yael. 2012. *The Make-Believe Space: Affective Geography in a Postwar Polity*. Durham: Duke University Press.

Nazpary, Joma. 2002. *Post-Soviet Chaos: Violence and Dispossession in Kazakhstan*. London, Sterling: Pluto Press.

Niethammer, Lutz. 2000. *Kollektive Identität. Heimliche Quellen Einer Unhemlichen Konjunktur*. Reinbeck b. Hamburg: Rowohlt Verlag.

Nikiforova, Elena. 2005. "Nationalizing Post-Soviet Borderlands: Reterritorialization of Social Space in Narva on the Estonian-Russian Border." *Paper presented at the annual meeting of the American Sociological Association*. http://citation.allacademic.com/meta/p_mla_apa_research_citation/0/2/3/1/0/p23106_index.html.

Nimmerfeldt, Gerli. 2011. "Sense of Belonging to Estonia." In *the Russian Second Generation in Tallinn and Kohtla-Järve, the TIES Study in Estonia*, edited by Raivo Vetik and Jelena Helemäe, 203–29. Amsterdam: Amsterdam University Press.

Nora, Pierre. 1989. "Between Memory and History: Les Lieux De Mémoire." *Representations* 26: 7–24. doi:10.2307/2928520.

Novikov, Andrei. 2017a. "Krasivyi Gorod, Kotorogo Net." Accessed March 09, 2020. http://www.pkzsk.info/krasivyj-gorod-kotorogo-net/.

Novikov, Andrei. 2017b. "Severnogo Kazakhstana 'Bronza' Po Rostu Tsen Na Kommunalku." Accessed March 09, 2020. http://pkzsk.info/u-severnogo-kazaxstana-bronza-po-rostu-cen-na-kommunalku/.

Nowicka, Magdalena. 2007. "Mobile Locations: Construction of Home in a Group of Mobile Transnational Professionals." *Global Networks* 7 (1): 69–86. doi:10.1111/j.1471-0374.2006.00157.x.

Nozhenko, Maria. 2006. "Motherland Is Calling You! Motives Behind and Prospects for the New Russian Policy on Compatriots Abroad." *Lithuanian Foreign Policy Review* (18): 77–94.

Oldenburg, Ray. 1999. *The Great Good Place: Cafés, Coffee Shops, Bookstores, Bars, Hair Salons, and Other Hangouts at the Heart of a Community*. New York, Berkeley, Marlowe; Distributed by Publishers Group West.

Ong, Aihwa. 2011. "Introduction: Worlding Cities, or the Art of Being Global." In *Worlding Cities: Asina Experiments and the Art of Being Global*, edited by Ananya Roy and Aihwa Ong, 1–26. Malden, Oxford, West Sussex: Wiley-Blackwell.

Ostrovskii Efim, and Petr Schedrovitskii. 1997. "Rossiya: Strana, Kotoroi Ne Bylo." Accessed May 12, 2018. https://gtmarket.ru/laboratory/expertize/2006/466.

Paasi, Anssi. 1995. "Constructing Territories, Boundaries and Regional Identity." In *Contested Territory: Border Disputes at the Edge of the Former Soviet Empire*, edited by Tuomas Forsberg, 42–61. Aldershot: Edward Elgar Publishing.

Paasi, Anssi. 1999. "Boundaries as Social Practice and Discourse: The Finnish-Russian Border." *Regional Studies* 33 (7): 669–80. doi:10.1080/00343409950078701.

Passport of North Kazakhstan Region. "Socio-Economic Passport of Petropavlovsk." Accessed March 06, 2017. http://petropavl.sko.gov.kz/page.php?page=socialno _jekonomicheskii_pasport&lang=2.

Pavlenko, Aneta. 2008. *Multilingualism in Post-Soviet Countries*. Bristol: Multilingual Matters.

Peyrouse, Sebastian. 2008. "The Russian Minority in Central Asia: Migration, Politics, and Language." *Kennan Institute Occasional Papers* 297: 1–28.

Peyrouse, Sebastian. 2007. "Nationhood and the Minority Question in Central Asia. The Russians in Kazakhstan." *Europe-Asia Studies* 59 (3): 481–501. doi:10.1080/09668130701239930.

Pfaff-Czarnecka, Joanna. 2011. *From "Identity" to "Belonging" in Social Research: Plurality, Social Boundaries, and the Politics of the Self:* DEU; Bielefeld.

Pfaff-Czarnecka, Joanna, and Gérard Toffin. 2011. *The Politics of Belonging in the Himalayas: Local Attachments and Boundary Dynamics*. Governance, conflict, and civic action series v. 4. New Delhi, London: SAGE.

Pfoser, Alena. 2014. "Between Russia and Estonia: Narratives of Place in a New Borderland." *Nationalities Papers* 42 (2): 269–85. doi:10.1080/00905992.2013.7 74341.

Pfoser, Alena. 2017. "Nested Peripheralisation." *East European Politics and Societies* 31 (1): 26–43. doi:10.1177/0888325416665157.

Picker, Giovanni. 2017. "Rethinking Ethnographic Comparison: Two Cities, Five Years, One Ethnographer." *Journal of Contemporary Ethnography* 46 (3): 263–84. doi:10.1177/0891241614548105.

Pilkington, Hilary. 1998. *Migration, Displacement and Identity in Post-Soviet Russia*. London: Routledge.

Pilkington, Hilary, and Moya Flynn. 2001. "Chuzhie Na Rodine? Issledovanija 'Diasporalnoi Identichnosti' Russkih Vinuzhdennih Pereselencev." *Diaspory*. http://mion.isu.ru/filearchive/mion_publcations/russ-ost/diaspr/12.html. Accessed March 06, 2020.

Pilkington, Hilary, and Moya Flynn. 2006. "A Diaspora in Diaspora? Russian Returnees Confront the 'Homeland'." *Refuge* 23 (2): 55–67.

Pilvre, Barbi. 2017. "Mets on Eestlase Kirik—Eesti Ekspress." *Eesti Ekspress*, October 10. Accessed March 09, 2020. https://ekspress.delfi.ee/arvamus/mets-on -eestlase-kirik?id=79738194.

Pink, Sarah. 2008. "An Urban Tour." *Ethnography* 9 (2): 175–96. doi:10.1177/1466138108089467.

Platt, Kevin. 2019. "Introduction: Putting Russian Cultures in Place." In Global Russian Cultures, edited by Kevin M. F. Platt, 3–18. Madison: University of Wisconsin Press.

Pollini, Gabriele. 2005. "Elements of a Theory of Place Attachment and Socio-Territorial Belonging." *International Review of Sociology* 15 (3): 497–515. doi:10.1080/03906700500272483.

President of Russia. 2014a. "Address by President of the Russian Federation." Accessed May 12, 2018. http://en.kremlin.ru/events/president/news/20603.

Putin, Vladimir. 2001. "Vystuplenie Prezidenta Rossiiskoi Federatsii V.V.Putina Na Kongresse Sootechestvennikov." Accessed March 09, 2020. http://old.nasledie.ru/politvnt/19_44/article.php?art=24.

Rees, Kristoffer and Aziz Burkhanov. 2018. "Constituting the Kazakhstani Nation: Rhetorical Transformation of National Belonging." *Nationalism and Ethnic Politics* 24 (4): 433–455.

Rees, Kristoffer M., and Nora W. Williams. 2017. "Explaining Kazakhstani Identity: Supraethnic Identity, Ethnicity, Language, and Citizenship." *Nationalities Papers* 45 (5): 815–39. doi:10.1080/00905992.2017.1288204.

Relph, Edward. 1976. *Place and Placelessness.* Research in planning and design 1. London: Pion.

Richardson, Tanya. 2008. *Kaleidoscopic Odessa: History and Place in Contemporary Ukraine.* Toronto: University of Toronto Press.

Ries, Nancy. 2002. "Anthropology and the Everyday, from Comfort to Terror." *New Literary History* 33 (4): 725–42.

Riley, Robert. 1992. "Attachment to the Ordinary Landscape." In *Place Attachment*, edited by Irwin Altman and Setha M. Low, 13–32. New York: Plenum Press.

Roberts, Les. 2002. "Welcome to Dreamland: From Place to Non-Place and Back Again in Pawel Pawlikowski's *Last Resort.*" *New Cinemas: Journal of Contemporary Film* (2): 78–90. doi:10.1386/ncin.1.2.78.

Rodman, Margaret C. 1992. "Empowering Place: Multilocality and Multivocality." *American Anthropologist* 94 (3): 640–56. www.jstor.org/stable/680566.

Rosaldo, Renato. 1989. *Culture and Truth: The Remaking of Social Analysis.* Boston: Beacon Press.

Ross, Kristin. 1998. *Fast Cars, Clean Bodies: Decolonization and the Reordering of French Culture.* 3rd print. Cambridge: MIT Press.

Ryden, Kent C. 1993. *Mapping the Invisible Landscape: Folklore, Writing and the Sense of Place.* American land and life series. Iowa City: University of Iowa Press.

Sandomirskaya, Irina. 2001. *Kniga O Rodine: Opyt Analiza Diskursivnikh Praktik.* Vienna: Wiener Slawistischer Almanach.

Sandomirskaya, Irina. 2004. "Rodina V Sovetskikh I Postsovetskikh Diskursivnikh Praktikakh." *INTER* 2 (3): 16–26.

Sassen, Saskia. 2006. "The Repositioning of Citizenship and Alienage: Emergent Subjects and Spaces for Politics." In *Displacement, Asylum, Migration*, edited by Kate Tunstall, 176–203. Oxford: Oxford University Press.

Schatz, Edward. 2010. "What Capital Cities Say About State and Nation Building." *Nationalism and Ethnic Politics* 9 (4): 111–40. doi:10.1080/13537110390444140.

Schulze, Jennie L. 2010. "Estonia Caught Between East and West: EU Conditionality, Russia's Activism and Minority Integration." *Nationalities Papers* 38 (3): 361–92. doi:10.1080/00905991003641954.

Schulze, Jennie L. 2017. "Does Russia Matter?" *Problems of Post-Communism* 64 (5): 257–75. doi:10.1080/10758216.2016.1239541.

Schulze, Jennie L. 2018. *Strategic Frames: Europe, Russia, and Minority Inclusion in Estonia and Latvia.* Pitt series in Russian and East European studies. Pittsburgh: University of Pittsburgh Press.

Schwartz, Katrina Z. S. 2006. *Nature and National Identity after Communism: Globalizing the Ethnoscape.* Pittsburgh: University of Pittsburgh Press. http://www.loc.gov/catdir/enhancements/fy0666/2006015726-b.html.

Seamon, David. 1980. "Body-Subject, Time-Space Routines, and Place-Ballets." In *the Human Experience of Space and Place*, edited by Anne Buttimer and David Seamon, 148–66. New York: St. Martin's Press.

Seliverstova, Oleksandra. 2017. "'Consuming' National Identity in Western Ukraine." *Nationalities Papers* 45 (1): 61–79. doi:10.1080/00905992.2016.1220363.

Seliverstova, Oleksandra. 2018. "Consumer Citizenship and Reproduction of Estonianness." In *Identity and Nation Building in Everyday Post-Socialist Life*, edited by Abel Polese, Jeremy Morris, Emilia Pawłusz, and Oleksandra Seliverstova, 109–27. London, New York: Routledge.

Sen, Arijit, and Lisa Silverman. 2014. "Introduction." In *Making Place: Space and Embodiment in the City*, edited by Arijit Sen and Lisa Silverman, 1–19. Bloomington: Indiana University Press.

Shapirova, Dina, Aziz Burkhanov, and Alma Alpeissova. 2017. "The Determinants of Civic and Ethnic Nationalisms in Kazakhstan: Evidence from the Grass-Roots Level." *Nationalism and Ethnic Politics* 23 (2): 203–26.

Shevel, Oxana. 2011. "Russian Nation-Building from Yel'tsin to Medvedev: Ethnic, Civic or Purposefully Ambiguous?" *Europe-Asia Studies* 63 (2): 179–202. doi:10.1080/09668136.2011.547693.

Shukurov, Sharif, and Rustam Shukurov. 1998. "O Vole K Kul'ture." *Tsentral'naya Aziya i Kavkaz* 1: 163–72.

Simakova, Olga. 2016. "Emigratsiya Russkih: Priglashenie K Razmyshleniyu." *Kazahstan Spektr* 1 (75): 99–109.

Simmel, Georg. 1997. "Bridge and Door." In *Simmel on Culture*, edited by David Frisby and Mike Featherstone, 170–74. London, Newbury Park: Sage Publications Ltd.

Siseministeerium. 2016. "Rahvastikustatistika." Accessed March 06, 2017. https://www.siseministeerium.ee/et/tegevusvaldkonnad/rahvastikutoimingud/rahvastikustatistika.

Smith, Anthony D. 1999. *Myths and Memories of the Nation.* Oxford: Oxford University Press.

Smith, David. 2002. "Framing the National Question in Central and Eastern Europe: A Quadratic Nexus?" *The Global Review of Ethnopolitics* 2 (1): 3–16.

Smith, Graham, Vivien Law, Andrew Wilson, Annette Bohr, and Edward Allworth. 1998. *Nation—Building in Post—Soviet Borderlands: The Politics of National Identities.* Cambridge: Cambridge UP.

Smith, Neil. 2010. *Uneven Development: Nature, Capital, and the Production of Space.* 3rd ed. London: Verso.

Soja, Edward W. 1996. *Thirdspace: A Journey through Los Angeles and Other Real-and-Imagined Places.* Oxford, Cambridge: Blackwell.

Solska, Magdalena. 2011. "Citizenship, Collective Identity and the International Impact on Integration Policy in Estonia, Latvia and Lithuania." *Europe-Asia Studies* 63 (6): 1089–1108. doi:10.1080/09668136.2011.585762.

Solzhenitsyn, Aleksandr. 1995. *The Russian Question at the End of 20th Century.* London: Harvill Press.

Somers, Margaret, and Gloria Gibson. 1994. "Reclaiming the Epistemological Other: Narrative and the Social Constitution of Identity." In *Social Theory and the Politics of Identity*, edited by Craig Calhoun, 37–99. Cambridge: Blackwell.

Stedman, Richard, Benoni Amsden, Thomas Beckley, and Keith Tidball. 2014. "Photo-Based Methods for Understanding Place Meaning as Foundations of Attachment." In *Place Attachment: Advances in Theory, Methods and Applications*, edited by Lynne Manzo and Patrick Devine-Wright, 75–87. London: Routledge.

Stedman, Richard, Tom Beckley, Sara Wallace, and Marke Ambard. 2004. "A Picture and 1000 Words: Using Resident-Employed Photography to Understand Attachment to High Amenity Places." *Journal of Leisure Research* 36 (4): 580–606. doi:10.1080/00222216.2004.11950037.

Stenning, Alison, and Kathrin Hörschelmann. 2008. "History, Geography and Difference in the Post-Socialist World: Or, Do We Still Need Post-Socialism?" *Antipode* 40 (2): 312–35. doi:10.1111/j.1467-8330.2008.00593.x.

Stoler, Ann. 2013. "Introduction 'The Rot Remains': From Ruins to Ruination." In *Imeprial Debris: On Ruins and Ruination*, edited by Ann Stoler, 1–39. Durham, London: Duke University Press.

Strathern, Marilyn. 2002. "On Space and Depth." In *Complexities: Social Studies of Knowledge Practice*, edited by John Law and Annemarie Mol, 88–115. Durham: Duke University Press.

Strathern, Marilyn. 2004 [1991]. *Partial Connections.* New York, Toronto, Oxford, Walnut Creek, Lanham: Altamira Press.

Teliya, Veronika. 2001. "Kontseptoobrazuyuschaya Fluktuatsiya Konstanty Kul'tury 'Rodnaya Zemlya' V Naimenovanii 'Rodina'." In *Yazyk I Kul'tura: Fakty I Tsennosti*, edited by Elena Kubryakova and Tatyana Yanko, 409–21. Moscow: Yazuki slavyanskoi kul'turi.

Terkenli, Theano S. 1995. "Home as a Region." *Geographical Review* 85 (3): 324. doi:10.2307/215276.

The Doctrine on the National Unity. Accessed April 09, 2018. http://assembly.kz/ru/docs/doktrina-nacionalnogo-edinstva.

Thomassen, Bjørn. 2012. "Revisiting Liminality: The Danger of Empty Spaces." In *Liminal Landscapes: Travel, Experience and Spaces in-Between*, edited by Hazel Andrews and Les Roberts, 21–35. London: Routledge.

Thomassen, Bjørn. 2014. *Liminality and the Modern: Living Through the in-Between.* Farnham Surrey, Burlington: Ashgate.

Tiesler, Nina C. 2018. "Mirroring the Dialectic of Inclusion and Exclusion in Ethnoheterogenesis Processes." In *Changing Societies: Legacies and Challenges. Ambiguous Inclusions: Inside Out, Outside in*, edited by Sofia Aboim, Paulo Granjo, and Alice Ramos, 197–219: Imprensa de Ciências Sociais.

Tilley, Christopher Y. 1994. *A Phenomenology of Landscape: Places, Paths, and Monuments.* Explorations in anthropology. Oxford, Providence: Berg.

Tishkov, Valerii. 1993. *Russkie Kak Men'shinstva: Primer Estonii.* Moscow: Institut Ethnologii i Antropologii RAN.

Tishkov, Valerii. 2003. *Rekviem Po Etnosu: Issledovaniya Po Sotsial'no-Kul'turnoi Antropologii.* Moscow: Nauka.

Todorova, Maria. 2010. "Balkanism and Postcolonialism, or On the Beauty of the Airplane View." In *In Marx's Shadow: Knowledge, Power, and Intellectuals in Eastern Europe and Russia*, edited by Costica Bradatan and Serguei Oushakine, 175–97. Lanham: Lexington Books.

Tolz, Vera. 1998. "Forging the Nation: National Identity and Nation Building in Post-Communist Russia." *Europe-Asia Studies* 50 (6): 993–1022.

Tonkiss, Fran. 2005. *Space, the City and Social Theory: Social Relations and Urban Forms.* Cambridge: Polity.

Torbakov, Igor. 2017. "What Is to Be Done About the 'Russian Question?'." *Eurasianet*, October 27. Accessed March 09, 2020. https://eurasianet.org/what-is-to-be-done-about-the-russian-question.

Trimbach, David J., and Shannon O'Lear. 2016. "Russians in Estonia: Is Narva the Next Crimea?" *Eurasian Geography and Economics* 56 (5): 493–504. doi:10.108 0/15387216.2015.1110040.

Tsing, Anna L. 1993. *In the Realm of the Diamond Queen: Marginality in an Out-of-the-Way Place.* Princeton: Princeton University Press.

Turner, Victor W. 2008. *The Ritual Process: Structure and Anti-Structure.* New York: Aldine de Gruyter.

Unwin, Tim. 1999. "Place, Territory, and National Identity in Estonia." In *Nested Identities: Nationalism, Territory and Scale*, edited by Henrik Herb and David Kaplan, 151–73. Lanham: Rowman & Littlefield Publishers.

Urazova, Dinara. 2014. "Kazakh Statehood Is 550 Years Old: Nazarbayev." *En.tengrinews.kz*, 2014. Accessed March 09, 2020. https://en.tengrinews.kz/politics_sub/kazakh-statehood-is-550-years-old-nazarbayev-257056/.

Valdur, Mikita. 2013. *Lingvistiline Mets: Tsibihärblase Paradigma Teadvuse Kiirendi.* Tallinn: Grenader.

Valentine, Gill. 2008. "Living with Difference: Reflections on Geographies of Encounter." *Progress in Human Geography* 32 (3): 323–37. doi:10.1177/0309133308089372.

Vallimäe, Tanel, Mikko Lagerspetz, and Liisi Keedus. 2010. *Venekeelsed Kodanikuühendused Ja Eesti Kodanikuühiskond: Paralleelsed Maailmad Või Vaikne Integratsioon?* Tallinn: KUAK.

van Gennep, Arnold. 1960 [1909]. *The Rites of Passage: A Classical Study of Cultural Celebrations.* Chicago: The University of Chicago Press.

Veser, Reinhard. 2015. "Fast normale Staatsbürger." *Frankfurter Allgemeine Zeitung* February 26. Accessed on July 23, 2020. https://www.faz.net/aktuell/politik/ausl and/europa/die-russen-in-estland-suchen-ihren-platz-im-land-13450349/estalnds -praesident-toomas-13448720.html

Vihalemm, Triin. 2007. "Crystallizing and Emancipating Identities in Post-Communist Estonia." *Nationalities Papers* 35 (3): 477–502. doi:10.1080/00905990701368738.

Vihalemm, Triin, and Veronika Kalmus. 2009. "Cultural Differentiation of the Russian Minority." *Journal of Baltic Studies* 40 (1): 95–119. doi:10.1080/01629770902722278.

Vihalemm, Triin, and Anu Masso. 2003. "Identity Dynamics of Russian-Speakers of Estonia in the Transition Period." *Journal of Baltic Studies* 34 (1): 92–116. doi:10.1080/01629770200000271.

Vitkovskaya, Galina. 1999. "Vynuzhdennaya Migratsiya V Rossiyu: Itogi Desyatiletiya." In *Migratsionnaya Situatsiya V Stranah SNG*, edited by Zhanna Zaionchkovskaya, 159–95. Moscow.

Vorkachev, Sergei. 2006. "Slovo 'Rodina' Znachimostnaya Sostavlyayuschaya Lingvokontsepta." *Yazyk, Kommunikatsiya i Sotsialnaya Sreda VGU* 4: 26–36.

Warriner, Doris S. 2007. "Language Learning and the Politics of Belonging: Sudanese Women Refugees Becoming and Being 'American'." *Anthropology & Education Quarterly* 38 (4): 343–59.

Werbner, Pnina. 2015. "Introduction: The Dialectics of Cultural Hybridity." In *Debating Cultural Hybridity: Multicultural Identities and the Politics of Anti-Racism*, edited by Pnina Werbner and Tariq Modood, 1–26. London: Zed Books.

Wierzbicka, Anna. 1997. *Understanding Cultures Through Their Key Words: English, Russian, Polish, German, and Japanese*. Oxford studies in anthropological linguistics 8. New York, Oxford: Oxford University Press.

Wiles, Janine. 2008. "Sense of Home in a Transnational Social Space: New Zealanders in London." *Global Networks* 8 (1): 116–37. doi:10.1111/j.1471-0374.2008.00188.x.

Williams, Raymond. 1980. *Problems in Materialism and Culture: Selected Essays*. Radical thinkers. London: Verso.

Wingender, Monika. 2015. "Einführung: Sprachenpolitik Und Identitätsdiskurse in Den Russisch-Türksprachigen Sprachgemeinschaften Kayachstans Und Tatarstans." In *Sprachpolitische Diskurse in Russisch-Türkischsprachigen Sprachgemeinschaften: Sprachen Und Identitäten in Tatarstan Und Kasachstan*, edited by Mark Kirchner and Monika Wingender, 1–39. Wiesbaden: Harrasowitz.

Włodarska-Frykowska, Agata. 2016. "Ethnic Russian Minority in Estonia." *International Studies. Interdisciplinary Political and Cultural Journal* 18 (2): 153–64. doi:10.1515/ipcj-2016-0015.

Wolfel, Richard L. 2002. "North to Astana: Nationalistic Motives for the Movement of the Kazakh(Stani) Capital." *Nationalities Papers* 30 (3): 485–506. doi:10.1080 /0090599022000011723.

Wright, Sarah. 2015. "More-Than-Human, Emergent Belongings." *Progress in Human Geography* 39 (4): 391–411. doi:10.1177/0309132514537132.

Wunderlich, Filipa M. 2010. "The Aesthetics of Place-Temporality in Everyday Urban Space: The Case of Fitzroy Square." In *Geographies of Rhythm: Nature, Place, Mobilities and Bodies*, edited by Tim Edensor, 45–59. London: Routledge.

Yeltsin, Boris. 1997. "Poslanie prezidenta Rossii Borisa Yeltsina Federal'nomu sobraniyu RF: 'Poryadok vo vlasti—porjadok v strane'." Accessed July 21, 2020. http://www.intelros.ru/2007/02/05/poslanie_prezidenta_rosii_borisa_elcina _federalnomu_sobraniju_rf_porjadok_vo_vlasti__porjadok_v_strane_1997_god .html

Yessenova, Saulesh. 2003. "The Politics and Poetics of the Nation: Urban Narratives of Kazakh Identity." PhD dissertation, McGill University.

Youkhana, Eva. 2015. "A Conceptual Shift in Studies of Belonging and the Politics of Belonging." *SI* 3 (4): 10–24. doi:10.17645/si.v3i4.150.

Yuval-Davis, Nira. 2006. "Belonging and the Politics of Belonging." *Patterns of Prejudice* 40 (3): 197–214. doi:10.1080/00313220600769331.

Yuval-Davis, Nira, Georgie Wemyss, and Kathryn Cassidy. 2017. "Everyday Bordering, Belonging and the Reorientation of British Immigration Legislation." *Sociology* 52 (2): 228–44. doi:10.1177/0038038517702599.

Zabrodskaja, Anastassia. 2015. "'What Is My Country to Me?': Identity Construction by Russian-Speakers in the Baltic Countries." *SOLS* 9 (2–3): 217–42. doi:10.1558/ sols.v9i2.26885.

Zabrodskaja, Anastassia, and Martin Ehala. "Chto Dlya Menya Estoniya? Ob Etnolingivstichekoi Vitaln'nosti Russkoyazychnyh." *Diaspory* 1: 8–25.

Zerubavel, Eviatar. 1991. *The Fine Line: Making Distinctions in Everyday Life.* New York: Free Press.

Zerubavel, Eviatar. 2006. *The Elephant in the Room: Silence and Denial in Everyday Life.* New York, Oxford: Oxford University Press.

Zevelev, I. A. 2000. *Russia and Its New Diasporas.* Washington: United States Institute of Peace.

Zevelev, Igor. 1996. "Russia and the Russian Diasporas." *Post-Soviet Affairs* 12 (3): 265–84. doi:10.1080/1060586X.1996.10641425.

Zimmer, Oliver. 1998. "In Search of Natural Identity: Alpine Landscape and the Reconstruction of the Swiss Nation." *Comparative Studies in Society and History* 40 (4): 637–65.

Index

Italic page references indicate figures.

Victory Park, in Petropavlovsk, 81
Virgin Land Campaign, 35

walking tours, and act of walking:
method of urban ethnography, 16,
69–70, 79–80
Wierzbicka, Anna, 120–21
Wright, Sarah, 3

Yeltsin, Boris (former president),
101–102

Yessenova, Saulesh, 43
Youkhana, Eva, 9
Yuval-Davis, Nira, 10,
20n6

Zabrodskaya, Anastassia, 7, 32, 34
Zhumabaev, Magzhamn, 37
Zimmer, Oliver, 85
zone of stasis, 25
Zusammengehörigkeit (belonging with),
20n6

About the Author

Alina Jašina-Schäfer is a post-doctoral fellow at the Federal Institute for Culture and History of the Germans in Eastern Europe (BKGE), Oldenburg, Germany In 2015–2019 she conducted her doctoral research at the Graduate Center for the Study of Culture at the University of Giessen, Germany.

www.ingramcontent.com/pod-product-compliance
Lightning Source LLC
Chambersburg PA
CBHW050655280326

41932CB00015B/2917